Letters from 500
Portal

Robert Lee Potter

BrightWire Publishing
Warren, New Jersey, USA
To contact us about this book, please visit our site and blog at
www.lettersfrom500.com

ISBN 978-0-578-08984-3
1. The Future. 2. Consciousness. 3. Spiritual Life. I. Title.

4 6 8 11 12 10 9 7 5 3

Contents

Acknowledgments v

Author's Note vii

Poem Two xi

Letter Twenty-Eight   Vehicle of Awakening............................1

Letter Twenty-Nine   Transiency of Form.................................9

Letter Thirty   The Void and Formlessness.................19

Letter Thirty-One   Resonance, the Key.............................27

Letter Thirty-Two   Black Point of Light............................37

Letter Thirty-Three   Place of Memories.............................45

Letter Thirty-Four   Elders 51

Letter Thirty-Five   Not Finished...61

Letter Thirty-Six   Body 75

Letter Thirty-Seven   The Grace of Freedom 87

Letter Thirty-Eight   Portal 97

Letter Thirty-Nine   Young Man 111

Letter Forty   Lens   123

Letter Forty-One   The Bridge and the Stars 135

Letter Forty-Two   Naïveté   151

Letter Forty-Three   The Great Storm................................... 161

Letter Forty-Four   Knowing the Oneself.......................... 173

Letter Forty-Five   Oneness Does Not Manifest 183

Letter Forty-Six   Glimpse of Awakening....................... 195

Letter Forty-Seven   Faith and Magic................................. 211

Letter Forty-Eight   Fire   223

Letter Forty-Nine   The Ark and the Covenant................ 235

Epilogue   Why Souls Leave the Earth................ 253

Acknowledgments

Stefan Bright and Judy Welder have been with me every step of the way in these books. They have shared my amazement at times, and listened compassionately when I complained and doubted myself. "Where is all this going?" my ego would whine. Judy and Stefan always answered with confidence that the material just needs to get out there. They often could see more clearly than I, what the bigger picture was.

High on the list to acknowledge are always the wonderful muses who have brought the material through. I have grown to know them quite well, at least in the context of receiving these *Letters*. The ones who assisted most often and directly are Clio, Caliope, Urania, Polymnia and, of course, Musagetes, leader of the muses.

My warmest thanks go to the members of my Monroe Institute Local Chapter group as well, for their constant support and feedback, and their presence at the inception of key scenes in the story. The field of rapport we have established together provides an ongoing source of inspiration. By name they are, Martha Monroe, Cindy Johnston, Brooke Steytler, Mark Waas, Bob Waas, Magda Helena Dineen, Nick Ife, and Steve Winchester.

I offer special thanks to Felicia DeRita Hueber for her generosity and unique inspiration, while we sat watching Eckhart Tolle together. I would interrupt with sudden ideas for the narrative, particularly the whole poem for volume three. My good friend, Loic Barnieu, in addition to correcting my stumbling French, has also been helpfully 'critical' of the books, giving me a 'real world' perspective on how they might be received.

Of course, I must recognize and thank my dear "future" friends, O, OM, B and others of the group. I truly delight in their presence during the writing and at any time I call out in their direction—whatever that direction may be.

I am also abundantly grateful to Lulu Publishing for making this whole process so accessible and financially feasible. Producing a book is still a major undertaking, but it is far less daunting than it once was.

At last, my greatest appreciation goes to you, the reader, again. You perform the invaluable role of receiving and grounding the material that would otherwise remain floating in the ethers of imagination. Whether you buy into all the notions and suggestions is no matter. It is the act of receiving them that enables simple appreciation to move forward. Thank you abundantly.

Author's Note

For a while last year, I thought the first book would be an only child. It came to me suddenly and unannounced, and then it virtually wrote itself, in an uninterrupted flow. When it was over, I could only shake my head and wonder. Yet, as time passed, something began stirring again. Eventually, I asked O if there might be another book.

While I do not characterize *Letters from 500* as 'channeled', I have to say I do occasionally ask O a question or two. I've even submitted questions from friends; I guess that *is* a form of channeling. But I don't make a big deal of it. To me, all artists 'channel' the muses in order get their creative juices flowing. And everyone does a lot of *natural* channeling, I think. We follow hunches and intuitions, sudden 'bright ideas' or encounters with coincidence and synchronicity.

By now, O has become a real person to me, a person from a real place. I can't prove her existence, nor can I *disprove* it. There is an undeniable vitality and 'otherness' in her messages that is way beyond my normal self; I know that much. When I'm getting impressions from her, I have a very particular, uplifting feeling. That same feeling returns when I re-read passages. Others tell us they've felt that too.

So, I asked O about a second book. Her response was at once tantalizing and perplexing. She said that from their future perspective, there were two divergent timelines. One portrayed just a single book being written. However, another timeline showed three books—a trilogy.

If the first path were chosen, the one book would be sufficient to fulfill the original purpose of the project. If the second were followed, it would open us all up to further development and revelation. The two additional volumes would build upon the first.

I then asked which timeline would it be. How would I know? O told me that the whole matter was under consideration by her group. If there were going to be second volume, another introductory poem would come through first. That's how I would know.

Then months passed, with no inspiration, and no *musing*. I began to think I was on that *singular* timeline after all—where there would not be a second book. If so, then *so be it;* I could just get on with my life. In the course of this, it was interesting to observe the difference between 'inspired' times and those which are not. The muses are just *absent* at these 'down' times. Trying to write without them is like slogging through deep mud. But when the muses come, words and ideas flow freely. Any concerns I might have just vanish into the air. This does not mean I don't do a lot of editing and refining afterward. But that's all part of the work of *translating*.

While I was waiting to see how the fates would lead, Stefan began setting up our web blog. He promoted the book far and wide. He made contacts with people across the country and around the world. Gradually, a dialogue developed—mainly between Stefan and the others. I occasionally make contributions to it.

At last, one day I detected a shift. Glimpses of the future began slipping into my thoughts and meditations. Then the second poem arrived. That was the signal. Within a few days, I felt that surge of buoyant energy, lifting me up from the inside. The first chapter— Letter 28—started with a burst. It came with a feeling I hadn't ever felt before in the writing—strong, authoritative, and 'collective'. The source of that initial message turned out to be the spirit of the whole group entity, not just O.

Exactly as before, this book started on the first day of a month and ended on the first of a month—five months later to the day — December 1, 2010. I don't know why this is. But the numerology of it is clearly '1' and '5'.

This edition of the *Letters* is somewhat different from the first. It has more of a storyline. I understand now that each book will have its own particular character. Volume one laid the groundwork and introduced the vigilan system of looking at the world. The second book is more experiential. It takes me through my paces— visiting a difficult past lifetime, then shooting off to the far, far future before sling-shooting me back here again. There's a lot more traveling and encountering this time. O even makes several appearances in this time zone, through private sub-dimensions.

I see this book fitting in with the other two as a bridge and a doorway—hence its title, *Portal*. I don't know much about the third book yet, but I feel it will be much lighter and ephemeral, perhaps even lyrical. This portal will take us from the ground-base of book one, into etheric realms of spirit in book three.

Volume two, curiously has many 'water' references in it. Water is 'transition', I've been told. It is mutable, mysterious; it seeks its own level. And it is the basis of life on our planet. Water, of course, also represents the unknown, the formless. I never actually asked O about these references directly, though I sense she might say it's a mystery that needs its own silent integrity.

For both the second and the third manuscripts, I was given visions of the beginning of the book slightly ahead of writing it. Each vision came during an 'inner journey' with a group of friends, listening to Hemi-Synch®. This is the sound technology of Robert Monroe, founder of The Monroe Institute in Virginia. His system helps induce profoundly altered states of awareness, especially effective in group formation.

Under the influence of the soft droning waves, I sank into a deep, incubational state. Gradually, out of a mist, I saw, or felt, O's group, assembled around a large stone slab. I was moved into the circle, floating like a dream. The group delivered a packet of ideas, a 'seed-link' to me to consider at another time. Then later, when I started writing, that experience flowed up into my memory. The 'link' began unfolding.

While this book's account may seem to be *my* particular story, I've been told there are openings in it for anyone—thresholds, if you will. These openings imply a grand, universal saga—the path of pilgrims toward a new species. They lead through dark waters and stormy seas, to the bottoms of rivers and oceans, down to the fluid foundation of our very bodies, soul and civilization. These portals are doing their part to open a passage through the clouds, through the tempest, and even through the sky itself—that ancient *Akasha*.

This second volume is about movement through the Great Storm that is raging deep down in each of us. Many people are still busy denying it—out of fear, no doubt. Would that they could but deny it away! Be assured that this Storm is there; it is everywhere.

We feel it intimately when we're alone in the night, or swept by unexplainable anxieties. We see it projected out upon our modern world, with all its toxic mix of 'gory' and 'glory'—the rising, falling, writhing of a civilization near its end. We have reached the heights and the depths simultaneously. I know this is the way it is *supposed* to be. The dark and the light are one.

The degree to which we are awakening, is the degree to which we admit this Storm exists in us, around us. And it is the degree to which we admit it *into* our consciousness, and *own* it. It is the awakened *danse macabre*—life and death—with all its revelation and apocalypse. *Conscious Evolution* is happening in each person, and in the *whole species*—right now. If we would pass through the Great Storm intact, we must see it for what it really is, and *where* it is—inside us.

We are asked in *Portal* to take up our stillness and see it growing, gathering momentum to move us far into the single moment of Now. We are invited to see it pierce the turbulence of our times with its fiery peace. May you, dear reader, find this of assistance on your journey into the bright unknown.

R. L. Potter,
Chester, Pennsylvania, July, 2011

Poem Two

Open eyes upon the world,
our vision now begins.
Down under,
core of Source
is stirring, molten, swirling
like a lava,
like a lake of stinging fire
on the veil.
It is arising, and it's burning,
churning,
dawning from the depths
of innocence through jaded
tempers of the mind.
Who is this mind
who thinks he rules the world?
Who thinks he can control
the Source of Power
down within?
What inevitable surprises are in store
for those who fear,
and wish to denigrate the heart!
There is a withering upon us now
that will endure and multiply
until its burning hour is done.
It will not pause nor cease until
it has devoured the ancient calumny
of indignation, shallowness and shame.
The world of change has come
into the countenance of men.
Seek not for refuge
in the passing vestiges of time.
It is not there,
the succor you would find.
It is not there
within the frozen, turning, sliding into dark—
the world that's fast eroding
into epochs of the
once before
but gone.
Seek not at all of anyone or anything.
who lures you to a form,

nor any who would offer you
a place upon that ground.
Release the clutching, catching
and the distance
now
that keeps you from the freedom
of your formless one,
the child of peace,
of home.
So, let the forms within you move
from deep down in
and far below
the Earth.
It's there that comes,
what is,
to surface in the moment of the pulsing
of an age—the end,
the culmination
and fruition of
the hapless world
that never
was.

— the Author, July 1, 2010

Letter Twenty-Eight
Vehicle of Awakening

To the One It Does Concern,

"We speak to you—as you, friends. Our voice comes from the deep Source that lies within us all. It speaks to the Oneness within and around you. It is the wake-up call of the still, small voice that lives beyond all individuation and separation. Our voice is joined into the web of the living word. Why should it be thus? Why is the Oneness speaking to itself through you? Why is it living itself through you?

"There is no answer to the question 'why'. But in asking it, we invoke the mystery of our shared being. The question is the presence, stretching out into wakefulness and wonder. Know that the circuit must complete itself through you. The electromagnetic—and *electro-magical*—forces must use *you* to come full circle into all the dimensions. Be of use! This is our injunction to you all, to *us* all. Make the best and clearest use of the portal you have been given. *You* are that portal, as surely as you have a mind to ask the question 'why'. Make clear your way into the moment. There is no greater blessing than being the opportunity that you are."

"Well, well, is that you, O? You sound a little different."

"This is the voice of our group speaking to the wider group of humans who are coming to their wakefulness now. We begin this way, that there may be a volume of energy poured forth into your presence, and in a way that will not be mistaken for anything less than the urgency of your age. We speak with Oneness, for Oneness, to the Oneness lying within you all. It is time to allow the ways to open, and to know what you know, what you have suspected for ages and kept hidden in your silence."

"Your group is speaking to humanity?"

"Only to those with ears to hear; that is, with their fields of resonance tuned to our frequency. Many will not hear these words at all. They will receive other words, other voices. But *hear* you shall— each and every one. You are all hearing now; though not all are yet listening. You are all touching the Apocalypse; but not all are yet feeling what is touching them in return. What is happening now in your time is the ancient, perennial 'quickening' of awareness. You can feel it in the waters of your flesh, in the pulse of your breath. It is rattling the molecular foundations of your species."

"Yes. I *think* I'm hearing and listening to what you say. Though I never can be quite sure. Sometimes I reread your materials and discover new thoughts I didn't see before. I think I get it, and yet I still miss so much."

"Such is natural. These words, from Source, are living. They come from deep down, under all; they move within themselves and vibrate endlessly. They change their form and wavelength in response to the listener and to the outpouring waves of magic and magnetism—in-breath, out-breath, in, out, pause. They are washing you alive. They will naturally transform and increase themselves in your mind, as Life continues to flow within them. Come and be nourished by this tide."

"May I ask a question?"

"Certainly, brother."

"What does 'Oneness' really mean to you? Why do you use that word so much? How are we to relate to it?"

"Thank you. Oneness is the vehicle for awakening. There is no other way to move beyond your current state of consciousness and your ego-world, than by entering and riding this vehicle. It is the presence of us all, united, sharing and grouping. And yet, it is far beyond that as well. It is union before union, the center before the circle; it is formlessness before the form. Verily, it is the form *of* formlessness. All radiance comes within its spark. Its fire ignites the passion of our charge. With Oneness we will cross the great divide and find the passage through the eye of the Storm.

"Oneness touches everything, feels everything, is everything. Yet it is not just this. It is also the Void and the Source and the Presence and the Voice. There is no concept that it is not. And yet there is no concept for what it truly is. In the meat of paradox it converges, albeit glancingly, with our earthly comprehension. To know it, to experience it, you may fly to the farthest reaches of your imagination and wisdom, or you may dive down into the fibers of your essence, in the moment, the ordinary station of your steps upon this Earth. It is everywhere you would seek to find it. But beware, what seems to be, is not real. Your seeking keeps you from truly seeing.

"Let go all your preconceptions of what Oneness is. Long have you sought it by *not* finding it. *Find it by not seeking it.* Now is the time to *know.* What a joy to share this time with you all. It is the wonder of the passing of a Great Age. You are, as one, passing into the history of Now. All history lies in the moment of creation. All passages lead into themselves. They are each, Source and destiny."

Suddenly I am seeing the field outside your home, near the ocean coast, the dunes and ponds. Seabirds are calling in the wind. Mists are carried overhead against the blue, in thin spiral wisps, dissolving as they move. I smell the salt air, feel the breeze on my skin. Loose robes of indigo brocade flutter hypnotically on me. The grasses wave with the dancing air and ripple out across the expanse. Your group has gathered outside, near the house with no roof. I see them clearly; they are seated in the field around a wide, flat stone. I look down on it and see strange markings from a former, ancient time.

I am observing the group, but I am not part of it. I seem to be hovering slightly above, floating. I see you all join arms and begin to sway in unison. First slowly one way then the other, unhurried, intentional. You are dancing with the breeze in the grasses. Or perhaps all is dancing together, in a concert of slow-motion grace. I am floating higher now. I see the shore and the ocean waves. The beach dissolves away in the mists both north and south.

"Look now into our world. Look everywhere. You are all most welcome here. Ride the waves of Oneness. Leave your separation behind. You do not need it ever more. Curl yourself around this, our planet, our chosen home—together. This is both ours and yours. Come and enter."

To the east, bright sun is drenching the tawny fields and the green vegetation farther on. Suddenly my vision seems to rocket forward, eastward, flashing over landscapes at irrepressible speed. Across the mountains, the deserts, the plains and forests. My vision—beyond bodily constraint—is soaring out over the far coast and the other ocean. It flashes on to both Europe and Africa in a stride, as sun is setting into night; then to Asia and India, China, Australia, to the islands of Japan.

In the passage of my senses over all the Earth, I feel the exquisite wonders of your world. I feel the souls, living, breathing, playing and working everywhere below. Now across the wide Pacific and the sun is rising. Through gray clouds, I fly over swelling, rolling waters and the inscrutable ocean deep. Back to here. I am floating calmly above the misty shore.

"This, our precious child and forebear, is the world you will come to know and embrace as your own. It is yours now, as we speak the living word. Come and feel your being here beside us, in us, as your own flesh and blood—you, our genetic forebears and ancestral love. We are one."

Below someone is chanting—a single, piercing voice of such beauty that I am pinned against the sky. The rest of you below echo back some of the words. I feel drawn down again by the power you are generating, hovering over the stone slab, right in the center of the circle. I am being moved by the sound, and by the momentum of your ceremony. You, O, are now looking at me. All around I turn and gaze back into each of your eyes, full circle.

"We take the gift you are giving us, have given, will give; it is the root and groundwork of our race. Your essence, spirit, wonder; your imagination and genius; your quantum imprint, evolutionary force and physical form, are still within us. They are alive and breathing, across the centuries to here. We are closer than family. We are one and the same creation!"

It is Black's voice I have heard from far above, that drew me down. She sings again and the sound is inside me, cutting through my defenses and senses, right through the flesh of my heart, down deep into every organ, gland and chakra. My body structures are all awhirl, effervescent, glowing with their own light. I see seven shining, spinning disks, openings in my body, all in vertical alignment. The energy reaches up through me, down through me. I link with the Sky chakra above my head. I plunge to the Earth chakra below my root. I am bound to Earth and Sky. My energy is theirs. I have become, for this moment, their portal.

A realization dawns on me: This is the *future past*. It is the time *before* you first came and contacted me. I'm witnessing the ceremony that you used to find me, and to cross the 500-year temporal divide.

"Watch now and know our ways, dear friend. Listen to the movements and the mudras that have borne us together."

The man in green robes lifts his hand high. Pointing upward, he seems to scoop his fingers into the sky. Sitting next to him, you follow his gesture with your own hand. One by one around the circle, each of you lifts one arm and takes a bit of the heavenly sphere to your touch. I see electricity interlacing the spaces between of your hands. The image flickers in my eyes and I see an emptiness behind your hands. It's like your hands are there and then they're not, then back again—flickering in and out of existence in that magical space just beneath the sky. The electricity spirals between your fingers, down around your arms slowly, gracefully; now upon your heads and necks and bodies, down into the ground. The soil lights up with a silver fire, golden fire, pulsing toward the stone.

I am completely mesmerized and cannot move except to waft gently on the breeze of your incantation. It is my part, I sense, to be treated thus. I release my desire to be in control of anything. I am ignorant and naïve. This too is part of the ritual. I know I'm intended to be aware and yet unaware. I am waking from the dead and dying both. Something has gripped me totally from the bottom of my being—my center peg; it holds me fast. I am both here and far away.

At one high and airy note of the song from Black, the group in unison sounds a hard and earthy grunt—a deep, guttural burst of rock-like sound. Then silence. Poised stillness. All is waiting, holding, vibrating to the moment. Something is shifting in you all, and in me. I feel like the patterns of my physical structure are rearranging and merging, placing themselves into new configurations. I have felt this sensation before, on the edge of the new universe, on the threshold of Hunab Ku.

Silence. The air whispers across the grass. It speaks a language I can almost understand. Arms are raised all around. The ground is shaking and rumbling, answering the guttural call. I notice something I hadn't seen before. At the center of the stone wheel—a calendar, I would say—is a pool of invisibility. I gaze upon it in awe. It is pure emptiness. There is nothing there. No surface, no depth, no light nor dark—a scintillating absence of all. This is an embodiment, in form, of the Void itself. Am I going there? It is calling me again. I can feel it in my bones.

All your hands begin to move. They have touched the sky and, having gathered essence there, are now descending. Each in turn, they fall toward the center of the stone. Though each of you is seated at a distance from the wheel, your hands, still pointing, are moving to the center, in a great arcing gesture over the Void. One by one, each hand is placed together. I can see the Void right through, as if the hands are now transparent. The Void is real; the hands are not.

Now your dozen hands are melding into one hand. *None of this is possible,* I can hear my mind reproaching. Hands do not stretch out from their bodies; they do not become transparent and merge. The Void does not appear in time and space! My eyes are taking it all in, but my mind refuses. It reels and spins and I within it spin.

I look again around the circle, at all your eyes. You each are pouring your souls into mine. I can feel this flow. It is as though you are creating me with those eyes—the windows of the soul. I am coming into existence for the very first time. The last I see is your eyes, O, piercing into me, holding me fast even as I slip away.

Void. Nothing. No space. No time.

"Where am I?" I whisper. My own voice sounds like an echo to me, a ritual voice rising up from far away. Wherever I am, my asking the question has a creative power. I know this without a doubt. I am creating whatever will be the answer to my question. I am creating a form right before me. I see it as a swirling, glowing flow of energy, curving off into space and away. I cannot tell where it is going. But I know I am here now, at this end of the path. It is a path. I have created it out of the knowing of it, out of the asking. What I ask, I know, I create. Whatever I see before me is, in reality, my own manifested self, no matter the form.

I realize quickly that I am being held in a very sacred and magical space. This is not my normal, physical world. It is my place of power, the center of me. It is where I can create the whole universe that I will experience. It is the Void and Threshold, where creative forces come to be born. I am one of these forces now. I have somehow transferred my presence into the flowing pathway of orange and golden light. I am the path and the power. This feels vaguely religious to me. I can sense my own true virtue. But I also feel the ego lurking nearby, watching for an opportunity to slip back in.

Where does this lead? I ask. With my deeper sensation, I answer my own request and see the destination. I follow the flowing colors, down to Earth, into my time upon this planet. It feels as though I'm being poured, as a fluid, into my old form. It is so hard and tight, encrusted with a thousand shuttered windows.

What is this? I stir, suddenly feeling the taste of fear. It is the fear that my old separateness is returning. I shudder and know this world for what it is—a binding, blinding illusion. It has no power, but paradoxically, it has *control.* I bow down and cry. I have passed away. I am dead to your world. I feel it all so much more than I ever did before.

"What is this, O? Please answer me! I have lost my power."

Letter Twenty-Nine
Transiency of Form

"Ouch, that was abrupt! It feels like I've just put on an old, tight pair of shoes. Are your there, O? Can you help?" I'm at my desk, shaking.

Without any words, I now see a gossamer vision of you appear across the room. You walk from the window and sit down before me. This is the first time I've seen you in my own time and space. It sends a thrill into my senses.

"O, you're here. That's wonderful. I'm better already. I didn't know you could appear here!"

"Well, I could have done this all along. But it would have disturbed you unnecessarily before. So, hello soul friend, I am here at your request. How can I help?"

I stare into your face and your eyes for a few long breaths. "Just seeing you again is a big help. I really like having you here. I can't believe you're doing this. You must be aware of what I just saw at your house, in the future."

"Yes," you smile.

"Well, at the end of it I was suddenly feeling so powerless. A moment before that, I felt all the power in the universe at my fingertips. Where did it all go? Why can't I feel it now?"

"You *can* feel it, if you turn your attention to it again. The physical world is a mighty distraction for you humans. Yes." You look sympathetically at me. "Sometimes it can be difficult to 'turn' your attention; I understand. But you can learn to see through the distractions, into reality. The trick is to remember how to see nothing—the Void—behind the forms. It's like tuning into a radio signal. Or rather, it's like tuning into the carrier wave behind all radio signals. Look first to the spaces between the stations. Remember your talent for Source gazing."

"Yeah, that. OK. You've been telling me this before. 'Read between the lines.' The Void is there all the time, behind everything.

No thing is behind *every* thing. My mind doesn't want to comprehend though, not really."

"Your mind wants the world to be fixed and solid—no mystery; it wants the outside, physical experience to give you all your answers. It wants the 'concrete' world to handle your enlightenment. The mind doesn't trust the deeper you, which it cannot see. It wants to fabricate a controllable belief system."

I again find myself staring at your eyes. They seem to be directing this whole conversation. I mumble, "My mind wants me to be enlightened?"

"Yes, in its way. The mind and ego do want enlightenment. All your being wants this. The desire is an upwelling from the core of consciousness. As the pure desire rises through the layers of your manifested body on Earth, the various aspects of illusion distort it. But at the heart of each thought and emotion you feel, even as humans, is the desire to expand your awareness. That is precisely what thoughts and emotions are—expansions and projections outward from your inner spark of consciousness into the world.

"I have told you before that you can start your journey into awakening even from the platform of the mind. Here's the reason it can work." You lean forward over my table and look intensely at me. "You can trace your own essence backward, down into its Source—down from the mind's eye. From wherever you are, you may begin the journey to enlightenment—even while immersed in distracting thoughts. You may realize enlightenment from any state of consciousness or unconsciousness. It's all a matter of persisting on the path to Source. If this were not true, there would be no evolution at all."

"That is comforting," I admit. "Let's backtrack for a moment. I know that the Void is a wonderful, even essential experience from my own encounters with it. But why should this be important for humans in general? Don't we have more urgent matters to pay attention to?"

"Being able to see into the Void is the most urgent matter of all in the coming years of your time. Your illusion will be crumbling all around you in many ways. It obviously needs to. This is happening right now before your eyes—in your news media, in your politics, in your personal lives. Behind all the crumbling lie other illusions, ready to replace the one you're currently in.

"If you do not comprehend what lies behind *all* the illusions, you will simply substitute one of these others for the current one. It may perhaps be fresher, shinier and more comforting for a while. But it will still be an illusion. The opportunity you now have, as a species, is to realize *reality!* To enter true empowerment, you must be able to touch the Source of your power. That means knowing the Void!"

"Would you please tell me, then, how can we see the Void more clearly in ordinary life?"

"Here is a simple way. It requires no great technique or practice. Relax. Breathe. Hold your gaze on a single object, one that is not moving." You point to a paper clip lying in front of me. I look at it intently.

"Do not blink your eyes as you stare at it for a minute or so. Blinking or moving your eyes is a reset button. Do not reset your eyes or mind.

"As you gaze at the object, notice what happens to your vision of it. Notice the distortions that begin to appear around it. It is partially your motor-perception making this happen, of course. But soon the distortions will be apparent within the object itself. The image will fluctuate as it comes into and out of focus. It is not *just* your eyesight creating this phenomenon. The quantum physicality itself is fluctuating, coming and going, vibrating in and out of existence continuously.

"You are observing the transiency of form—both in your eyes and in the object before you. You saw this in our hands upon the altar outside my house. If you were to stare long enough at any object, it would disappear completely. Without the continual 'reset' to physical reality, the forms of the world would be much more transient and transparent. This is the way vigilans see reality. The Veil of Forgetfulness, the curtain between the realm of spirit and mind, is the mechanism for circumscribing your incarnate awareness. The Veil is programmed, in your species, to continually reset itself.

"Now, back to the object. As you see the fluctuations in the image before you, understand it as a portal beyond form. The opening is there right before your eyes, right within the object itself, and right inside your eyes as well. *The Void is in the eye of the beholder.* Take only one small step toward that portal, and there you are—in the Void, feeling the Void, sensing that it is all around you, beyond time. This exercise can be speeded up, with a little practice, to mere seconds." You pick up the paper clip.

I blink and the image is suddenly reset to solid. "Thank you, O. That worked for me. I wonder if it will work for anyone else. The Void is right there in front of me, and *within* me. I like being able to sense it like that."

"Sense it and *use* it, my friend. Use it to touch your power and find your presence. Knowing the emptiness that embraces all things is to know the Source and destiny that embraces all things. This can be known by anyone with a strong enough resonance to do so.

"You are now ready for one more clarification. Going *within* is actually not what the mind thinks it is. We say that reality—truth, power, the whole Cosmos—lies within you. What that means on a more subtle turn is that within you is a *portal* into reality. It is not that the universe is actually contained by your individuality; the individuality archetype is your icon and access point into the great, 'undivided' nature of creation.

"Lying deeply within us all is the Oneness, wholeness and emptiness. This is accessed by means of portals. Study of portals is a major science for vigilans. These portals exist at the quantum level everywhere—non-locally. They are the thresholds to formlessness. In truth there is only one portal everywhere."

You gesture broadly with your hands. Your facial expressions are captivating me in a way I haven't sensed since we were with the old man in the far future.

"I guess that makes sense. So, when I enter the Void within myself, or perhaps have any transcendental experience, I am really passing through that portal. I sort of get it. Can you explain a little more about how that works and how it is relevant to us now, during the Great Storm?"

"That portal is, of course, how I communicate with you. You have felt it before as a tiny, subatomic point within yourself. This has been described by some of your scientists as microscopic black holes, lying at the center of every atom.

"To repeat myself in other words, it is actually the non-linear, non-local Threshold of the Void itself. There is no distance you have to travel to reach it. You do not have to seek it 'out there' somewhere. It is everywhere—in all space and time and matter. It has no form and, therefore, is not bound by any of the laws of the form world. It is the presence and point *of you* in each manifestation of consciousness. When any creature realizes this point, it awakens—the creature awakens, and the point awakens!"

"I guess I have not truly realized this point yet in myself, since I still have ego reactions. I still feel fear—and, therefore I'm not awakened. Correct?"

"Correct." You grin and lay a hand on my arm. "But you know the path you are on. You saw that path, and created it in your recent vision of the future. You were awakened temporarily, as many humans are now. But then, by following your path to Earth again, you triggered the reset button."

"Yes, I understand now. It was exhilarating and empowering, and then ultimately disappointing." I frown. "You allowed me to witness the process of our first contact. It was a stirring ceremony. Thank you for that. But, of course, I have more questions."

"But of course."

"What I saw—do you call that *technology?* What was happening behind the scenes? My mind imagines some sort of machinery would be needed to travel in time."

"Once again, science-fiction—and your industrial mentality— has led you a little astray. Not that there is anything wrong with science fiction, mind you. That's what you and I are writing together here. Right?"

You tilt your head and almost wink. "It was a useful tool for stimulating and enhancing human imagination. We have forms of entertainment and education similar to it still in our day."

"Really," I inquire.

"We no longer call it 'fiction', however. For our vigilan minds, thoughts and even fantasies are linked to creative power; they reflect factual possibilities and potentialities. If not linked in this way, they hold no interest for us."

"Well then, are you saying you didn't use any machinery for this? And, in fact, do you not have any machinery in your world at all?"

"The machinery we have in physical form exists only to focus our intention and inventive capacities. Yes, we have machines. But they are not like human machines. They are primarily iconic for us, and extensions of our own Life force. They allow us to easily channel our creative energy for particular, applied purposes. The travel map in my house is an example of that. Moving the map pieces initiates the protocol in our psyches and dimensional networks for projecting our forms."

You raise your hand to stop my question. "Here is an opportunity to examine another clue, hidden within the words you commonly use. Look back to the origin of the word 'machine'. The root in Sanskrit is *magh*, which means 'to have power, to enable, to make'. Of course, this is the same root as your word 'magic'. Our ultimate *machine* is the magical, empowerment from Source, within."

"That's interesting. So, how does your transposition technology actually work? Was there more to it than I witnessed in the ceremony?"

"Yes and no. Your deeper being witnessed everything, even though your mind could apprehend only a fraction of what was taking place. The group was functioning with powerful intention, grounded in years of preparation—decades in my case. We built up an intense clarity of Oneness and intent amongst ourselves. This was our vehicle for moving deep into the Now, and the means by which we sidestepped normal functions of time and form.

"As you may recall from the previous book of *Letters*, the way that transposition works is through *repositioning* one time frame upon another. We do not move through time; time moves through us. Transposition is only possible when consciousness is expanded to the intensity of Oneness itself—the Now. Without such an intensity and dimensional offset, lesser laws of physics and physicality prevail. This is our reason for engaging the group entity."

I watch entranced by the slow, graceful movements of your hands and arms. Your short-cropped auburn hair is gleaming from some unseen source of light. "Gathered minds, highly concentrated and embraced by the union of their souls, is a requirement for bringing about the altered physics. Such a union amplifies exponentially our capacities. In this way, we evoke formlessness, non-locality and, finally, timelessness—in that order. It places within our hands, literally, the power to move time."

"Now I understand why you need the group energy for these talks of ours. And your hands seemed to be an important part of the exercise." I smile, gesturing to your hands, still in motion. "What about the hands? And the stone slab?"

"The hands are the instruments of karma—action—and of releasing karma. Joining hands, as you have experienced yourself, can generate dynamic effects. The stone wheel was another iconic representation, intended to guide our attention. The stone itself is not actually anywhere near my house. It is in its true power location in another part of the world—Central America. What you observed was a *projection* of the real object."

"I understand. Is it the Mayan Calendar?"

"Yes, one of them. This one, with much more accurate annotations was discovered after your time."

"Well, that brings up a lot of questions for me. What about the predictions that many in my time ascribe to the Maya? What about December 21, 2012? Is that the date you're referencing as the center of the Great Storm? If so, what's important about it?"

"I will not short-circuit your grand revelation, your Apocalypse, by telling you the details. The *mystery* you are living through today is of utmost importance. Dates are merely pointers. They exist inside the illusion. But they point to the deeper movements within timeless stillness itself.

"Profound mysteries are necessary. They are the question 'why'—unanswerable, but essential. They draw you out, beyond your limitations. But be assured the years around 2012 AD were a very powerful period of transition. These dates, again, are only icon-ic—a projection and metaphor for great inner workings of the spir-it, the psyche and the transformation of our species. It is not a date *in time* that this is all about, as I'm sure you know. It is about trans-cending the illusion of time."

"You said *our* species? I recall something about a 'merger' of our two species in the last book. But I have to say I never really under-stood what that meant."

"Quite simply, our two species realized their Oneness as you and I crossed the galactic threshold into the new universe. That awakening sparked our crossing. I will address this in subsequent letters. I will also illuminate what I have discovered about our new universe, and how it affects the old one. The beginning of it is right here, now. As we embark on its description and exploration, we are *divining* it; we are manifesting its expression in our consciousness and in the physical world. We are literally creating this universe as we speak."

"Wow. Am I really going to believe that?"

"Why not? But remember, belief is not what we ask of you. You may choose *not* to believe, and at the same time you can still *allow*. You may take it into your awareness and resonance without formu-lating any beliefs at all. This is what we ask."

"I'd like to go back to 2012, if we may."

"Which is it? Backward or forward?" You grin mischievously. "Please excuse a little humor."

"Yeah, I'm chuckling. I do appreciate your humor—*any* humor about what humanity is going through these days. People seem to be taking things so seriously. Either they're seriously cynical about the future and the government and the human race, or people sink into serious denial and bury themselves in frivolous distractions."

I continue, "On the other hand, there are those who believe something *really* serious is already happening that will change the world, perhaps destroy it. Conspiracy theories abound. Some be-lieve we're going to be lifted into a higher dimension, and civiliza-tion will start over from scratch there. I guess I can relate to any of those perspectives at times myself."

"There is indeed some truth to every perspective—even that of denial. Your fluctuating beliefs and defensive reactions are well justified. The Great Storm is still, fundamentally, an internal affair for each individualized entity—whether it be a human, a community, or a nation. This is where all resolution of conflict must come. There is much disturbance in the fields for you all right now. It will persist for a number of years to come, well beyond the year 2012 AD. That date, however, was emblematic. It pointed to the end of the age, and to a crescendo of energies spinning out from the galactic core. Most importantly, 2012 manifested the opening of a portal to empower our species' transmutation.

"During that period, the solar system crossed the plane of the galactic equator. This happens every 26,000 years. During such times, the Earth, the sun, and all the planets around us are subjected to acute energetic impacts. On this gargantuan table, the galaxy serves up a cocktail of gravitational and electromagnetic forces far beyond human comprehension. These forces stimulate severe change in all solar and planetary functioning. They are especially relevant to any life form that is ready to shift its evolution. That would include, of course, us."

"One more question, please. Why do you say 'why' is an unanswerable question? Surely, there are times when we *can* answer it. For instance, let's take a simple question. Why does the sun rise? Answer: Because the Earth turns. Isn't that an answer?"

"Indeed it is, in terms of language. But behind the answer is always another 'why' question. Why does the Earth turn? There are many explanations for this—scientific, romantic or otherwise. But an explanation is not the answer to 'why'. It simply illustrates that there is a mind addressing the question. If you would engage the full opportunity of this, you must realize the spiritual and mystical implications. 'Why' opens up the mind into ever-expanding mysteries. These can never be *closed* by a mere series of explanations. Once opened, the mind relinquishes control and passes into the consciousness beyond understanding, and beyond answers."

You get up from your chair and slide it back under the table. It makes a scraping sound against the floor—a very physical presence, I register. It prompts me to ask, "How did you do that? How are you able to move objects in my space, if you are just a projected image here? And how can I feel your touch?"

"You experienced these same effects on your travels into my time. I don't pretend to understand all the physics myself. But, to put it simply, I am keyed into your specific frequency and the objects in your immediate vicinity. When you see me, we're both projected into a sub-dimension—close to the one that is normal to you.

"You and I, and this chair," you clasp the back of it firmly, "are focused in the sub-dimension. This is all part of our shared projection. For the purposes of our writing, I will not visit you this way too often. I would prefer not to distract you from your work," you smile, pointing to my keyboard.

"Bear in mind that a kind of projection technology stands behind all creation in our form worlds. Every form, no matter what its dimension or universe, is a projection from subtler realms. This is true even in the strictly physical sense: Raw quantum energy projects atomic particles, which project molecular structures, which project matter. These projections, of course, tie back through the portals I mentioned. An example of this is the projection technology behind many crop circles and UFO images in your time."

I want to ask about crop circles. But you bow and turn, giving me a look. As you do so, your image morphs into a brilliant orange and silver sphere, the height of your body. You are gone. The sphere remains, and divides within itself. The divisions continue and become moving geometric patterns. It's a breathtaking, three-dimensional kaleidoscope. After a few seconds the patterns stop changing. They hold in a radiantly beautiful design, illuminated from within.

The patterns resemble shapes of sacred geometry—in three dimensional depth and transparency. Now the lines begin to move again, curling toward the center of the sphere, withdrawing like fractals into the hub. As the formations condense, the sphere shrinks with them. Down. Down. Finally the whole of it is but a tiny, bright point of light that dissolves into nothing. I am left alone, smiling.

Letter Thirty
The Void and Formlessness

I'm sitting at my keyboard, wondering if you will come through today.

"Look for a sphere to manifest for you in the near future."

"What? Hello, O? You're back—in voice at least."

"Of course."

"What were you just saying? Look for *what* to manifest?"

"A sphere," you reply.

"You mean the one you left for me last time? That was beautiful! Are you saying it will come back?"

"I knew you were thinking about it. You have a rather clear impression of it in your aura."

"It left an impression, all right," I grin. "Incredible. Why did you do that?"

"I wanted to demonstrate projection and form building as we view it in my time. Images like that are art forms for many here. We inject our own vision and life force into the sphere, and then let go, so it will create its own continuing expression, often in fractals. These forms can be dazzling and amusing to watch, highly stimulating. They bring into the world, geometric essences that nurture and elevate us. I sometimes work with them for hours at a time."

"What do you mean I should look for a sphere to manifest?"

"A small globe of some sort will come to you. Look for it; manifest it."

"OK then. Why would this be happening? Who is making it happen? Are you? Am I?"

"Yes," you say. "It will be a little 'project' for the two of us; manifesting this form will help enhance the communion between our two timeframes. We will build a stronger link, if we do this."

"I'll try. Yes, that sounds fun. Just what should I be looking for then?"

"Notice a small sphere in your environment in the next few days; it will be ours. That will be sufficient."

I'm a little confused. But that's nothing new. I ask, "Last time you implied this sphere had something to do with crop circles. What exactly did you mean?"

"I meant to give you a hint, which is what I did. I will not explain crop circles more than that, except to point out they are projected forms, using the same technology we use to communicate and visit with you. Some of these forms are projected through humans, the so-called 'hoaxers'; some of them, however, come through direct energetic transfer."

"Why does it all have to be such a mystery?"

"Because mystery is a key to appreciation and wonder. Mystery triggers the engine of imagination and transformation. It is the inscrutable unknown that delights vigilans so much. Allow yourself to be drawn into that vortex, my friend."

I pause to take in what you've said. "Just an observation about crop circles, in passing. Part of me believes that people are making all of them—under the cover of night. They are obviously well thought-out and laid down; whoever's making them is doing an amazing job.

"My mind says that only humans would be capable of such things. And yet, at the same time, I realize that this is human vanity—to think we're the only beings with a sense of design or math. So, another part of me finds it *hard* to believe that people are making them all, especially the more elaborate and sacred ones, the ones that appear out of nowhere in just a few minutes. I guess I don't know what to believe."

"This is a good way to be. It is paradox. The two opposing beliefs will cancel each other out. *Mystery defeats belief,* ultimately. All the mystics knew this—even though their *followers* usually wanted to create belief systems around what the teachers saw and reported. They took the messages in the opposite direction; they wanted belief to conquer mystery. This was only because the followers were not awakened; they wanted to have a form to identify with. But the mystics were actually teaching *freedom from form*—through mystery.

"Again, the lesson I would ask you to take from this is that mystery—the unknown—is the great projector of manifested form. Think about what this means. The unknown is what generates all form and illusion. All of what we know derives from what we do not understand and cannot see; light emerges from darkness and sound derives from silence.

"Form is temporary and transient; all projections are creations from subtler levels of awareness into denser ones. The subtler levels are normally not known to the denser ones without some kind of awakening. We must appreciate what lies behind all this illusion, if we would resonate with truth and the subtle nature. We do not need to understand it with our minds, but with our hearts—open and empty, supremely receptive. The basis of all projection then is the Void, the essential formlessness."

"Well, this brings up a question," I remark. "My friend, Stefan, has been reading the first two letters of this book; he raised a concern about the way we are using those two words. He feels that readers may be put off by the concepts of 'Void' and 'formlessness'. They might see them as negatives—even, potentially, generating fear."

"What did you tell him?"

"That I would ask you about them, and raise his concerns with you."

"And what else did you tell him?"

"Well, that the Void itself does not generate fear, but rather it seems to bring our fears to the surface, where they can be exposed."

"Very good. You're learning."

"But I can understand his concern. The Void does seem to be a negative space, especially from the human, physical perspective. It is the removal of all things, all forms. In such a place, we lose everything we have, everything we know. We are as nothing there. It is totally unknown and unknowable. That *can* be fearful, to say the least."

"All right. Fear also can be a stimulus to awareness. The Void does not have to bring up fear, however—far from it. Look back and tell me what you've experienced in your trips into the Void; you've made trips consciously several times now."

"Yeah. That's true. And I have to say, the first time, I felt like I was falling a very long way down a hole in your living room floor. That was a little disturbing. Wait. There were actually a couple of other times before that, before I ever met you."

"Did you feel fear in those situations?"

"Not exactly, no. While I was a little alarmed, there was also a powerful feeling of peace and acceptance in that space—utter still-ness. I remember a wonderful state of vastness and bliss. I felt like I was at the hub of all creation."

"And you were. If you all could but realize it, you are there right this moment—Now—in the center of all creation. That center is the Void."

My mind responds, "Nevertheless, Stefan was wondering if it might not be prudent to say something less threatening to our audi-ence. Why do we have to call it 'Void'? That is such a negation. Why isn't 'Source' or 'Cosmos' good enough?"

"Do you want to know the truth? Or do you want to be cod-dled? Only the ego is frightened of the Void. It does not want to contemplate being without itself, without its identity in the form world. The ego knows it has no identity in the Void. Its world of things is turned inside out. Negation is an issue only if reality is a *thing*. The mind, embedded in the illusion that *things* are *real*, will of course see negation. This is where the fear comes from, where ego leaps in. It comes up from deep in your subconscious minds, brought to the surface by the pure vacuum of emptiness. But, in essence, the only negation here is the negation of illusion."

You continue rhetorically, "How is the Void relevant to our or-dinary, earthly lives? What does it offer us, other than a rather dis-turbing abstraction? Basically and incredibly, it offers you *everything*. Nothing else can do that. It offers you the entire life you live. From its Life comes our very existence. Without this mysterious and, per-haps, frightening presence, no love or wisdom would exist, no intel-ligence or power or manifestation; there could be no awakening or growth.

"Forms *must* rest upon the formless, as paradoxical as that is. There is no form inclusive enough or powerful enough—by many multiples—to contain *all* other forms! It is simple logic then, to conclude that all forms must be contained within something else— some *non*-container. If that something—to use a word—isn't a form, a thing, what is it?"

"It's formlessness. Exactly. I'm sold."

"You suggested we might use the term 'Cosmos'. One might view the Cosmos as a great *container* of all things—hence a 'thing' itself. But rather than containing everything, it is actually the *formless* integration of all things, local and far distant, inside us and out, tiny and expansive. If we consider Cosmos thusly, it *is* in fact the Void."

"You don't have to sell me. I do get it, finally. But let's not dismiss this question entirely just yet. I think there's something more we can learn from pondering it.

"I'm listening."

"If we are to deliver our message in a way that receives the optimum acceptance, then we might want to understand how referring to the Void and formlessness makes people uncomfortable. And hence unwilling to accept what we offer. Do you get what I mean?"

"Yes. And I am feeling good about your intuitive progress. You and Stefan are seeing into this issue with compassion and clarity. You are generating precisely what is needed for this letter. And I would do nothing to dissuade you from your concerns. Only allow me to make again the case for deep appreciation. What you and I are calling the Void is, on the one hand, emptiness, nothingness, *Evam* in Buddhism. On the other hand, this *Evam* is the origin and fullness of *everything*, every *form* in existence—before it becomes a form—and *while* it is being a form. It is the field within which Source enters into existence. Out of this alchemistry derives creation, evolution and eventually *Conscious Evolution!*"

"I asked this in the last book. But how are Source and Void different?"

"As you have pointed out, formlessness is a negation; Void is the ultimate negation. Source is the ultimate affirmation. But it is beyond both form *and* formlessness. It is the Absolute, 'about which naught may be said,' according to the ancient wisdom."

I feel a twinge of frustration at this level of abstraction again. I challenge, "So why try to talk about it at all?"

"Our audience is ready to sense the truth, whatever that truth may be. They are ready to let go of the old beliefs, attachments and false notions. The last 26,000 years have prepared them for this, if for nothing else. Our message is destined to rally and to serve those who are ready to awaken—no more, no less than that. It is fundamentally a message of appreciation. It proclaims the opportunity to look deeply—abstractly—and more inclusively than most humans have ever imagined looking before; then, having looked, one can choose the direction of one's own destiny. In the act of choosing destiny, consciousness is born. The child is awakened, open-eyed and ready to grow out into the world."

You fall silent. The last words echo around my head. Then you continue, "From where I view it, the deepest, most profound underpinnings of Life and consciousness—the spring of abundant waters—is the most interesting and attractive vortex in all creation. It is the center of all that appreciation can touch and reveal. There is no word or name that can adequately describe this wellspring. You may call it many names—non-locality, spirit, God, Allah, the Absolute, Alpha and Omega. You may call it the Void. I *will* call it the Void."

I gulp, "Er, well. I would be happy to continue calling it this, in that case. You know, I think we've covered that topic to my satisfaction. If someone is still offended or pushed away by the sound or implications of this word, then that's just the way it's going to be, the way that it is.

"All right. I accept what is. Nevertheless, I will continue to be vigilant to observe the way we use any and all words, especially 'Void'. I'll do my best to convey my understanding and appreciation of the Void, whenever that subject comes up."

"I love your assertiveness." You smile. "I, of course, will do the same, friend. I, too, will be *vigilant*." Your smile turns to a laugh.

"OK, now. You mentioned our message is to serve those ready for awakening. Is this the purpose of the present book? Could you spell out for me what you would like to accomplish with these new *Letters*?"

"*Accomplishment* is not the result I would choose for our work. Allowing and acceptance is as far as I would go."

"Semantics, I think. But have it your way. What would you have us *accept?*"

"That all this creation is a projection! It is no more substantial than the most delicate, abstract and fleeting idea in the universe. All objects, individuals and constructions are ephemeral; they are patterns of energy and consciousness, woven into the fabric of space. We are each working the threads of cosmic energy, weaving the world *screen*, participating in the creation and evolution of it all. Our awareness of the nature of projections determines how we react, learn and evolve. As we awaken, we unfold the electromagnetism of formlessness and Oneness."

"So, please tell me how we can use the information you're sharing? What is so important about knowing that everything is a projection?"

"I am assuming you are asking because you feel others will raise this query, not that you do not grasp what I mean. *You* do intuitively know. I will say it simply, again. What you project into the world becomes the world. You are responsible for that. We must know and accept our responsibility for creating the world we see before us, what we *project* before us. This is the key to awakening evolution within ourselves. Awakening is what we're up to here."

"Yes. I couldn't have said it better myself," I quip. "Just kidding! So 'awakening' is the purpose of this book?"

"That, my friend, is the purpose of *all Life*. Our purpose, in this writing, is something a little less ambitious. We offer, nevertheless, to assist Life in its natural unfoldment. You will recall that at the beginning, my project appeared to be no more than experimentation with electromagnetic fields of the Earth. As we moved forward, we soon realized it was more than just that. We found we had touched a nerve of deep evolution and beyond.

"Certain forces came awake around and within us. They took hold of our understandings and turned them inside out. It might seem, to a casual observer, that this was mere accident or luck. But no. We were drawn into this like a gravitational vortex—with intention. In the beginning, we had chosen our own purpose for the project. But in the end, the purpose came to life itself, and chose *us* for *its* project. This was a new and deeper revelation of destiny in us.

"There are several ways we can describe our purpose in this work. Time is now running short for the human race on Earth. We, and all of you, must act expeditiously, be clear and concise. There is no time to dawdle. You are moving rapidly into the revelation times—the end of the Great Age. It has been called the Apocalypse! This again, means 'revelation'. There is a Great Storm brewing within the planet. The purpose we have been given is to harness certain electromagnetic and gravitational forces that are already drawing you swiftly forward. Our mission of revelation is to conduct souls through the portal at the eye of the Storm.

"We offer our services, to those who have ears to hear—those who are attuned to this frequency. If there is a resonance in you, dear reader, notice and allow it to be. Let go of resistance, but be discerning. Find your deep authentic being and ready yourself to act. For our part, my group is working to help you all open the passage a little wider.

"First, *see through the eye;* then marshal your inner resources and cross the threshold. Enter the Storm with a sense of wellbeing and confidence. If you remain centered in your true being, you will pass through these times unscathed. In fact, you will pass through with grace and power. You will be blessed beyond measure. The time of that blessing is Now!"

Letter Thirty-One
Resonance, the Key

I turn the page. And there you are, saying simply, "Would you mind coming with me on a little adventure?"

Your words vibrate through my mind like a sudden gust of wind. There in front of me is the sphere again. It's a transparent silver-orange as before, with many circulating shapes and lines—swirling crystal geometry. Then your body begins to appear inside, standing calmly amidst the oscillations. Once your form has stabilized, you lift an arm and reach forward. Your hand breaks through the bubble.

"Please take my hand."

I start, but then instinctively hesitate. "Just where would we be going?"

"Trust me. Let it be a mystery."

"All right. But strange things happen when I hold your hand."

As soon as I feel your fingers gripping mine, I am drawn into the bubble. It surrounds the two of us, much larger than I expected. In fact, the surface seems to be expanding. Or perhaps we are shrinking! Yes. We are now riding a fractal thread down toward the center. Then there is nothing. Blankness.

"What is this space? It seems like the Void. But it doesn't feel that way," I whisper. "It feels, hmm, rather ordinary."

"Yes. It is quite ordinary," you reply out of the dark in a normal voice. "We have shifted into a sub-dimension very near your own. It's one that is completely empty. Nothing exists here. But, you are correct. It is *not* the Void. It's a formless form, a simple and direct projection of the Void. We vigilans often come into spaces like this to begin creative work."

"An empty dimension? I've never contemplated such a thing. Are there many such places?"

"As many as you can imagine. The imagination actually creates them."

"So, what are we doing here?" I ask.

"I want to demonstrate how to create a whole universe from scratch."

"Really? You can do that?"

"*You* are going to do it, my friend. Just imagine making a 'scratch' on the emptiness. Go ahead."

"Humph. This is weird. Make a scratch? You mean we're literally making it from *scratch?*" I hesitantly follow your instructions, imagining my fingernail scraping down a blank screen in front of me. Upon the darkness, a thin, white vertical line appears.

"That was easy." I continue to whisper.

"Now get closer to it. Go right up and tell me what you see."

My vision moves forward at your request. "It's widening and opening, shimmering along the edges. It looks effervescent, like thousands of tiny bubbles. They form the boundary all the way around."

"Look into your creation and keep telling me what you see," you urge.

"There's depth. I can see into it, like space. Something's happening in there." I stare for a few moments, not quite understanding what I'm seeing. "It looks like molecules being created, or maybe atoms. I guess I can't tell the difference."

I'm amazed to see such depth inside the void. Everything outside this 'scratch' is just flat. Inside, the orbs keep popping up, dividing, multiplying, connecting. OK, now they seem to be shrinking, or maybe my vision is pulling back. It's hard to tell. The opening is getting wider. I can see more now. There are surfaces, formed from millions of the combined orbs. They're like waves, sheets of gossamer material. Above is a kind of ceiling, in motion, like the surface of an ocean, viewed from below.

"Wow." A sudden flash of light from above; everything is stirred up and agitated. My voice starts again. "The molecules are shaking fiercely. Sheets of them are tearing and curling, flying all around."

Another flash, and there is more agitation. My vision is rising toward the ceiling. It breaks the surface. *This* is *an ocean*. Rolling waves swell around me. Somehow now, I'm inside this world. There's a horizon in the distance, and on it a sun is rising—just a tiny sliver at first. It is not the Earth's sun, though. It's blue. Everything in this world is tinted with that color.

I can no longer see the edges of the slash I made. The flat emptiness is gone. I'm inside the new world. Another flash of light, lightning strikes the water. Another strike. And another. Thunder roars close by above. Over and again, the lightning pounds the surface. Great clouds roil the sky. Blue rain pours down; the sun is obliterated. I feel the ocean teeming, aroused. It is Life! *The ocean is alive. The clouds are alive. The lightning is alive.*

"I'm feeling an incredible exultation. This is *my* creation," I realize, shouting. "*I've* created this world! Forgive me, but I'm feeling like God here. Whatever I imagine comes to be. I sense the direct link between my imagination and it's creation. This is amazing."

"If you want forgiveness, you'll have to ask it of yourself." I sense you winking. "After all, you *are* God."

"Cute, O. Now tell me what this is all about. Why are you having me do this?"

"I want you to know that you are God. We are *all* God. Now give your blessing to the world you've just created, and come back to me. Let this universe go its own way. You may return at any time to check on its progress. It will always be part of you. It will always draw its projection from your channel of divine energy. In this way you are responsible for its destiny."

I'm again in the void, looking at the scratch from outside. Yet I can still see into it. Rapid evolution is taking place. Already single-celled organisms are forming and multiplying throughout the living ocean. That ocean is shepherding and nourishing its life forms. I send in one more generous blessing and withdraw completely.

Now I'm back at my keyboard. The sub-dimension is gone and so is the orange sphere.

My questions are coming up with force. "So, tell me. Just what is my 'responsibility' for that world I just created?"

"Your essence will guide all evolution within its realm. As your consciousness is, so will be your creation. If you would have your world be beautiful and benign, alert and authentic, then you must be that in yourself. This world will be everything *you* are—with all your personal qualities. So, be good, for goodness' sake," you laugh sympathetically.

"That's no small responsibility!" I cringe. "Why did you want me to know that I am God, O?"

"What a silly question! Who in their right mind would *not* want to know such a thing?"

"Well, yes, of course—a good thing to know. But why is it part of our communication right now? How does it fit with your purpose for this book?"

"This book will illustrate many forms of *projection and creation*, using imagination, sub-dimensions and portals."

You settle into a more instructional tone. "We ourselves are projections, passing up through portals from deeper levels to come here. We begin at Absolute Source, as a singularity, and move out through the field of Oneness; we eventually project ourselves into the duality world. This progression results in the *opposite* of Oneness—call it 'many-ness'. This swamps humans in a morass of complexity, illusion and separation—nothing seems connected; you do not see the etheric web that weaves it all together.

"To the awakened mind, however, this same projection triggers something quite different—the appreciation of paradox. With it we know what is real and what is not. We see the multitude of forms in the Cosmos as *Oneness in disguise*. With a discerning eye—living within the sensation of paradox—we can look straight through all the manifestations of things, right to the Source."

"OK. But that is beyond the capacity of most humans. For instance, my creation was pretty unconscious. I didn't even realize it was me doing it."

"In duality, everything shares existence with its opposite! Each *thing* contains a portal into its opposite. Thus, all forms are linked with formlessness; within duality lies the portal to Oneness. Your ego is constantly *en guard* against that portal opening."

"Really!" I react. "I can see that. Ego wants to be the *one-and-only.*"

"You were indeed working blindly in that little adventure just now. However, you sensed the reality, without having to think about it. That is what we're asking each of you to do in your lives over the coming years: Feel the reality *below* the illusion; feel the formless below the form and the Oneness below the many-ness. I'm saying this quickly and in passing here. But I will elucidate each aspect of it in the coming letters. Take this statement as an overview of our objective. As our group voice declared, 'Oneness is the vehicle we will ride through the passage of the Great Storm.'"

"And just what does that mean? It sounds so abstract and metaphorical for me. How do we 'ride Oneness' like a *vehicle?*"

"Perfect question, my friend. How does one ride any vehicle? It might be a flying device or flying animal; it might be on the ground or in the water. One can ride inside or outside, within or upon. There is one thing in common, no matter what the form. It is that you must give yourself over to the thing you ride. You must trust and surrender, or it will come to naught. At the same time you must take the reigns and direct the vehicle where you would go.

"And what is a vehicle, after all? Let's look at the root of that word. In Latin, *vehere*, means 'to carry'. In Sanskrit, *vaahana*, means 'transport'. A vehicle carries us, when we need or desire it to, when we know how to enter and command it. It lifts us above the plane we have been walking on; it moves us at greater speed and protects us from untoward elements on our path; and it propels us through time. It actually takes on and abbreviates the path we follow, transporting it into its own portal nature. In a word, a vehicle is a *portal.*"

"Great. It all sounds great," I sigh. "But how do we climb aboard this 'vehicle of Oneness'? That still doesn't make sense to me."

"Let's look to one other kind of vehicle for an answer. That vehicle is your own body. It is the vehicle for your soul in this incarnate world. Your soul has projected the physical, emotional and mental bodies into the world, to be *carried* through a lifetime here. Your body is a formal representation of the individuality archetype.

As we discussed earlier, that means 'undivided'. Of course, undivided means 'one'."

"I'm following you, sort of," I murmur. "Are you saying that our individual bodies are symbols of Oneness? That makes sense. But how can our bodies be the vehicles you were talking about? Are they going to carry us through the portal—through the Great Storm? If that's the case, why bother telling us all this? How can we make sense of what you're saying?"

"Don't 'make sense'. Let sense make *you*," you pronounce.

"How does that happen? How do we know what we're looking for? I've gone within my being many times before. All of us have. So what's new here? I've never seen any portal like that before."

"Ah, but you have, my friend. You called it the Threshold to the Void. Others have seen it as the presence of God, the ground of being, or the eye of Vishnu. There are many other names for this space. But names are irrelevant. That so-called Threshold holds all the secrets of the most profound truths of creation—the *Akashic* records. It holds all the portals of Oneness and freedom. They are many and yet there is only one. Right there on the edge, at the brink of creation and annihilation, lies the fundamental portal of truth. There lies the fulcrum of duality verging into unity.

"Look into your body. Sit still and become even more still. Find the ultimate stillness within you. Just for a tiny moment, faster than the blink of an eye. That's all you need in terms of time. Find that stillness and know its truth. Root sensation. Feel its vibration. Lie with it longer if you can, and let it surround you with its shimmering essence. Feel the vibration turn to resonance and alignment. Feel the resonance turn into connection, integration and dissolution of all separation. Feel it reaching out into the Void and into the Cosmos. This is timeless and formless. If you feel it for only a tiny moment, you will feel all eternity within you. It is the form that formlessness assumes for duality's sake. This is Oneness! This is your precious vehicle."

"O, excuse me. But this is getting very abstract here. Can we make it more concrete?"

"I was just coming to that. Thank you. Here's the bottom line, as you humans like to say. The vehicle lies within you—at the 'bottom' of you. It is not in your outer world. Oneness will never be found there, amidst the complexity and *many-ness* of manifestation. Humans have tried for thousands of years to impose Oneness on the outer world. There is no need for this; and there is no possibility of attaining it. The purpose of the outer world is to be as illusory as it can be, to be *unreal*. Let it be as its nature is."

"All right. So, the short version of your message here is that portals lie within us, not without; and the world is an illusion."

"Yes. The outer world does not negate Oneness, however. It *fulfills* Oneness. Christ consciousness said, 'Think not that I have come to destroy the law or the prophets. I have not come to destroy, but to fulfill'. Incarnation fulfills the truth of its Source. It does not destroy the projection, nor that which projects it forth. *Christos* is the soul of us all—'teacher alike of angels and of men'. Thus does all the illusory, outer world *fulfill* the reality and the soul lying within it.

"The fullness and fulfillment do not always appear as you might like. Your outer experience in the world reveals this. Many are trying hard to create Oneness in some outer formation or other, such as your United Nations, your great religions, your New Age convergences. These can be beneficial in their ways. They will not succeed in reversing natural authenticity, however. They will not manifest Oneness where it cannot be. Nature must manifest multiplicity and duality. That is its function and its way. If you doubt me, just look at the millions of species evolution has created in our world.

"We look upon your human attempts at unity and solidarity as icons for inner truth, not for outer transformation. Their creators mean well—all the multitude of them. The more of these unity groups there are, however, the less unity actually manifests; they end up competing with each other. It is all natural, your nature. Know this—*Oneness does not manifest in form*. Its integrity is maintained at the brink of creation. Do not look to your outer, human groups, therefore—as noble as they may or may not be—to be portals for your safe passage through the Storm."

"OK. But are you saying—O and vigilans—you have the *only* way through the portal to the future? This is beginning to sound a little exclusive."

"I am not saying that. There are many approaches. I'm only saying that for them to be effective, they must provide you with an *inward* path of Oneness. Certainly, the way we are offering here is only one of the many ways. These ways appear numerous and diverse in the planes of manifestation; that is natural. Ultimately, they all converge at the portal."

"Why has it taken so many words to communicate this simple message to me?"

"The principles of multiplicity are applying here, I'm afraid," you chuckle. "We required many words in order to build up gradually to this point, to prepare the way for you and your readers to receive the message clearly. Resonance is the key again. Find it in your bodies. It will lead you to alignment with the portal. However, realize this: Resonance, in and of itself, is *not* the portal; resonance is the key.

"Resonance with Oneness is more or less accessible for all humans through their own bodies. You have felt it in your cells and tissues, as a kind of subliminal humming. I advise, first, that you learn to be still enough to feel that vibration. This opens the way to resonance.

"Once you find the resonance, and concentrate on it—in a *concentric* manner—you will begin to feel yourself dissolving, becoming ever more subtle within. Use your imagination to follow this thread, and to plant a seed in this resonant field for the portal you seek. Then stop seeking any further. Allow the portal to draw you *into it*. Imagine this is happening while you are sitting in stillness. It is not difficult to do, because *it is real*. Reality will use the imaginary to draw you into itself. This is, pure and simple—after a lot of build-up—all you need do to enter the vehicle of Oneness."

"You mean we don't have to imagine the Void or the Threshold or projection, or any of that stuff you were describing?"

"No, you don't. All you need do is feel deeply within and allow the opening to come to you. I needed to use so many words though, to give you the sense that this in fact *can* work—and to connect the process with its underpinnings. There will be more details on all this as we move forward with the letters. Rest easy. The passage is opening now and you are near."

"What about ego? Won't it try to defeat our awareness of this?"

"It will. But the resonance is much more powerful than ego. It is pure and profound. If you persist, ego will grow very quiet. This is a process of realizing your true power."

"By the way, O, I found a little sphere the other day, while I was meditating with a group of friends. When I got up, I noticed a beautiful little silver marble behind my chair. Is that what you wanted me to manifest?"

"Yes. The link is strong! Carry it with you as a reminder."

Letter Thirty-Two
Black Point of Light

I'm lying in my bed, very still. The room is dark and I have some soft music playing in the background. I've decided to try the exercise you gave me. First, I will feel the sensation of faint vibration inside my body, in my hands and arms. Yes, there it is. That was easy. Now I feel it in my chest and legs. It's that 'humming' feeling. I lie very still, while random thoughts fire in my mind. Gradually, they calm and recede into the distance. I focus on the vibration.

Now, I take the next step—from vibration to resonance. I'm not sure what the difference is, really. I lie still for many minutes, probing my innermost sensations. Then I begin to understand. I feel it. The vibration sinks down and opens up; it contacts something 'other', something very expansive. This vibration in my body seems to link with the Life force around me; it stretches out into the world and universe. It is the tip of a very deep iceberg.

My mind dreamily wanders the deep, around the globe and out into the stars. Extraneous thoughts start to creep up on me, tantalizing my attention. Stop. I catch myself. The mind has already slipped in again. I watch it raise thoughts that will vie for my attention. *Why does this always happen?*

"Don't program yourself to believe that, dear friend."

"O, you're here again. I was trying to do this without you."

"If you assume this will 'always happen', it will—especially in such an impressionable, meditative state. Be cautious not to plant beliefs in your subconscious that do not serve you." Your voice disappears into silence. Then, "Would you like me to go away?"

"Well, uh, of course not. You're welcome anywhere, any time with me. But are you now monitoring my thoughts?"

"I knew you were trying the exercise; so I tagged along. I couldn't help but read that thought because you entered a subtle level of awareness. Do you mind?"

"No, no. Not really. I just wanted to do this alone, so as not to bother you. I know communication between us takes a lot of your group's energy. This seems like such a trivial matter."

"It is hardly trivial. This exercise is the point of power for you, and for us all. Our shared destiny is activated by coming to this level."

"What level? I don't think I was anywhere but in my mind. I got lost there."

"Not true. You caught yourself. And in that realization you moved deeper. You are now very near the Threshold. Look around; feel around. Your mind knew you were here. That's why it tried to distract you. Just go a little deeper now and you'll see what I mean."

At your suggestion, the stillness seems to pull me more into itself—from the inside. Every cell and molecule of my body moves in unison toward the center of being—deeper, smaller, into the tiny-ness. I flow into a field I know very well, though I haven't visited it for some time.

It feels like I'm floating in a spaceship over the surface of some vast, featureless planet. But this is no planet; there's *nothing* here. And yet I know viscerally that this is not the whole truth. In paradox, *everything* is right here. For the first time, I sense the power of the Void, the potentiality and endless rapture of it. It is the essence of literally everything in the universe, in all times of creation. I find a new appreciation surging through me.

The understanding comes up into my heart and mind. We conscious beings have an intimate relationship with this emptiness. We draw not only our Life from it, we use it for anything we choose to manifest. We are the creators. The Void is the raw *non-material* out of which we create materiality. I sense that without the creative impetus of consciousness, this space would remain forever inert.

I imagine the Void as an infinite lump of clay. I break off a chunk and hold it my hands. It is Life, full of potentiality. By moving it between my fingers and pouring my vision and intention into it, it takes on form. It moves out from formlessness. The clay begins to breathe. Life becomes alive.

I look from the form back into the formless and see the power that derives from it all, the power that enables us to be creators. There is no separation except that which lies in the capacity of appreciation itself. My mind suddenly boggles: *Appreciation is the origin of separation.* And to come full circle, appreciation must now become the agent of Oneness. It is all a magnificent shell game. The grandeur I feel both humbles and exalts me. *How can this all be so intimate within me?*

"It is beautiful, is it not?" your voice whispers me out of reverie.

"Yes. Wonderful... blissful. The peace and power transfix me. I could stay here forever. I hear your voice, but I don't see you. Where are you, O?"

"I'm not exactly here. I can watch through your eyes right now. You and I have a unique bond, I'm sure you realize. Your appreciation is like a beacon to my awareness."

"Were you tuned in on my last thoughts there—about appreciation and separation? That seems almost blasphemous. Can it be true?"

"You *are* surprising me, friend. That insight of yours is worth everything. You know now how it all works! 'Blasphemy' is just another word for paradox. Appreciation, paradoxically, is what indeed stirs the creation of separation and form. That's why it's the key to awakening—the realization of *non-separateness.*"

"Thank you. I am in awe, truly."

"Hold that feeling in your heart. However, now let's return to your purpose for coming here. Remember, the exercise?"

"Oh, yeah. I got distracted. It seems easy to forget things here."

"Ah, but it is equally easy to remember. In fact all memories, of all times, come here to incubate."

I turn my attention to the resonance again. Immediately it's all around. It has continued to tug my little spacecraft along. *Where are we heading?* As I stare into the spaciousness, ephemeral forms emerge and dissolve. Colors, like rainbows, solar flares, swirl in the abyss. *Am I creating them with my imagination, or are they real?*

"Allow me to answer that, if you don't mind."

"Sure. Speak up, Madam Orange, mind reader."

"At this sacred level of existence, our consciousness behaves in ways not possible on the physical planes above. We are so near the fields of dissolution and insemination of form that we can feel the breath of Oneness itself upon us. It infuses our duality with direct creative and intuitive presence.

"What this means, practically, is that whatever we encounter here, we create—in the very act of encountering it. To encounter means to create. But, be mindful, I speak not of the little, individuated self. It is the collective, universal being in us. We are blended almost entirely with the universal here. If we were any more merged with it, we would lose all independent orientation. You know this from your past experiences crossing that veil."

"Yes, quite. But does that mean I'm just making up an arbitrary illusion when I see something down here?"

"Illusion, yes; arbitrary, no. All forms are illusions, as you know. Your powers of creation in this place are totally synchronized with 'what is'. Look there. See the points of light coming this way? *They* are your creation. But at the same time, they have been here forever. You and we, in all our transcendent glory, have just now created them in their forever-ness."

"That doesn't make the slightest bit of sense. But I get it somehow."

I see lights, like stars, coming toward us across the greater field. Or perhaps we're moving toward them. I guess there's no difference. Beyond them lies the inscrutable, silvery emptiness. The lights are arrayed in clusters mostly, though each has a slightly different form and presence. As I look more closely, I see they all have different shades of color and texture, different auric fields.

"I know what you mean while I'm down here, O. But I'm afraid I will lose this understanding when I go back to the surface."

"That's just the way of it, my friend. Sacred awareness requires sacred space. This is where peace becomes your understanding."

I'm beginning to sense more forms out there in the field—like openings to other worlds. Even landscapes and cities exist here, I feel. There are many beings that seem to inhabit this plane. *Who can they be? Angelans,* I guess. *That would make this place a form of heaven.*

"You will come to know more of this very soon. Some of it you already know," you whisper.

The clusters of light stream nearer. The resonance is apparently guiding me to one cluster in particular. I approach and am in the middle of it very quickly—inside the circle, surrounded by a dozen points. They are all various shades and hues—tan, green, orange, blue, black. Yes, one of them is a *black* point of light, strangely enough. I can't describe how this is possible, except that I must be *feeling* more than seeing it. The resonance has increased hugely in this cluster. But I still don't see why I was drawn here.

A very long, peaceful moment passes. An ardent joy wells up in me. I'm watching intently. Suddenly a human body appears before me. It's just there, out of nowhere, just floating serenely. Then, shockingly, I realize it's my own body. This is eerie. I look into my face closely. My eyes are closed. The apparition appears to be sleeping, arms at its side, breathing peacefully. This is like an out-of-body experience; except my body is hovering over me. *What is this?* You remain silent, though I know you're listening.

OK. I'm here for a reason. Yes. I'm here to plant a seed for my portal. *What kind of seed? Is this the place? Where else would it be?* I decide to be still again—even more still than before. Silent stillness. It dawns on me: There is no end to how still one can be. And, likewise, there's no end to how still *Oneness* can be! This is it. I know it. This is my portal to Oneness, floating right here in front of me. All I had to do was be still enough to know it. My body is the seed—or at least the image of it.

So, what are these other points? Black? How can there be a black *point of light?* I know in an instant whose portal this is. As I gaze at the point, I see Black's form emerge—just a shimmery impression, barely visible. Quickly I look around at the other points. Each of them is a member of your group, with an apparition floating around it like an aura. I get it. I look around at the orange point and see your image materialize slowly, lightly. I look at your eyes. You blink and dissolve away to near invisibility. I turn back to my own body. It still hovers there. It has no point of light like the others. Its eyes are still closed. But the form has become more visible, with a distinct indigo hue.

I know inwardly that this is where I must plant the seed. *But is this my portal? Why don't I have a point of light like the others? If this is my portal, can I pass through it into the future?*

"Not so fast, my friend." Your voice is forceful. "You have prepared the field for your seed. But recall what I said. You all must wait and allow the portal to draw you into itself. There is more work yet to be done before you are at that stage. You are not yet *allowing* enough. Let us unfold this in you over the coming months."

"But I don't want to wait that long," I whine. "Why can't I just allow it from here, right now. This is the timeless *Now*, isn't it? Why didn't my point of light appear?"

"This is indeed the Now. And the Now will tell you when you are ready. You must be patient. As long as you see the Now as separate from yourself, the Oneness has not yet arrived. Relax. Your portal will appear, and you will plant the seed, when you have released some important limitations from the past. It is your destiny now to reveal and release them. This is your Apocalypse!"

Your image appears again out of nothing, and takes my hand. Suddenly Black is with you this time, holding your other hand. All our forms are ghostly apparitions.

"Come with us, child." Black reaches toward me with her empty hand.

"*Child* is it? All right. OK. Whatever. Say, why are you both here?"

"Don't let this go to your head," you smile. "But I don't have the same talents as you. I still need some help coming to this level. So I asked Black to bring me along." Black smiles into my eyes with a soft ferocity.

Despite her eyes, she speaks warmly, "Welcome back, brother. We have missed you in our hearts and minds. Thank you for returning to our destiny."

"How could I not return?" I grin. "It's sure good to see you too, B."

She continues, "You always have a choice, my friend. The first book of *Letters* could easily have been the end of it, at least for your old universe. The initial intention was fulfilled there. Now, because you are willing, and since you have come freely to this holy space, there is a deeper intention." Black brushes her long white hair from her face and gazes into my eyes.

I sense something is happening, but I don't know what it is. My impulse is to try and distract her, to regain my composure. "And how about the *new* universe? When are we going to talk about that? Just what's it all about?"

"We will satisfy your curiosity about that soon." B answers. "But that time is not now. Suffice it to say, we are all more open in that universe and ready to move swiftly through the Storm. We will set a pattern—a projection pattern—to be sent back to the old world from the new."

Your face floats close to mine. Your eyes look deeply into me. "Right now, we want to propose a little trip together, since we're already in the Threshold."

"Yes." Black resumes. "In fact, we three are the only activated members of the group at the moment. Remember, three is a magical, manifesting number."

I glance at each of you and say, "I *knew* there was some other reason for you both being here. Wait. What did you just say? Three members? You mean, I'm a *member* of your group?"

"Of course. What other group would you be a member of?" you laugh.

"Well, it just never occurred to me. I'm honored, O. And Black. Thank you."

I sense you're both ready to move me along. "But I do want to know more about the new universe, when you feel like telling me."

I take a deep breath. Silence. "So, where are we going?"

"Into one of your past lives—a major one, to be sure," you state flatly.

"Really? Why would we do that?"

B replies, "We all have some important unfinished business there."

"All right. So, which lifetime is it?"

Again Black answers, "The one that still holds the contract with your ego."

"The *contract* with my ego? What the hell is that?"

"Hell is just the right word for it!" she mutters. The two of you laugh. I, for my part, begin to grow anxious.

Letter Thirty-Three
Place of Memories

"Where are you, brother? You've disappeared."

I hear your voice. *But I can't see you. I'm in darkness. Is it another empty dimension? Or is it some kind of limbo?* I try to speak, but no words come, no sounds. I drift for a long time, not knowing my own senses. Fear.

"Where, where am I?" I shout at last. I hear my voice echoing from a thousand miles away.

"Here he is." It's Black's voice, very softly, very near. I look, but see nothing.

"B, if you're here, please help. I'm lost."

Then before me in the darkness B's shape appears, blacker than the darkness—but only slightly. I see only her faint silhouette—black on black. She whispers, "Take this."

Projecting from her is a shiny black disk. It floats slowly toward me, toward my heart, and seems to flow into my body. *Do I even have a body here?* Suddenly a jolt of unformed awareness rocks me from head to toe. I know I just received something. But what is it?

"Relax, friend. You are safe. The awareness will catch up with you slowly. Allow it to unfold at its own pace."

"B, where are we? What's going on? Why am I always in the dark?" I sputter.

Laughter erupts all around me, at first just from B. But then, your voice joins hers. The laughter seems to be carrying me back into the light. Gradually, I'm with the two of you again. The Threshold is as it was, spreading out infinitely over the Void. I look to you, furrowing my brows. "What was that?"

Still brimming with mirth, you reply, "It seems that you slipped away a bit, inside some kind of ego bubble. It was a sudden, blank sub-dimension, yes. You certainly had a strong reaction to our last suggestion."

B interjects, "We must be on the right track, I would say. The ego is very tender around this. We shall have to proceed with care. That disappearance was very interesting. It took me quite a while to find you in there, child." B smiles comfortingly and pats my hand.

"OK. I guess I'm a bit jumpy."

Your voice comes in, "Yes. You *jumped* right out of this dimension. Let it be a caution. As talented as you may be at shifting levels, you have very little training. These shifts can come upon you without warning. Be mindful. And *we* must work with you. Black will take the lead, of course." She nods at you and smiles, still amused by my predicament.

"So, tell me, B. What was that black disk you gave me?"

"It is a what we call a 'seed-link'—a complex of thought forms and stimuli that you can receive into your being in a quick dose. I think it is a 'download' in your human language. These seed-links open up into your awareness gradually, when you're ready to receive the messages contained in them. They also can contain portals that link you to other thought complexes, ideas and dimensions."

You look intently at me. "This one will be important as we proceed on our little journey, I sense. Connections and understandings will open up to you as you need them. Do you feel composed enough now to continue?"

"I think so. But can you please be gentle with me?"

You both laugh again. B answers, "Another thing about the seed-links: They sometimes have minds of their own. Pay attention to where they come from. In your world, there are many with strong negativity attached to them. In the disk I gave you, there are several layers of protection built in."

I frown. "Are you saying I'm going to need protection?"

B continues, "You can summon it when you feel you need to, or it will open for you on it's own if you get into trouble."

You assure me, "You will be in no *real* danger. Nevertheless, you may feel apprehensive at times. Black and I will not be with you in there—at least not in the way you might expect. You will be on your own for the most part."

"In where? Just where is it I'm going? I seriously don't like the sound of this, O."

Black pulls lightly on my elbow, distracting me from my resistance. "Come, it is time."

We move away from the field of clusters, somewhat horizontally. There is a sensation of great speed and yet slow motion. I see a horizon ahead, and something else. *Is my imagination making this up?*

"Yes," you answer my thought.

"What is that out there? If I'm making it up, why don't I know what it is?"

"That's a very good question. Maybe you should ponder that in a meditation later. You're making this up as we are, as *it* is. This form has its own life and individuality, to be sure. But what your awareness makes of it, will be the form that fits most accurately into your own nature and conditioning."

"Wow. Do you see that?" What I see approaching us is grand and beautiful. The first impression is of an enormous glowing cloud. There are multi-colored filaments, arching up and cascading down like light-curtains. It could be a mountain range or an undulating forest, radiating light from within. It sits silently in the emptiness. Within its iridescent surfaces are shimmering eyes, like peacock feathers.

"Yes. We see what you see, through your eyes," Black whispers next to my ear.

There are innumerable openings in the surface—like glowing caves—that become visible, as the mountain range gets nearer. We float up to a very large one. The entrance is well over fifty meters in diameter. And the space has a floor to it now. We float down and stand upright on it, as if there were gravity. The space is awesome—huge and glorious! Great corridors wind off and disappear into far distances, all around, above and below, levels upon levels.

Everything is slightly transparent, but solid enough to walk on. So we walk. Strolling past a long, delicate filament, ornate with tiny spheres of pastel light. I gasp, "This is so beautiful. I can't believe it. Is it *real*, O?"

"As I've explained before, it *is* real. However, you are making up the form it takes. Someone else might see this quite differently. Black and I are seeing it as you see it, because we have entered your imagination. The form is indeed beautiful. You are an artist, my friend."

I stare into the caverns, all illuminated from within. I feel as though the illumination is inside me as well. When I look, I see this *is* the case. You and Black are shining with the same light.

"This is all *your* vision—based on your deep, unrealized appreciation," B confirms. "We are here to reveal what is yet unrealized in you."

And now I see something else that surprises and delights me. There are angelans here! *Am I making them up too?* They are suddenly visible everywhere—or should I say *invisible* everywhere? Their shapes are so subtle and transparent, that they blend almost completely into the multi-colored curtain walls and peacock feathers. I see them and yet I don't. *How curious—to see something that's not there.*

"O, Black, what is this marvelous place?"

"It is the Place of Memories. In Sanskrit, it is called space, ether, *Akasha,* or the Akashic Records. Within these indestructible halls are portals to all the universes and dimensions of time, creation, and space."

"Impossible!" I cry. "All creation? All here in this one place?"

Black answers, "Each of the tiny globes of light is a portal in time and space, held as what we call memory. But we are in a near formless space here. All memory and action, from anywhere is *Now.* We have access to all living experience in this place—as long as some consciousness somewhere is living it. Reach out and touch one of the lights with your finger and see for yourself."

And so I do. My finger does not stop at the surface, but passes inside. Suddenly, my whole awareness is pulled in. I find myself floating in space above an alien planet. It has great rings like Saturn, except they are interwoven on numerous different planes. I am inside a glass bubble. Outside, great rocks are hurtling past at high speed. When I turn to see where they're coming from, I'm aghast. A gigantic form, looking like an animated, green starfish, is throwing these boulders—at me! Just as I begin to feel alarm, I notice a small point of light on the bubble surface. I waste no time in pushing it.

"I'm back. Thank God! Black, what was that?" I'm standing again between the two of you next to the strand of light balls.

"That, my friend, was someone else's lifetime. I, personally, have no idea what or where that was."

I exclaim, "You mean to say that we can just pop in and out of anyone's life memories like that?"

"Well, you just saw it for yourself. There are *some* limitations. Did you notice the glass bubble?"

"Yes. What was that about?"

"When it's not your own memory, there is normally some device to indicate it. The device your mind chose was the glass bubble."

"All right. That makes sense. But how do you ever find your *own* memories here? There must be billions of trillions of these little globes."

"Quite a lot more than that, actually. We are here to show you one particular lifetime. The angelans are the keepers of this place. They will find that memory for us."

"I thought the angelans were inaccessible to you vigilans."

"Not at all. We interact with them when there is a need. This is such a need. Our limit is that we cannot travel in their world."

Now there is a very tall, gossamer figure towering over the three of us. He or she—I can't tell which—is indicating we should follow. I suppose Black has communicated our intentions already. The angelan goes out silently ahead, flowing like sheer drapes in a light breeze.

"Do they ever speak?" I whisper to B. She smiles back, but says nothing.

We slide easily through the great space—down one long hallway after another. The walls and spaces vary considerably from one cavern to another. A few are dark, and inscrutable. Others are cheery and joyful, full of active feelings. Still others resemble wide-open landscapes, with rivers and mountains, full of nature. Most commonly, however, the caverns appear as gardens of light. There are occasionally other people here and there as well. They seem to be researchers, or perhaps just tourists.

We do not tarry with any of the visitors, but move swiftly toward our destination. Here now we have entered an area of rather gloomy aspect. A sense of foreboding is palpable in my throat.

"O, just what did you mean by a 'contract' on my ego? I've never heard of such a thing."

You chuckle, "Not a contract *on* your ego, *with* your ego. For each of you humans, and for any being with a dominant self identity, there is one particular lifetime where the ego becomes a master of its domain. For all other ego-bound lifetimes, it establishes the reference point for expressions of separateness in incarnation. It is the holder of the key to unlocking ego's grip on your mind. It is like a contract the ego has made with your soul."

"Well, isn't that just swell! What do you propose to do about this contract?"

"We can do very little for you in this matter. But *you* can do much. We are escorting you to the bridge. You will make the decision whether to cross it or not. If you do, you will enter one of your past lives, and discover for yourself the contract you have made. In fact, you are making it still to this day."

At last we halt in what resembles a shaded, box canyon. High above, an arched roof and many stalactites, glisten. We have arrived here through a veritable maze of alleyways and warrens. This cavern is a dead end; it has no exit save the way we entered. Black steps aside while I creep forward into the gloom.

"You certainly have our best wishes and intentions to back you up." B smiles serenely—like a coyote.

Letter Thirty-Four
Elders

In the center of the cavern, we come to a halt. I gulp deeply, a sweat breaks out on my astral forehead. This hall is one of the darker ones. And before us is literally a bridge. It sags to one side, as though bearing the weight of an eternity of neglect. It crosses over a dark ravine, deep, empty and lifeless. Where is all the beauty I saw everywhere else? I suck in a deep breath.

"Well, I suppose I must cross this alone. Right?"

"Not entirely. We will wait here, on this side. The angelan will go with you. Call on her if you need any help in there."

"That's good to hear. She's a female then?" I quip, trying to be cheery.

"Who knows? I'm just projecting." You stare straight into my eyes, smiling, and squeeze my hand.

"Remember to use the seed-link once you're inside." B pats me on the chest, reminding me of the black disk she lodged there. She then pushes me forward onto the rickety bridge. I stumble and the angelan grabs my arm.

"Thanks." I look up into the impassive, compassionate face, glowing with a divine fire. A soft twinkle in the eyes tells me more than I can process right now. This is a being I can trust implicitly. No judgment, no distance; in fact, no separation.

Together we cross the divide. If anything, it's now getting darker. Near the end of the bridge I see a scraggly branch, hanging low out over the abyss. There is but one dim globe on it. I know instinctively that *this is it.* The light pulses slowly, erratically, almost glowering; it seems to have been waiting all these years for this encounter. I gulp again. *Am I ready for this? Whatever* this *is?* A voice comes up from the abyss into my brain and tells me, *"It is time!"*

Glancing quickly back across the bridge, I see your shadowy forms planted, unmoving. I turn and slowly, hesitantly, press my finger into the pale bulb.

Instantly I'm in another world. A marble temple, with high columns open to the blue sky, surrounds me. The marble is white and translucent, like alabaster. The floor is a pattern of black and red stones. All is suspiciously tranquil. A subtle fear washes through me. I'm wearing colorful robes of red-orange and gold silk. On my hands are large gold rings with many jewels. I know this place. I've had dreams of being here before. This is a past life, for sure. I shudder.

My large, robust body reclines on a wide, ornamented bench with many soft pillows. I sigh and feel my presence melding with the personality of that time. For his part, this man seems to be momentarily aware that I have invaded him. He—I—jumps to his feet and looks around warily. I am now fully *him*.

I shout to the house soldiers. "Who's there?"

A very tall man in metal armor strides forward from behind a column. Long, blond hair cascades around his silver breastplate. "Your excellency?"

"I felt someone, something. You didn't hear that, Arithne?"

"I heard nothing, excellency." The captain stares impassively. An aged servant now appears and stands a respectful distance behind him.

"I don't like this. Something's wrong. Call Mestiphius," I command.

The servant scurries away on his mission, without a word. I walk to the edge of the outdoor room and peer around one of the wide columns. Below is a garden courtyard with lush vegetation, paths and fountains. Beyond that and below, the city lays spread out like a coarse-woven blanket. Knotted threads weave into patterns of bulk—streets and squares, alleys and markets, green parks and blue waterways. Beyond the city wall, the land reaches out to the south in a broad agricultural plain. The grid-work of canals recedes into the far distance. I am uneasy, even though it is a peaceful scene.

I recall how Mestiphius has warned me repeatedly. He is wary and does not speak directly to me of negative forecasts. He knows my temper. Still, I am aware that he has seen our imperial state in decline. He believes that the persistent earthquakes foretell a great cataclysm that may be bound up with my ambitions. I cannot allow his version of the future to prevail. Besides, he has been wrong in the past. He *must* be wrong this time.

The earth tremors are signs that we must act now to claim what is ours! How can we not be victorious? We have a far superior force. There is no doubt. The world, to the east beyond our shores, is weak and impoverished. My generals and troops are well tested in numerous campaigns. They are ready for battle. The war clans to the north have long been seeking our movement. I have visions of glorious conquest—treasure, power!

The clearing of a throat interrupts my musing. "My lord, you sent for me?"

In the entry way stands a grizzled old man in dark robes. Mestiphius. His hood is low on his forehead, but I can see his black eyes shining nonetheless. I don't trust him. And he doesn't trust me. I sneer. But he has been useful to me.

"Yes, I did. There was a sound, a feeling."

"Sire?"

"I heard something, like something came in here." I realize I'm clutching my chest, and immediately throw my hands down. I don't know. Damn it. Can't you rattle your magic bones and tell me what it was?"

The priest bows and reaches into his pouch. In his hand I see the sorcerers' bones. He raises them to his forehead and whispers an inaudible incantation. He then throws them to the floor. They sparkle with light as they bounce and tumble. I watch, feeling anxious. Suddenly he lifts the dark hood, exposing a ghostly white visage. His brow is knitted tight above the sunken eyes. His mouth is open.

"What is it? What do they say?" I pant.

He hesitates, not looking up. Finally, his shallow rasp of a voice rises. "They say that you, my lord, are... uh..."

He refuses, at first, to speak further. I grow impatient, and erupt, "What! They say I am *what?* You imbecile."

"Sire, the bones say you are *possessed!*" he blurts out in a nervous rush.

"What?" I cry. My temper flairs. "How dare you suggest such a thing! What is this nonsense?"

The vizier cringes and steps back. He has seen my temper many times. He knows I hold his life in my hands. I grimace. A heinous thought crosses my mind. How I love making people feel pain and fear, watching them cringe and squirm. How I love the power, and the force of will I press upon them. This is a delight to me! I feel a surge of pride and arrogance. I am in my prime—physical, mental and political. Few are the men who would dare challenge me.

And yet, right now, something *is* different. *What has changed? I am the one feeling fear. What is this?* An impulse Almost makes me draw my sword and separate this crumpled old man from his head. My hand is on the hilt. But—a presence is in me, holding me back, staying my anger. I shout for him to leave.

"Say nothing of this, or you will pay dearly. Go."

I dismiss the hapless creature from my thoughts. I will gather my generals. We must act soon. The war plans must go forward in full fury, before the moment is lost. Another anxiety suddenly arises in my mind. I still need the formality of approval from the Elders. I've been avoiding that convention for weeks. *All right,* I growl to myself. *This must be dealt with straightaway.*

I summon my palanquin. Servants scurry about, bringing me sandals and the mantle of my authority. As I stride down the steps to the street, soldiers are at my side. They glance at me with typical apprehension—and rightly so. I am a most ruthless and relentless master. My mind is quick and hard. I never compromise.

Ah, my mind, I muse, climbing into the ornate carriage. My pride flushes. Part of me is observing from a distance. The pride I associate with my powers of thought almost makes me swoon. *It is a powerful machine, this mind—so clever and deviously brilliant!* With it I have risen above the masses, above the teachers and scholars, equal to the generals and courts and priests, indifferent to the law itself! I am full of my own illustrious self—full to bursting. *No one can take this destiny from me!* I gloat.

The Temple of the Elders is not far. We move quickly through narrow alleys and broad avenues. In minutes I arrive. We enter the Great Square, where I have delivered glorious speeches in the past, to assembled citizens and leaders of society. A delicious recent memory takes hold of my mind. I was standing high on the palace steps, roaring in my strong, persuasive voice. Below, in the square, was half the population of the city. They were cheering and chanting approval for the violence I am inciting in their feeble minds. Their passion stirred me to grant them a blessing. I dramatically raised my arms overhead and shouted an incantation I stole from Mestiphius.

As the words congealed in the air around me, I swept my arms down and around. Out from my hands flowed an orange mist. It rose out over the mob, hovering; then it descended upon them all. The dust blanketed everyone, seeping into them as they breathed. Their voices rose into a frenzy, screaming and cursing in malevolent delight. I continued to rant and bend the crowd to my will, conducing them to demand the blood of our enemies, to demand the fulfillment of empire! "It is our *destiny*, and we must claim it."

The palanquin moves roughly across the cobbles; it jostles me back to the task at hand. At the base of the grand steps, I descend from the car and march up the stairs. My entourage stops with me before the huge wooden doors—symbolically one of the few remaining obstacles to my ultimate power. Arithne pounds heavily on the thick, imposing wood with the butt of his dagger. Silence.

They make me wait. It's not the first time. *I will not forget this when my ascendancy comes. They will change their song when my army returns victorious. They think they're the only voice for the gods. But they're wrong. The gods have spoken directly to me more than once.*

At last the portal creeks open, only wide enough to allow me to squeeze through. This is all designed to insult and anger me. I seethe, thrusting the doors wider, with strong arms. The great hall stretches back into darkness. I see three figures at the far end. There are Beneth, Sarites and Morjiln. *The other four are absent. Why?* That is the question in my mind as I stride up to the dais.

"Your august highnesses." My voice scarcely disguises its contempt. "Permit me audience. Where, may I ask, are the others?"

"We knew you would be bringing your anger with you, Levati-col," Beneth speaks solemnly. "The others chose to remain in chamber. We are here to represent them and to hear your request."

"This is less than the respect I am due, your eminence. But I will proceed. As you know I have marshaled our generals, our armies and navies, and gathered our allies among the northern cities. The time has come to claim a grander place in the world. I am persuaded that our nation must act soon to maintain the advantage foretold in the heavens. This is the time we must go out and place our yoke upon the world. The hour of our glory is at hand."

Sarites, the old man—clearly past his prime—speaks in a withered whisper, "Levaticol, you still have given us no sound reason for expanding our nation, or for subjugating other peoples. The world is at peace. Our citizens are content within our islands. We already have a grand nation; and we have good relationships abroad. Why do you say we must send forth our navies? What do we need of empire?"

I am not pleased to have to explain this once again. "It is our *destiny*. The gods are indicating that our civilization should be established abroad. The many earthquakes of the past decade are speaking to us of this destiny. If we do not heed their message, they will grow worse, until they destroy us. Ours has long been the most advanced nation in the world. Primitive tribes populate most of the eastern mainland. They live in wandering clans or isolated city-states. But more than this, our national prosperity and prestige demands growth across the sea."

"You are thinking of your own, *personal* prosperity and prestige, more like it!" Morjiln challenges. "And just *which* of the gods has indicated the path of empire that you and your cohorts advocate, administrator?"

She dares to call me that? I grimace and shout, "The prophets of old have adjured us to go forth and prosper abroad!"

Morjiln raises her voice to match mine. "Nonsense! We have heard no such prophesies, Levaticol. You distort the truth to achieve your own aggressive ends. Only you and your cohorts dream of empire. And let us be clear. The Elders are the speakers for the gods. Not you! You exceed your authority. Call off your war machine before it is too late. No good can come of this for the islands of Atlantis."

My fists tighten, and I laugh menacingly, "It is already far too late to call this off. And no one stands in our way. Certainly not you, little woman!"

The three Elders rise in unison to this insult, their long black robes forming an imposing sight above me. I feel a tinge of apprehension. Quickly I force it down. I replace the feeling with outrage, as I watch the three old ones turn to leave and dismiss me. *I cannot allow this.* I feel heat rising to my face. *No one can treat me this way!*

In a fit, I spring upon the dais and bar their passage with my large frame.

"Administrator, you are out of line!" Morjiln exclaims.

"There is no such thing. *I* will define the lines." I sneer indignantly, pushing her back with force. The other two rush upon me, in a vain attempt to restrain my force. I swiftly repel them with powerful arms. Enraged, I pounce on Morjiln. *Let this, then, be the end of it.* I declare to myself. I grab her throat in my hands. *I will silence this impudent voice once and for all!*

"Stop at once," commands Sarites. But his words are frail and rattling. "This cannot be. This can never be. You cannot defy the gods and the Elders in this way."

I ignore the old man, and stare upon my prey. All pretense has evaporated. "You will die, hag. Here and now!"

My large fingers press hard into the soft, white tissues of her neck. I am beside myself with wicked ambition. Strangely, Morjiln does not resist. She seems to absorb my fingers with mystifying plasticity. My hands should be tearing away her flesh. But instead I am witnessing a calm smile, looking up at me with profound pity. A small black disk suddenly appears out of the medallion at her throat, between my hands. *What is this sorcery?* In a flash, it has surged forward into my chest.

My body begins shaking like a mouse. I look desperately around and see the other two holding their hands aloft, invoking the gods. A potent shaft of fear severs my being in two. The universe rips open. Losing control, I find myself writhing on the floor uncontrollably. Retching myself up, I spin around and flail my arms. I have now two minds, in one body. I remember myself at last. Levaticol is stunned to find me here; he somehow realizes I'm from another life. We both know that we cannot survive this way. We must reconcile or die.

At the moment a battle is raging. Two dimensions are pressed together within me. I cannot yet stop what is about to happen in the old form. In that universe, Levaticol rushes upon Morjiln once again and finishes his grizzly task. In the end, all three Elders lay dead on the dais. Blood drips from his sword. Even Levaticol realizes the odiousness of the crime. But, for him, there is no turning back. He rushes down and across the hall in furious abandon.

Now, however, there is another universe. I am its arbiter. I must come to my senses—and to my own redemption. I call upon the angelan—who at last I remember—and force myself back to the heinous scene. She is there immediately, hovering over. I ask, with all my heart, for forgiveness and for a redressing of my folly.

"Forgive me, Morjiln. Elders, all, forgive my trespass. I humble myself before you." I fall to my knees, head bowed, weeping. Suddenly the three are alive again, healed of their injuries. The angelan stands tall above us all with arms spread wide—a full three meters wide! Golden energy radiates from her hands, down upon us. The Elders look at me, silent, struggling to their feet. They turn to the towering figure, and bow. *This is a god to them,* I realize. I look at each Elder's face. Immediately I see into the distant future. I see that Morjiln is an earlier incarnation of Black. Beneth is you, Orange. And Sarites is the Old Man. *I should have known!*

Now, as I stare, humbled and defeated, and yet miraculously released, there is another, deeper healing rising up. I feel it stretching up and out, far beyond this sorry, little lifetime. It moves swiftly into one life after another, swinging like a needle and thread sewing a new garment. With each stitch I am asked to repent from my ignorance, separateness and pride. I am being asked to join this mantle of opening, beyond my empire of ego and little mind. I eagerly accede, again and again—endlessly it would seem.

Then, retuning to the life as Levaticol, I bear witness to the unfolding remainder of that incarnation. Flying at a near distance overhead, I watch as his forces sail forth upon the sea, and then sweep across the continent. He lays waste to cities and towns, pillaging and destroying as he moves. Easy victories are to be had at first.

But this story is being told in two parts now—his and mine. In his, he is still intent on establishing the empire. But he is deranged, defeated already from within, though he does not recognize it. My universe is prevailing upon his, undermining it at key intervals. His fierce and fiery victories turn to ashes in his hands. The land is too extensive to be occupied and controlled in the way he has imagined. His force is weakening with each new conquest. In each battle he has fewer soldiers to marshal and is farther from home. To make matters worse, a civil war has begun back in Atlantis.

At last, near the end of his tether, he encounters a foe more formidable than any before. A great and bloody battle begins; it continues for over a year. Levaticol is finally defeated. He must withdraw, and begin to face the inevitable. Athenian forces chase him across the Mediterranean, all the way to the Pillars of Heracles, decimating his armies with each progressive month.

The once great navies—mightiest in the world—are reduced to harried bands of exhausted survivors, scrabbling in darkness over land and sea. The high administrator at last slinks back to his island homeland, utterly broken. His remaining warriors disband wearily into the hinterlands. Levaticol retreats to the northern mountains and tries to hide himself within the clans who now oppose the southern cities.

For the last time, I enter the body of this ancient self. I feel his profound anguish and, yes, even a measure of remorse. As this man, I live furtively in the mountains for many years, a miserable exile and fugitive. However, in the end, I am discovered and carried back to the ancient city of temples in the south—a criminal in disgrace. I am brought again before the Elders. This time the circumstances are very different. Morjiln speaks sternly to all the crowds assembled before the temple, where I once held sway. Her voice is at one with the gods.

That voice is thunderous. Its message is not a pleasant one, neither for me nor for the citizens of the nation. The gods are most displeased by our collective actions, by the civil war and national divisiveness, by the ambition to empire. There will be enormous prices to pay.

"Levaticol," she declaims. "To you, the gods direct a special distinction. You are condemned to judge *yourself.* No other than you knows the inhuman depths to which you have descended."

Without ceremony, I am struck down from within my own heart. My anguish feels boundless. The judgment is indeed left to my own soul to determine and proclaim. Swiftly it comes. It appears as a curse upon myself—never again to possess a pride and intellect such as this vicious man has had. It has led to vast death and chaos, and has left his destiny in ruins. Within my own full, disembodied consciousness, I decide, for recompense, to condemn my future incarnations to be weak-minded and powerless, living lives of service and subservience, for the span of thirteen millennia.

But I have not acted alone in all this. The whole consciousness of Atlantis affirms for itself a fate not unlike my own. Incomprehensibly, our collective choice, directed from our own gods, is to be *forgotten* from the face of the Earth. The time span of this oblivion will be the same—a half turning of the Great Zodiacal Wheel, or 13,000 years.

For my part as the former high administrator, I am now an outcast, shunned in my own land, far and wide. The nation descends into shame and denial, still battling itself. Clearly, our days are numbered. In the final vision of this devastating lifetime, the earthquakes have become convulsive, in every corner of the planet. The intensity increases; and fires rage across the skies. For months, comets and meteors fall and decimate our world. They return again and again, relentlessly. All civilization is perishing, collapsing into itself before our eyes. At last, my nation, my body and all my sense of self, are swallowed up whole, into the Earth and the tormented, angry sea.

Letter Thirty-Five
Not Finished

I sit bolt upright in bed, gasping for air, cringing and cowering as though objects are falling on me. I'm terrified and shaking. My body is twisted inside and out. Many minutes pass while I try to calm my nerves. I slip out of bed and stumble to my studio. I'm in shock, staring out the window into the night. Barely conscious, I finally turn to my keyboard and begin typing.

"O, help! Please." I stop and look into the screen numbly. It sits blank and empty on the desk; a gentle whir is my only answer. Silence surrounds me in a menacing way. *Was this just a nightmare?* I shake my head and lower it into my hands.

I hear a faint whisper in my mind. "Come back."

That is all. No more impressions, no urge to write anything from you. I listen and remember the words. They don't seem to make any sense to me. I'm so confused, bewildered, wrenched within by the experience in the Akasha. *Was that really Atlantis? How could that have been me? No!* And yet it felt so real—almost as real as being here. I'm still divided between two lives.

Again, a whisper, "Come back. It is not finished."

Now I know what the voice is saying. I shudder. *How can it not be finished? I died. Levaticol died. It's done! I'm done! I don't want to go back!* I resist with all my might. But then a softer, humbler part of me notices my predicament. Within my separated, divided self, I reach down and take pity; I offer comfort to the cringing entity that is my ego-mind.

"I forgive you," I mumble. Then, with essence rising, I say it louder. "I forgive you." Again and again, I repeat the words and the sentiment, with the growing force of my soul.

In a trance, I stumble back down the hallway to my bedroom, back to the portal and the Void. Lying on my back again, my eyes closed, I sob. Tears stream down my temples. I cover my eyes with my hands and moan. This continues for a very long time, until I'm exhausted, purged of emotion. At last I sense a lightening, a feeling of freedom and gentleness lifting up through me. I sink down into it—a feather falling through clouds.

"So, you've decided to come back, eh?" You smile. You and Black are standing next to me in the Hall of Memories, back across the bridge. I look at you both and shake my head. Then I glance around over the bridge. The lone branch is still hanging there, with a single globe at the end. The color seems to have changed though. It's brighter and greener, but still slowly pulsing as before.

"Where is the angelan?" I ask. Before the words are out of my mouth, I realize she is standing directly behind me. Her hands fall onto my shoulders. I feel warmth coming into me. Her touch is healing and refreshing. It is a totally selfless gift, detached and without judgment.

"Thank you, all," I stammer. "You know, this was a most disturbing experience for me."

"We understand." B caresses me with a steady voice. "Be assured; we had a good reason for putting you through it. We only smile at your distress because we know the deeper side of these events. We know your soul guides us all in this revelation."

"So, please enlighten me," my voice grumbles. "Just what does my soul have in mind? What was the reason for showing me that past life? And what does it have to do with the Great Storm or with anyone else who might read this?"

"The Great Storm is within you all," you answer. "As you know, it projects out visibly onto the screen of your incarnate existence. But it all starts and finishes *within* you. All the dire and disturbing manifestations you witness in the world around you are projections of your own inner Storm. All humans are experiencing this together in your time."

Black's voice is firm. "Many still deny it and try to live so-called 'normal' lives, however they can. They erect elaborate façades and distractions, holding onto a hope of stability and 'business-as-usual'. But your species right now is bewildered and adrift inside. A great disturbance is plaguing you all. The more you refuse it, the more you *seethe*. But the more you accept it, the more you *see*.

"Look at the body politic. It does not yet see. It wrestles and contorts, divides and retches within itself, turning rapidly one way, then the next, never satisfied. Rage lies constantly just below the surface at all times. That rage erupts like a human volcano when the forces escape containment. And the foundations of civilization shake. The species body is nearing the point of no return. All humanity must remember its ego contract—the bargain it has collectively *made with the devil.*"

"The devil? What?" I ask. There's a sudden chill in the air of the cavern. And now a breeze moans against the walls and crevices around us. B's long, silver hair and jet-black robes rustle and curl. Crimson patterns in the fabric are like dark flames to my mind.

B speaks crisply. "The devil was created by *you.* It is the embodiment of your species' pain, the dark-side projection of you all that has become the essence of your evil. But paradoxically, this devil is also your own *soul* in deep disguise. Your essence takes on many guises in its quest to capture your attention and awaken you. Be aware that the vast scope of incarnation, and all the glorious, grueling and horrific dramas played out through it are an elaborate charade. It's all a wonderful, anguishing spiritual game of your soul's evolution, and of Source itself upon the physical domain. The Great Storm is the time for *seething and seeing* through the illusion. That is the Revelation and the Apocalypse!"

"I don't get it. Maybe I don't *want* to get it. Please tell me why we have to have this contract, this deal with the devil, as you call it."

"You know well the answer, son." B replies squarely.

"But wait. Are we making a deal with the devil, or with the soul? Who holds this contract anyway?"

You answer now, "It is all within you—the soul, the devil, the contract. Clarity only comes from opening up the whole game inside your appreciative faculty, and seeing it for what it truly is. Separation is the nature of the game, the contract. Seeing the *illusion* of separateness, seeing through it to your own soul, brings down the whole house of cards; it dissolves, and fulfills the contract. That is the grace of it. But this realization does not come easily, as you are experiencing now."

Black continues again, "Your soul has manifested all that you encounter here, all that you desire. What humans desire, they desire in separation, for themselves exclusively. They are possessed by their own *possessiveness*. It drives your race into deeper and deeper separation from the Life of nature, from your own essence. Your species is on a mission and a destiny, to explore and experience the farthest reaches of division and separation, and ultimately, to experience the depths of desperation. All creation on Earth, and beyond, is being subjected to your quest for separative might and control. Conquest! Desperation is the thing that will bring you back."

"Bring us back? How could it do that?"

"I'll get to that in a minute, " she continues. "In the meantime, your species has put evolution itself on notice. The urge to separation is never satisfied. It *feeds* itself into ever increasing hunger. There are those within your ranks who found they could use it to push themselves into supremacy over all other humans. They have manifested a controlling elite, throughout the world. At first it was an evolutionary experiment-in-progress. The question was, How much separation can we create? How expansive can we make our creation? How divided can we become?

"Over the ages and sequential incarnations, these separative ones began to take on the *body of pain* for the entire species. Deprivation, mistrust and fear are great tools of separation. The separative elite became intoxicated with their experiment. In order to maximize the pain, they grew to oppose all progress that did not result in further division. This opposition eventually came to be antithetical to all evolution, and to Life itself. Hence," she pronouces very slowly. "Evil!"

I shudder at her words, glancing around the dark cavern. Long tentacles of clustered globes hang down from the rugged ceiling far above. They sway in the wind, and pulse ominously. A roiling mist rises up out of the abyss as Black speaks of this subject. Somehow I know these spheres are the memories of millions of malefic lives. They are the likes of my Atlantean self.

Her voice rises again. "There seems no power that can restrain their rapacious greed. They have manipulated their way toward controlling all the wealth and resources in the world. They influence all governments, all religions and politics. They seek to control all information entering your minds and emotions. They, being drunk with so-called *power*, have come to think of themselves as gods. *They* decide who can live and who will die, who can starve and who will consume—and *be* consumed.

"The mongers of separateness decide who will go to war and who may remain apart from it, in arrogant disdain." B continues with passion, spreading her arms toward the hanging tendrils, "They have even enflamed those who oppose war, crafting intricate strategies of deceit and divisiveness among the minds of all mankind. In the name of peace, they have learned to forge opposition and rancor. They have maneuvered themselves into control of finances for endless war, by enabling all parties—both for and against everything. In their lordly remoteness, they contrive to never allow any side to actually *win* in the end. They only want *war* to win. They invented war—the greatest device of separation ever to be imagined—and have amassed enormous control over Earth systems."

"I *don't* want to imagine such things. I don't want to think about them, B." I gather my folded arms tight against me. The wind brings the mist closer. The light of the cavern is ever dimmer.

"You and most humans! And *they* don't want you to imagine it. They want you to dream the illusion, and remain asleep. In their secret enclaves, these separative ones, brokers of a broken world, have their own vicious, horrid dream. They choose to become the *embodiment* of human evil. And this is not confined, alas, to only one period of history. Such hubris came again and again into the ranks of men, perpetuated through incarnate bloodlines. It happened in all ages, at the brightest and the darkest of times—even in Atlantis, at the height of human spiritual-mental development. And it rose to a crescendo again in your own age—at humanity's *lowest*, most material-mental ebb."

"This is an awful story you're telling, B. It sounds so hopeless."

"We understand," you interject with a more soothing tone. "The root of the word 'desperation'..."

"...is 'separation', right?" I react sardonically.

"No. It is *desperare,* which means 'to lose hope.' Humanity needs to lose the hope it has founded within the illusion. You need to be driven to this state before you will be open to new options, beyond your ancient 'projected' world."

I shake my head, not quite getting it. B smiles and resumes, "Let me answer your earlier question now. Here is how desperation can bring you back. At the lowest ebb of spiritual awareness in your civilization—where you find yourselves now—something is different. Something is stirring in the depths of your being, forced by the loss of hope, and the loss of connection with your authentic being. You have been pushed and pulled to the extreme limits. An awakening, an enlightening, is coming up out of the profound darkness. It is rising with a silent fury that cannot be heard by the deaf and dumb, darkened minds of your race. The remote elite cannot feel it; they have cut themselves off from such sensitivity.

"But the stirred-up force of being cannot be suppressed by that handful of heart-denying, compassionless men. They stand for darkness and negation of heart, with their strange, perverted *ill-lumination.* The force that is rising is deeper than all material might, beyond the cleverest comprehensions of mind."

I try to catch my breath, and notice that you, O, appear to be amused at this lengthy diatribe from your mentor. "All right. I'm getting it, B. I can clearly see what you're saying about my past life. But what about that 'deal with the devil' you mentioned?"

Black raises an eyebrow. "Yes. Back to your past life. Atlantis fell under the spell of your age-old collective contract, though it was a beautiful and marvelous civilization. The likes of it had never before been seen on Earth—and never since, in that form. The Atlanteans possessed technologies of both heaven and Earth—land, sea and sky. Its people were strong, intelligent and comely, inventive and refined. Their culture lived for ten thousand years in peace, harmony and productivity.

"But alas, in the end they could not rise above the perennial nemesis of humanity. The ego grew beyond their understanding or control. It slowly wove itself into the fine fabric of their culture, as surely as it has in every other expression of *homo sapiens.* As mighty and high as Atlantis had risen, equal to that was the inglorious

depth to which it sank. Its curse was to devolve into ruin and dissolution for the ages. The great Golden Age of humans was forgotten
to the histories of man, relegated to myth, conjecture and doubt.
Barely was it remembered even in the heart."

I glance up at the angelan, and wonder what she must think of
this discourse. Her expression has never changed from that of detached compassion. Just looking at her, I am filled with wonder. *But
I do know what she's thinking!* It's a thought of service and appreciation. We are embraced by it, thoroughly.

I turn back to Black. "So, you're drawing a parallel here? Are
we, my modern civilization, like Atlantis? Is our fate going to be like
theirs? Just what are you telling me about the Great Storm? O has
implied, before, that we could move peacefully through it, if we stay
centered and authentic."

"Indeed, many are making such moves. But far greater numbers
are *not*. They are laggards, deniers and worse!"

B places her arm around your shoulder, looking squarely, magically, into your eyes. "Your first book of *Letters* laid the groundwork
for understanding this predicament."

She turns her gaze back to me. "But now is the time to realize
what the Storm means to the power structure of your world. My
friend, you are living through darkness rampant, the extremities of
desire for power out of all bounds. Fear is coursing in your cultural
veins. The forces of night are upon you in full measure. They are
hell-bent on thwarting your evolution into shared consciousness. At
the same time they, in their sanctimonious ranks, are disturbed and
confused as never before. They are unconsciously beginning to
sense their fate. But still they would rather deny, and project their
fears upon you than to let go and face the truth. They do not want
to believe their illusion could ever crumble.

"They shout within their minds, 'How dare these mortals challenge the gods?' But gods they are not. And *mortals*, you are not!
They have promulgated and lived their own lies for so long they
cannot see truth when it stands directly in front of them. There is
no truth for them. They do not recognize the tide sweeping up and
over. For thousands of years they have ruled and exercised their
raptorial will upon the enslaved masses."

Now the mists have gathered all around B in a large swirl. The tendrils of lifetime memories, arching down from above, are pulled toward her words. These words are like incantations to them. I think of the old saying that 'demons are summoned by the mentioning of their names.' Black, iconic to the color of her robes, is invoking the darkness, drawing it into her aura. It is as though her being is breathing it in for some deep purification ritual. Banshee screams and siren songs echo faintly from within each globe on the vine, heralding B's summons. I'm glad the angelan is with us. I sense you are too.

"These incarnations of greed do not feel the earth sinking beneath their trembling feet. They clutch to their bloody treasure, and will carry it avariciously with them into doom. They now, in your age, are secretly building underground shelters for themselves, expecting that the Earth will protect them from the Armageddon they have conjured. Little do they know that the ground does not *want* them. Their ignorance blinds them to knowing that the Earth is alive. And, rather than shelter them, it is ready to *devour* them."

"Holy cow, B. Those are strong words!" I exclaim. I gulp and breathe. "But I understand. What I don't get is what you mean about these people holding the contract for our collective ego? That's horrible. What can we do about this?"

"What indeed?" You step in front of Black now and look me in the eye. I feel the magic that B must have transmitted to you moments ago. "Just what has been learned over all these many eons of human adventurism? What have you, my friend, learned from encountering your own ego contract? In this parable of separation we can see a fractal image of the whole. Please follow us."

Suddenly I'm frozen. Your words have raked me into stillness. *What's happening now?* The Hall of Ancient Memories dissolves away. We're floating free again, above the Void. The field of clusters is returning. I'm paralyzed, carried along by your intent. In moments we're hovering in our cluster, seeing again my body there. I stare, fascinated and a little disappointed with the way I look.

"There is someone in that past life of yours you didn't recall earlier. We'd like you to return and meet with him. We want you to realize that you did not act alone in your avarice."

I start to protest.

"Don't worry. This time you'll be fully conscious of yourself in both worlds." Black assures me.

"Do I have a choice?"

You laugh, "You've already made the choice by being here."

"Outstanding!" I groan. "Do we have to return to the hell... I mean, the *hall* for this?"

"No," you smile sympathetically. We can induce your memory from here; you've made the bond."

Black reaches forward and touches my forehead with one finger. Simultaneously her other hand is on the top of my head. "This seed-link will help."

"Just relax and follow my words. Close your eyes. Sink down. Down. Back. Under..."

Before I know it, I'm in the body of Levaticol again. But I am still aware of myself this time. The old administrator is haggard and worn, much thinner than before. Clearly I have returned to a time after the war. I search his memories and realize the authorities have not discovered him yet. He is in a tiny room in a cottage in the mountains. With him is Mestiphius, the oracle.

"I need to see Allamorath," he is saying emphatically. "It's extremely important."

The old wizard is bolder now, less subservient. "I don't think he wants to see you, administrator. In fact, I know he does not."

"Have you seen him recently?"

"I have. He is very busy with his own affairs. He must find a way to defend himself before the Council. That will be no trifling matter."

"He's the high priest. Why should he have to defend himself before *them*?"

"Things have changed. You would hardly recognize the governor's palace. Everything's in disarray. Everyone is suspicious, plotting. No one can be trusted. And you know they're searching for *you* high and low."

Levaticol looks down and swallows hard at his next words. It comes at enormous expense to his pride. "*Please*, Mestiphius!"

The aged one cringes in surprise. A grisly smile creeps across his lipless mouth. He does not answer immediately. "Well, 'please' is it? Perhaps... I might be persuaded to do one last favor... *my Lord*." He drags out the last two words with years of pent-up contempt.

Now my vision flashes forward. Mestiphius is leading Levaticol down a long, arched colonnade, somewhere in the City of Temples. I am floating slightly above. Obviously, he has been smuggled in. He is wearing a long, brown-hooded robe that does not fit well. It drags across the red cobblestones, catching on uneven edges. He has to pull up the fabric above his ankles at intervals just to walk. His dignity is in shambles. The two hooded figures slink along, down long steps into another hall, buried beneath the great building above them. More gigantic columns, supporting high arches, retreat into the distance in every direction.

Suddenly, there is a faint sound behind them, a light footfall. He turns and catches a glimpse of someone disappearing behind a column. This is dangerous, he knows. Has someone followed them?

"Hurry," he commands in his old, impudent voice. Mestiphius ignores him.

"Is that one of your people behind us, wizard?"

"It's probably one of the High Priest's men. I spotted him several minutes ago."

It seems interminable, this journey into the bowels of the temple. They file down a narrow, winding stairway. Finally, at the crypt, he sees a dark silhouette in the torchlight. It is Allamorath. His shimmery white and tan robes are familiar to me. The bargain has been kept—at least thus far.

"Greetings, excellency. I am indebted to you for this meeting."

The blond man does not smile. He is shorter and younger than Levaticol. But he appears to have aged considerably since their last meeting. He grimaces at the site of his old associate, and whips his long tresses aside.

"I know why you have come, administrator. And my answer is 'no'. There is nothing I can do to save you, or your fortune. Your properties have long ago been confiscated or sacked by the rabble. Indeed, probably by your own troops—such loyal followers." He continues to snicker for a time. Mestiphius stands back, in the shadows, but Levaticol senses he, too, is sneering.

"Wait one moment, Allamorath." Levaticol summons yet some fire in his belly. "You are the one who started all this. You're the one who convinced me the value of war! You promised we would be rich beyond measure. You said it was our destiny to spread the empire." His tone changes abruptly. "You *owe* me, priest!"

"I owe you nothing! You were all too eager to seek your own personal gain. Do you forget you cut off communication from the field, once you had a few minor victories? I know you were thinking of a *personal* empire. You actually had me worried for a while," he chuckles sardonically. "But when I heard of your mounting problems, I knew you'd taken on too much. And you had no idea what was happening here at home. The unrest and bitterness were tearing us apart. We had little means of suppressing the rebels, thanks to your taking the army away. And there is still no end to it. Matters grow worse by the day. All the old ways are gone."

Suddenly the solid rock floor vibrates and groans. It shifts perceptibly back and forth. The giant edifice above rattles like a heavy, breaking sky. All three look alarmed. Then it is still again. Silent.

"This is happening more often," Allamorath mutters, looking up into the large stone slabs of the ceiling.

"Let us finish this then, Levaticol, and get out of here. I cannot help you. I can barely help myself. But I will see to it that you escape the city once more. I will keep that promise."

He grimaces, as if reconsidering. "I'll do it. Though there's nothing in it for me. Go. Hide yourself wherever you think you can. It makes little difference now. My pity is upon you."

The priest hands him a bag of coins. "These may yet be worth something to you. It is all I will offer."

On an impulse, I decide to intervene, from across the millennia. I take over Levaticol's body and voice. "Hold on, comrade. You must know something else about this matter before we are done."

The ground gives another lurch under our feet. I approach Allamorath, pulling back my hood. "Look into my eyes. See who I have become. I speak to you from ages in the future—some thirteen thousand years. My crimes have cost me greatly over those centuries. I have come here to settle this account with you. Now!"

"What nonsense is this? What dark magic are you conjuring, you pathetic wretch?" he says defiantly. But I can see the fear in his eyes. He sees something in mine that he cannot deny.

Sensing his weakness, Levaticol surges up in me one last time. He grabs the priest's collar and pulls his face forward. We smell his breath, close. Mestiphius' running steps echo loudly as he disappears into the dark. There are other footsteps as well, but I pay it no mind. "You will listen to me now. It is time. And then it will be done! Once and for all!"

Allamorath is speechless, helpless in my grasp. I am feeling my own power from deep within. Inside me, Levaticol steps aside. My soul speaks. "You have been living a lie. You and your cohorts thought you had power. But you only had what the people allowed you to take. We all naïvely surrendered our integrity to you. Without the people's sovereign power though, you are nothing. Without the hypnotic trances you have always pressed upon us, you can no longer persuade us, or control our minds.

"I must say that your kind are living again in my own time. In that future, they are attempting the same lying game of unbridled greed and control. But you will not succeed this time! We are reclaiming our power, here and now! We are leaving you behind, in the prison of your own making."

Allamorath struggles, but cannot free himself. I am in the body of a hardened soldier in spite of its gauntness. The priest shouts, "Guards!"

"Guard this!" Levaticol shouts with authority, taking over in a brief rush. He slaps the priest across the face with his fist. He crumples to the floor. No guards are coming. My mind flashes on the spy who has followed us. *Is he here? No. He fled with Mestiphius.* I smile wryly. It was the wizard's man following us after all. I feel indignant.

In that moment I know my own ego is flaring again. I stop and release it. It is clear, by comparison, how much stronger my ego once was. Slowly I manage to center myself and bend down, with my knees on the cobblestones. I bow before the man I've just struck down. I feel a profound humility embrace me, radiating from me. It washes over us—the high priest and me, with my ancient incarnation. Here now, I suck in the last of Levaticol, absorbing him into my being.

"Allamorath, I have come such a long way to seek you out. I did not know I would ever find you. I did not know I would even *need* to find you."

The helpless man lies on the floor, looking up at me in fear. He mumbles unintelligible words. I realize now he thinks I will kill him. "I'm not going to kill you, old comrade. I will do nothing to you. Our fate awaits us all soon enough. But I will offer you something—an insight. Perhaps you will not recognize it yourself for thousands of years. But here it is. *You are a soul!* You are my brother, a brother of us all, in a dimension where we all have come from. Let this awareness be a seed I plant in you that will take root and grow at its destined time. And, for what it's worth, I *forgive* you!" To my mind, this is almost an afterthought.

My eyes soften and stare into his. He is incredulous, absorbing my words, but not understanding. My soul speaks. "It is finished!"

I release my gaze from the fallen figure. I don't know what effect my words will have. But I have spoken from my heart across the gulf of time. I have performed my destiny. Suddenly I remember the blond man in your group from the far future. His face beams with wisdom and gratitude through a timeless space.

So, the images fade and disappear. All the memories are sent back to their distant origins, past and yet to be. And I am returned here, to you—O and Black. We stand for a moment in silence.

"Well done, my friend." You grasp my shoulders and bow. "Welcome back. A most satisfactory conclusion."

B is also smiling at me. I shrug, thinking, *I didn't do very much.* She continues, picking up my thought, "It may not seem like much right now. But small gestures ripple out into large effects over thirteen centuries. Simple forgiveness is magical for any who would find their own heart in these times. May others witness this and know that within them lies the humble power to open grand portals!"

I turn my eyes to the cluster of lights with its transparent body images, floating. I see my own body, lying serenely within the circle. A force I've never felt before suddenly seizes me. It feels like I'm *exploding* inside. My scope of vision has become enormous. There we all are—and me with two bodies. Yet I am as grand as the whole Cosmos. I embrace it all, as a child would hold a tiny doll. The great and wonderful Cosmos itself is but a small plaything to this vast awareness I have become.

"Amen!" a distant, intimate voice commands. Then within the greatness, I witness every human lifetime I've ever had, from humble and brief to high and mighty—peasant and queen, soldier and seamstress, thief and priest. There are more than a hundred such. I don't count. They hang like tiny globes on a single, winding branch of the *Akasha.* But each globe is its own world. Each has virtue and integrity, with contributions to make to my countenance of now.

I see the births and deaths of each life, the bodies of each. From all the wide array of individualities, I draw these bodies before me. I gather them in, layer upon layer, all of them. They fall together, inside one another, and begin to fuse into a single form. My divine vision is directing them to meld—from the many to the one—*e pluribus unum,* I am.

I sink back swiftly into my witnessing self in the cluster, standing between the two of you, compatriots of soul and of incarnation. My one, fused body now begins to twinkle with many tiny lights— one for each of my lifetimes. From every corner and molecule of translucent flesh they move toward the heart. The lights converge and turn into one bright point of indigo light in the center of that floating body. It gleams like a homing beacon.

I know now that my portal is ready.

Letter Thirty-Six
Body

I haven't said a word to O or B in several days. The events of the past few letters have turned me inside out emotionally. Something is very different, and I'm not sure I like it. The memories keep resurfacing whether I'm asleep or awake. Actually, I'm not sure which it is sometimes. *Is this a reaction to the portal I opened? Was all that just a bad dream?*

My mind has been running non-stop, flooding me with strange feelings and questions. Somehow I've remembered the silver marble in my pocket. I finger it absently as I think. *Just what is a portal anyhow? Is any of this real? If not, what part of me is generating the fantasy? Who can I trust? Does the future really exist already? Am I receiving real messages or am I deluded? Where is the truth?*

"It is right inside you, friend."

"Uh-oh. O, you've been listening to my thoughts again! I thought you wouldn't do that."

"Well, the way your mind is these days, it's hard *not* to listen. I don't want to pry into your private time, but I am aware that you are injecting a lot of resistance into your life right now. You're broadcasting it in all directions."

"Yeah. I agree. I don't seem to be able not to."

"Would you like some help with that?"

"My first reaction—admittedly an ego reaction—is to say 'no'. But now that I've said that, I know I don't mean it. Resistance just keeps forcing up inside me. I *do* want you to help. I just don't want to believe it's possible."

"What's possible? Do you mean my help, or *me?*"

"Both, I guess. This is so strange—talking to someone I can't see and whose existence I can't prove. And it's doubly strange to be explaining all this to that person."

You respond, "I'd say it's triply strange because, in addition, you feel comforted by that person's communication. You feel soothed by my presence. Am I right?"

"How did you know I was feeling that? Are you reading my emotions now too?"

"Yes. They're actually much easier to read than thoughts. I can feel your relaxation and calm when I help you."

"All right. Yes. When you come through into my writing, I always have a feeling of warmth and truth. I mostly don't know if what you're saying is true or not, but I know that it *feels* right. In fact, O—and I'm not saying this to flatter you—just now as you interrupted my thoughts and started speaking, I felt that deep peace inside. Just having you paying attention to me makes it better, like there's some *order* again that was missing."

"I understand. You asked the question, 'where is the truth?' The answer is 'within', always. Bear in mind it is *your* truth, not necessarily that of others. To go within and feel that truth, you need some calm and order. So, I'm supplying that. My observation of the human condition has shown me you cannot always supply that for yourselves. It's hard for you to stop reacting unconsciously and resisting what is, even when you realize you're doing it."

"Ain't that the truth!"

"Well, let me commiserate a little. I am feeling what you're feeling right now, and it isn't pleasant. The energies of the galactic crossing are very intense in your time. It's no wonder so many humans are frenetic and self-destructive under the pressure of it. The forces streaming out from the galactic center, and pulling back in, are irresistible now."

"So, tell me something, Madam O," I interrupt. "What can we do about it? I've heard this stuff before. But we seem almost powerless in the face of it."

"That's what it wants you to believe. But beneath every powerless situation there is a vacuum that accesses the deep recesses of power, Source power."

"What do you mean 'it' wants?"

"The forces of *disempowerment* have taken on a vast, complex personality across your world. They have become an individuated 'self'. It is a body of intense negativity and selfishness, to be sure.

Nevertheless this is, collectively, manifesting the energy of *divine* resistance."

"Wait," I react. "Now resistance is *divine?*"

"All things are divine when seen with 'divine' vision. All contrast is divinely designed. Step for step the darkness and the light must dance. Both have summoned up the emergency together, in response to the awakening of evolution on Earth, and by the surging galactic tide. The interplay of it all is gargantuan. It is sending out psychic-etheric waves, far beyond little Earth. The Great Storm of your world is becoming a grand, multi-dimensional attraction, cosmic 'high entertainment'. Species of many, many stripes are being drawn to this vortex, to witness the passing of the age. This has been such a potent event that it echoes strongly still in my time."

I rub my forehead. "All these waves and subtle influences, webs and streams and nets, crisscrossing one another, falling into vortexes, these things are making me more than a little crazy. How much can humanity take?"

"You will be able to take just what is given—just that, nothing more, nothing less. Remember, *you* are giving it to yourself in essence. What is to be done, will be done, is *being* done, as we speak. Destiny Now. The great game of *Conscious Evolution* is afoot in the Earth system. The waves from the Cosmos are provoking excitement in every individual and object in the entire solar system, great and small. They impact every planet, every nation and people. They touch deeply to the Oneness level, where you are all one people, one presence. These forces and fields, particles and waves, will continue to impact you mightily for some years to come. This condition happens for our planetary system only once in twenty-six millennia. So, it *is* a big deal!" Your smile is evident.

"Yeah. I hear you. But you're not the one having to live through these times." I smile back with a glower.

"Very few can maintain continuous balance amidst this kind of onslaught. The pressures aggravate the emotions and sensibilities of all creatures. This is the case for humans in particular, because you are the species most in need of evolutionary transfiguration. Time itself is caught in the energy flux and will soon be spinning in free fall. What can an individual do to maintain some equilibrium in the maelstrom? In the first book I gave some suggestions. But since then I've noticed it is not so easy for you to follow them, as simple as they are. The galactic forces are too disorienting and distracting for you."

"Well, maybe the suggestions were too abstract as well," I proffer. "It's not that they don't make sense. They do. But in the moment when I get distracted, or submerged in the tumult of daily life, I find it hard to put them into action."

"With this in mind, I'd like to give you three more suggestions, designed to address the situation you describe. I'll do my best to bring them down to Earth and make them more resonant with the forces you have to contend with right now."

"That sounds good. I, for one, could use some grounding. Will this help us understand portals better too?"

"Yes. That's using your intuition, my friend! It leads directly there. You will see in a moment. All right. Let's start with the first tier again—*noticing*. Notice, this time, with your *feelings*. Feel them. *Really* feel them—just as they are, whatever they are! In any situation of difficulty, do this first. Then realize that your feelings are actually located *in* your body. Please give me one of your feelings to use as an example."

"Uh, I'd say irritation at small annoying things around me. Is that what you mean?"

"That will do. Say you're feeling irritation. Something is annoying you. Perhaps you don't even know what it is. But you do feel the feeling. Go right ahead and feel it. Take it in. Don't try to stop yourself. Feel it especially in your body. Let your discomfort be the trigger to *feel;* then let the feeling be the trigger to be aware of your body, your head, your heart, your gut. Let your body do the noticing. Tell me how you react to what I've just said."

"Well, isn't this interesting." I look around myself. "Right now, I'm sitting outside with my keyboard. The neighbors' lawn crew is attacking the stillness; they're running multiple leaf blowers and lawn mowers all around me. They're loud and distracting. I find it *very* annoying and disquieting!"

"So, tell me what your body is saying. Pause and feel your whole body and tell me what's going on there."

"My body is scrambling to adjust itself to its environment. It's trying to find balance on the inside to counter this imbalance on the outside. Ah. Here's an insight, I think. I'm noticing my body seems to be *activated* by all this. I could even say it's using the noise as a means to *enliven* itself. Part of that is my irritability. One thing's for sure—my body *is* noticing!"

"All right. Good. Now take this noticing, this feeling, and go a little deeper. You don't have to intellectualize this at all. Go deeper into your body's feelings. Look at the whole of it, in your environment and in your body. Don't let the mind run off with itself, away from the feelings. Keep the whole package together. Feel holistically what is in this moment.

"If you feel annoyed, just feel it fully. Don't feel it *partially*. In other words, don't let the parts dictate the whole. The challenge here is to be your *whole* self, not a separated part, such as the mind or ego, or left foot. The annoyance is an honest emotion. Your system is being impacted in a negative way. Noise is a pollutant, a toxin in this case. Accept it as that. Acceptance is what happens when you stay *whole*. The whole constitutes full acceptance of *what is!*"

"Hmm. Is this some kind of trick?"

"Yes," you reply with animation. "You are intentionally tricking your mind into remaining part of the whole. Your *parts* are what get you into trouble, not your *whole*. The mind is just a part of you! But it pulls you away from the body and makes a *partition*. The *whole* being stays in tune with the environment. It calls upon its parts to perform their appropriate functions together. That being does not separate you—neither you from your environment, nor you from yourself and your appreciation; quite the converse.

"It is a matter of appreciation. Your body knows how to appreciate and accept. It also knows how to draw the line when the toxins are too great. If you remain in the feelings of your body, you will know when to stay and when to leave. If the noise is too much, you can always pick up your stuff and move. Appreciation is the full knowing of a situation. It is *feeling into the moment* and determining what action is right for you."

"It's curious to say that. I was assuming you were implying I should *zen* the noise and find peace through my body in spite of it. You mean, I could have gotten up and moved?"

"Of course. There are always options. You decided to stay and allow me to give you the exercise amidst the noise. There's nothing wrong with that. There would have been nothing wrong with your moving either. The noise gave us an opportunity to react and to see the elements of your irritation, however. So, in this case, for our purposes, staying helped more than leaving would have."

"All right. This is an extension of the 'noticing' suggestion. Can you summarize it then, and put it firmly in our understanding?"

"Feel the *whole* of a situation. Use your body for this. Your body is the mechanism for all feeling and sensation. It is a wholeness. There is no reason why the mind should be the only organ for understanding. The hands, head, heart, arms, legs, endocrine network, belly organs, sexual system, each have their own form of understanding—their essential gifts, contributing to the consciousness of the whole.

"Each part is a hologram that is endowed with unique integrity. And yet there is an intricate and dynamic balance that links to the entire system, as one. All together, these add up to a miraculously functioning creation. *Conscious Evolution* has created this miracle of Life. We are each and all derived from this blessing while we live in the incarnate world.

"Wholeness defeats separateness. *Disarming and defeating separateness* is the evolutionary leap you are making. That is what takes you beyond ego. The more you can embody non-separation in your daily experiences, the closer you will be to your transmuted being."

There is a silence now. I wait, absorbing what you've said. I can actually sense my future being very close. Then an intuitive spark pushes words to my pen. I ask, "I'm feeling it, O. And, no doubt, the *second suggestion* is related to non-resistance."

"Yes. Obviously, there is plenty of opportunity for resistance to creep up in the example we just used."

I answer, "You could say the whole thing started with resistance. Isn't irritation a form of resistance?"

"Remember that the root of the word 'resist' is *sistere*, 'to stop'. It is energy directed at stopping the existence of what is—that is, energy directed at negating *itself*. Irritation, on the other hand, is a reaction. In its direct, pure form, it is simply an *excitement* of the system. It does not imply a negative response until the mind is engaged and judging. The answer, thus, is yes and no. For the mind, irritation is separating and polarizing. But for the body there is no separation. And there is an opportunity here to expand awareness in the encounter. Irritation opens the awareness; resistance closes it down; it cuts off appreciation."

"All right. But I think we're getting a little abstract here again."

"Yes. Excuse me. Let's stay with the body then. The body takes in the irritation and begins processing it. You, as the body, have the opportunity to *observe* yourself in this process. You can see the environment prompt activation. You feel it viscerally. The mind comes in. You can observe this too. It immediately desires to take control of the situation, and to dictate an analytic, separative reaction. It sends its judgment out to the body system by means of emotion. Listening to the sudden barrage of noise, the mind could easily send out signals to the body to defend itself, complain about the intrusion, or flee from it in disgust. These are all separative reactions.

"This may all happen within you in a brief moment, a few seconds. But if you stay with your body, with wholeness, you can observe the parts in action holographically. Your awareness—beyond the mind and body—can be called into alertness here. It is always ready to cooperate with the wholeness in you. The greater awareness, at one with your body awareness, can move you through any situation with calm and order, with little or no resistance."

I wonder, "Is that so? How does it work?"

"My suggestion here is to allow the greater awareness to assume priority. Allow it to dissolve the tendency to waste your resources, pouring vital energies down the 'resistance drain'. Resistance is a *waste of energy*. It fights creation and evolution. This is the origin of the battle you feel inside yourself—as uneasiness, negativity and disease. These negativities result from separated factions within your awareness. Small parts of you, namely the ego or mind, have taken prominence over the whole being.

"You do not have to allow this; and you certainly don't have to *accept* it. Acceptance, as I've said, is the conscious affirmation of allowing. To engage this process of dismissing resistance, you must reroute it through the body of wholeness. Acceptance of 'what is' is the rerouting. It reclaims the parts into the whole, and is the key to being in the moment, the awakened state."

"Yes. I get it. I like the idea. I'm not sure I can actually implement what you're advising. But I'm sure it's worth a try. So what about the last leg on this stool? What about authenticity?"

"Body wholeness is again the link. Being authentic is being whole." You pause to let me reflect.

I question, "What about a physical body that *isn't* whole, say it's lost an arm or leg, a tooth or whatever. How does your notion of 'body wholeness' relate to that?"

"Wholeness remains integral to the body in any case. It is an infused hologram at the microscopic and etheric levels. This is literally *authenticity incarnate*. And believe it or not, I'm going to say that even your mind can be *whole!*"

"That *does* surprise me. What do you mean?"

"The mind is a part of your personal expression, part of your body experience on the physical planes. But it is also a part of a greater mind—higher *manas*. It holds within itself keys to wholeness and Oneness that have remained largely hidden throughout the evolution of *homo sapiens*. Feeling the body, as a means of holistic awareness, opens channels—portals again—into the higher, nondual functions of mind. Mind can be awakened to these portals as you evolve. This is wholeness of mind. It *will* happen!"

"And what about ego? Is there a higher correspondence there as well?"

"Yes, indeed. It is the spiritual Ego—the super-conscious oversoul. It has also been called the *monad*. The word 'ego' is Latin for 'I'. The higher, deeper Ego—the 'I am'—is the center of directive force for a wide group of incarnations. It wields the powers of will, love, wisdom and action. The Ego sets the initiative for creation and is the origin of your sense of individuality-in-duality. In its own domain, it is not separative, but it affords your little ego its illusion of free will; and from this *does* spring the ego's separation impulse.

"The oversoul works at the duality threshold with will, love and wisdom to manifest the image of Oneness in the duality worlds. This is the realm some of your spiritual teachers and interpreters are referring to when they say we are moving out of duality into Oneness. Let's save further comment on that subject for later. There is much confusion in the dualistic mind about that."

"I must say, I'm confused about it too. You said 'Oneness does not manifest'. I assume that's what you were talking about."

"Yes. I will address that in a future letter. For now, let's return to the subject of lower mind and authenticity. As the mind attempts to separate itself and dominate the body and emotions, you can catch it in the act. You can sandwich it between the body sensitivity and the greater awareness. This will stretch it out of its habituated conditioning. You are doing such a thing right now, and in fact throughout all these letters.

"You are taking the deeper, intuitive awareness and presenting it as *understanding* to the lower mind—from two directions, from above and below. The mind, of course, is just a tool. It does not have to react as it has been programmed to. It can be freed! It can be redirected to its true nature—an instrument of evolving awareness. This is greatly facilitated by bringing your body into resonance with your being and bridging that resonance through the mind and heart.

"The mind, employed as its destined function, takes its place within the holographic body. All together, the system is a marvelous instrument of wholeness and authenticity—which is to say, *Oneness*. Within its sensitivities reside all the elements of true being. But alas, by the nature of human incarnation, these sensitivities can be turned to the will of the lower mind and emotions, and separateness. They can become the instruments of regression and *devolution* instead of evolution. This is Black's definition of evil, if you recall."

"Ah, yes. Evil."

"Bear in mind though, even evil and devolution have their rightful places in evolution. They generate the contrast necessary for conscious recognition and realization. The so-called 'fall from grace' forms the platform for the 'rebirth to grace' into a higher, transmuted state. This is all part of the unfolding story—the great game—that is playing out in the Earth scheme.

"In spite of, and by virtue of the digression into ignorance, there have always been avenues of enlightenment available. The prime avenue is as close to you as awareness itself is—that is the *body*. The true value of your physical and etheric vehicle can easily be overlooked in the search for awakening. My third suggestion here then, is to return to the authentic wholeness of your body.

"The body holds within itself the power to move you toward goodness, Source, and divine manifestation—that is to say, authentic action. It has the ability to unite all opposites inside you, and bring harmony among divergent forces. You can feel this in the chakras of your body. Take the heart in this case. It is a *singularity* among the seven main chakras. It could be said to be the *One Chakra;* all the others are functions of it. All the chakras, when properly aligned and activated, function as one integrated portal.

"The very purpose of authenticity, with its subsequent action, is to foster evolution on Earth, in your world and in your body. This creative action goes out from you, and it comes back into you. Energetically, you originate the world and the universe that you experience. You send out your presence. It separates from you and then comes back to act upon you, as the 'other'. It is a cycle—out and in, forth and back—in a never-ending spiral of spiritual unfoldment.

"When the environmental self presents you with any situation, you have the choice to see what's authentically happening or not. You may choose to see through the projected forms, or you can react unconsciously, engaging lower mind, ego and resistance. What's really happening, though, is you the soul are moving through the extrapolated world toward your destiny. It is always an upward-inward spiral, a methodical, paradoxical expansion of awareness. It can come swiftly or slowly; it is your choice.

"Now is your time, humanity, to make this choice of expansion in consciousness. The first step is to feel the wholeness of your own physical vehicle, and then, using the energy of that feeling, to leap into the wholeness of awakening. This will acquaint you directly with the true vehicle—Oneness—and the path toward a new Earth.

"Let me summarize then, as we conclude this letter. Your body and your awareness are inseparably linked. They are complementary presentations of one purpose. The body is physical and earthy, easily seen to be 'real' in the materialistic sense. And yet, within it, are contained all the miracles of spirit and transcendence you could ever want to imagine. Using your body as a foundation for spirit enables the reciprocal process of your soul, grounding itself into physical action. This is the fulfillment of all the previous suggestions I've given you.

"Take care of your body and its presentation into the world. Allow it to be natural and giving, receiving and active, exploring and at peace—all in simultaneous harmony. Listen to it with all your senses. Learn to read your own 'body language'. You need no other source to tell you what's exactly right for you. No other individual or institution can tell you exactly what that is.

"Allow yourself to be fully in your body, as you would also be fully in your soul. You cannot be the incarnate whole without moving in both dimensions consciously together. Let this wonderful vehicle hold your awareness and your destiny on Earth. Realize it and accept it as it is—however it is. Take its blessings and challenges without resistance or judgment, and allow it to flow gracefully from one expression to the next. Let it be the portal for you, the unique individual, into the true and beautiful presence that stands at your profoundest depth."

A bothersome question rises in my mind. "O, speaking of bodies. How could both you and I have had lives at the same time in Atlantis—both Levaticol and Beneth?"

"There is no limitation placed on souls in that way. We may incarnate multiple bodies in a given time period, if we deem it to be useful. It is rare, but not difficult to perform. In Atlantis, our soul needed to have the powerful dynamic balance—clear dark and light—in order to fulfill our destiny."

I shrug. "Just thought I'd ask. Destiny. Yeah. I guess *so*. Don't think I'm not noticing that you got the easier assignment there."

"Hah," you retort. "Not so. I had to put up with the likes of you in that Levaticol body, remember. And, seriously, in the end, you and I have all the same soul memories. Don't worry. It's a complete balance there."

Letter Thirty-Seven
The Grace of Freedom

"The body is important," I agree. "No doubt about it. But modern, materialism wants us to believe the body and brain create consciousness, that there's nothing more to us than that. This, I know, is *not* what you're saying."

"Your society is ill-informed. But that doesn't matter; it does not negate the virtue of the physical-etheric vehicle. The incarnate body is integral with all deeper consciousness. It's own instinctual wisdom tells it of this connection; there is no real separation. The body knows it does not create consciousness; but rather is a vital, essential projection of it."

"Last night I watched a spiritual film that wanted to make the point that we are *not* our bodies. What do you say to this seeming contradiction?"

"We *are* what we are *not!* The only contradiction is in the mind. Acceptance of Oneness within us resolves all opposites, all doubts. What the message was intending, I'm sure, is that there is a transcendent aspect of our being that exists in its own realm, before and after the body exists. The body comes and goes in the flow, as a form. But while it exists, that form embodies and exemplifies our wholeness, if we would look for it there. Of course, we can deny it or abuse it; that is our prerogative under the system of free will. One does this at his peril, however. A body abused is a body divided from its authentic nature.

"The Life force cannot flow in a healthy fashion in a vehicle divided from its essence. Thus is the lot of most humans, sadly. Even for humans, however, all the lessons of evolution and devolution can be observed in the ways you behave toward your bodies.

"Wild animals offer an example for you. They are present in their bodies much more than humans. They instinctually honor and respect the wholeness and authenticity of the body. Without the interference of a dominant ego-mind they are living consistently in the Now, within the nature of themselves. Domesticated animals are another matter, however.

"You may study your own physical vehicle and find all the greatest spiritual teachings present there; nothing is left out. No other teacher is needed, if you choose that path. Such is the ancient teaching of Hatha Yoga, by the way. That approach teaches that spirit, at its deepest and most divine, can be accessed through this vehicle."

"Are you advocating yoga as a practice?"

"For those who choose that path, it can bring them to the threshold of awakening, indeed. But I do not advocate any practice or discipline other than looking within yourself for the truth of who you are. Now is the time when humanity is afforded the capacity to see truly—if you *consciously* choose it. You are given this grace for only a brief period in the Great Cycle. My advice is to choose the straightforward path while it is being offered."

"And who is offering this?"

"*Conscious Evolution* itself. If you do not choose this, it will not happen for you. Look around in your world today, at all the insanity and absurd levels of intolerance, rejection and intentional separation. These are choices being made by intelligent, evolving individuals. They are choosing a continuation of the old universe. They are denying, most vehemently, that the new universe is valid. For them then, it is *not* valid. Do not be persuaded by their impetuosity, unless you would accompany them into that future."

This makes me want to ask more about the times we're living through right now. "The world seems crazier every day. I can't believe what absurdities and outright lies are being shouted out as though they were true. And people are hearing and believing them! I feel the energy in the field of Life getting so intense I'm about to burst sometimes. I can't stand to read the news anymore."

"You are not alone, my friend. As Thomas Paine wrote, two hundreds years before you, "These are the times that try men's souls." He was speaking both of his times and yours. The soul is being *tried,* and called forth from its quiet world to provide heightened awareness and discernment. The times are reaching a crescendo of galactic electromagnetic flux. Rejoice and take enthusiasm from this, as strange as that may sound. All this pandemonium, distress and insanity is part of the birthing process. It is a guarantee of the changing times.

"Again, I will say, stay with your body. It can lead you true — through the chaos—if only you will let it. Allow it to be clear and pure, at least by way of intention. Let it be authentic and natural unto itself, without undue pressures exerted upon it from your mind and emotional upheavals. This refers also to all the social and religious teachings coming at you from others. Stay with your own truth about your own body. It *is* your truth in projected form."

"What do you mean? How can the body be such a thing? Please give me an example."

"The chakras, the *hara* or *dantien* centers, the meridians and subtle energy threads—all are representatives of your deeper, true being. Look at your blood, endocrine and nervous networks, the skin and other marvelous organs, the integrity and intercourse of molecules and cells. In addition, there are the essential fluids and forces, the robust electromagnetic fields, the sensuality and feeling, your senses and their underlying sensibilities. All these are representations of higher and deeper realities of being. They are all manifestations of the universal archetype of individuality.

"The fact that most of your physical bodies function so well, most of the time, is a miracle of creation and evolution. Even when they are malfunctioning, they are delivering spiritual teachings, if you would receive them. Look at your body, listen to it, feel it, know it! It is your closest teacher, your nearest portal into the authentic nature of your greater being. You need look no farther than this to find yourself!"

"Specifically speaking then, I had an accident on my bicycle a few days ago, and injured my knee. Can you tell me what message my body is giving me in this?"

"Certainly. It is telling you to be careful, to be aware of your blessing in having a strong and capable physical vehicle. It is saying, 'Appreciate me. Love me. I am yours. Use me to navigate the Earth planes, to your delight and enlightenment.' The knee is for bending and flexibility, and for standing and for kneeling. It is a powerful, action-enabling articulation of movement through the world. And it reminds you of humility. Accept its blessing and align with its message for you. Give thanks for the 'accident'. It was no accident, but a deliberate restorative to your alertness.

"It all comes down to *Conscious Evolution*, even on the personal and microcosmic levels. One could speak many paragraphs about this particular situation of yours, or any other body ailment. Ailments, whether acute or chronic, are signs to be read by your awakening awareness. For now, this example serves to show you what your body can reveal—in any direction you look."

"Wow, I had no idea it could go so far. So be it. Now tell me, please, about the cluster, and the bodies I witnessed converging from all my past lives. What do these bodies have to do with the portal I was opening?"

"What you observed in our portal cluster was a representation of the technology our group has developed for moving among various time frames and dimensions. This technology relies on the wholeness and Oneness lying behind manifestation. The body is the connector link between the projected world and the 'projector' world.

"The most powerful means of aligning your individuality with the undivided nature of creation, is your own body. In this light, you were given the opportunity to round up all your past vehicles into one space, and witness their own undivided nature. All the various parts of your manifested being were revealed in their non-separateness. The body—the individual—is a presentation of undivided wholeness. All the bodies together are the full statement of that.

"What you experienced in the lifetime that held your ego contract was a dramatized example of the forces and patterns at play in human incarnation. It was not unique to you; it is a form that resonates in archetypes throughout your species, and many other particular manifested lives."

I ask, "Does each person reading this, wanting to open the portal, have to search out their past lives, their ego contract, and fuse all the bodies like I did?"

"The specific process and form will be different for other individuals. Each will experience her or his own path. Look beneath the projections and find the essence that is real. Each path is unique to itself. This uniqueness, paradoxically, is another expression of One-ness. The word 'unique' derives from Latin, *unus*, meaning 'one'."

"So how do others proceed from here, having heard my story?"

"I say, let your intention be your guide. It will feel true or not, as the case may be. If it feels true, follow it to the ends of the Earth—the old Earth, that is." You smile. "If you set an intention to open the portal, and you follow that intention within, allowing your imagination to deliver information to your heart, you will be taken into your destiny. Explore it for yourself. Use the example described and dramatized here to know the deeper essence that ap-plies to whoever *you* are, in whatever form *you* may exist.

"The fact that each individual's approach is different is the guarantee and stimulus to fullness. Each contributes in this way to the greater path beyond the separated awareness. The seeming dif-ference is actually a projection from the Oneness. In duality worlds, Oneness is represented by opposites uniting, differences un-differentiating. Let this be a seed-link in your mind as we invite the topic of Oneness to unfold here soon."

I pause and wonder how this may sound to readers. "I suspect that people may be confused at this point. Could you explain a little more about what they can do to open their own portal?"

"The pattern set forth in your drama is quite simple really. It in-volves going as deeply within yourself as you can, and looking at the chief attributes of your own ego. These qualities will provide the target for your opening awareness. You will recognize them by their resistance. Once you recognize them, simply forgive them, forgive yourself."

"I'm sorry, but this sounds just *too* simple to me. How can it be that easy to overcome dozens of lifetimes of entrenched ego?"

"It is *not* easy. You saw that for yourself in Atlantis. Yet it *is* simple. It is as simple as setting the intention. Nevertheless, it is as *difficult* as finding and facing your greatest resistance. This is not about overcoming lifetimes of ego entrenchment, however. That will obviously not happen through such an exercise. This is about finding the immediate target for the creation of your portal. You are not overcoming anything here but your own ignorance."

"Well, I still don't see us humans being able to do that."

"Allow me to finish. Your deep-seated resistance to non-separation is our focus of attention. It is, believe it or not, your ego's weakest point. It is the very center of the ego structure. But recall, ego is all about defenses—that is, about *periphery*. Ego does not guard the center; it seeks only to protect the surrounds. Creating your vortex at the center will catch ego totally off guard.

"In creating your portal, there are three important elements—intention, identification and opening. Set your intention on, and identify your ego center. Once there, use intention to open the wholeness of your physical and etheric body, to push through to the heart. The body and the heart chakra are one; and the heart is the portal of the soul. This center is the locus of non-separation in all individuals. It is also where your greatest power lies. *Take your soul's greatest power and apply it to ego's weakest point.* This is the pattern for punching through your portal. This is what you personally achieved by returning to Atlantis."

I nod. "That makes sense. But what if people can't determine what their ego's greatest resistance is? After all I had you and B guiding me."

"Anyone can do this with a little self-examination. And believe me, there is no one reading these words that is a stranger to self-examination. Most importantly, each individual has inner guides, call them what you may. Some call them nature spirits or angels, or angelans. Whatever you call them, just be sure to *call them!* Ask for inspiration and guidance. There is no better time in your life than now! No one has to do this alone. No one *could* do it alone."

"All right then. Would you please give us a little more guidance right now about how to do this exercise, to find our greatest ego resistance?"

"Yes. Here's what I would recommend. Find your own way to enter the stillness and the deep emptiness. This might be lying down in darkness, sitting in a quiet room, or wandering peacefully in nature. Sit or incubate with this space. Feel its beingness. Sense that this is *your* beingness. You *are* this space, this Now. From here relax more profoundly than you normally do. Go beyond. Imagine the sensation of no ego, no identification with form at all. No form binds you. You are formless. Relax even more into that essence. This is the being that constitutes *everyone's* awareness. Wrap yourself in it and allow it to absorb you.

"From your selfless state, regard your *self*. It's the one who is still in the grip of ego. Look. That ego has characteristics. Begin softly to identify what your ego looks like. What are its favorite ways of maintaining its defenses and separateness—and above all, its identity with form? What forms does it use to relate to the world? Is it introverted or extroverted? Is it aggressive or timid? Is it mental, emotional or physical? What provokes it most?

"You may even ask your ego to help in this. In your silence, ask it to tell you what it is like. You might be surprised at what it reveals. What excites it and makes it react? What makes it uncomfortable? What pleases it? How does it identify itself? Who does it think it is? Know thyself! Your intuition will provide you understanding. Allow and accept this when you feel the truth in it.

"For you personally, my friend, your greatest ego force was *pride of mind*. You felt that issue most among all the separative issues in your Atlantean life. It was a mind that felt thought was the source of all power on Earth. You turned all your faculties toward the cultivation of control over others through the mind. This was the 'contract' you established that would become the dominant force in all other ego lifetimes."

"But wait. My memory of the end of that incarnation was that I decided *not* to have a mind between then and now. How could I have gone 13,000 years without a mind?"

"First, do not think of your incarnational history in linear terms only. The ego contract, once established in any one lifetime, covers the whole package of lives on Earth. It matters not which or when. Its effects can manifest in any time frame, before or after the contract; to the oversoul, lifetimes are all simultaneous. But specifically in your case, the pride of mind was present even when you were mentally handicapped. And this happened in a number of your lives—*our* lives. The pride was strong in its shadow form in these times, forcing you to bend to its will in an oppositional way."

"Yeah?" I react. "So you're saying that even when I had no mind to speak of, it was my mental pride that was forcing the issue? And its influence reached forward and backward throughout all my lives, even to this day?"

"Precisely. Your current life has always been poised to resolve the juggernaut—which you now have done."

"What are some other examples of ego contracts that people have?"

You pause, reflecting. "One very common type is the *victim* archetype. In this, ego sets up its defensive perimeter around a center of dissatisfaction. The world is seen to be hostile and displeasing. These egos thrive on being deprived, abused and disappointed. They invite oppression into their lives in order to build a stronger, more separate identity.

"Another common type of ego contract is the *charismatic*. This ego stakes its territory *across* the boundaries of others. It wishes to control through being appreciated. It usurps the soul's own attribute of appreciation, to its separative ends. This ego loves to be looked upon with devotion and envy—on center stage. But at the same time, it always stands apart.

"A third archetype commonly taken on as an ego contract is the *warrior*. In this form, the ego battles against the outside world. The battles may be physical, emotional or mental. But the chief characteristic in any of them is some sort of activism for a noble cause. This approach affords many opportunities to set up defenses and then project them out into the world.

"There are many other ego types, but this should suffice to illustrate what I'm talking about. If you or others wish to do further exploration, there are numerous teachings in your time regarding archetypes, ego and self-examination. Put two and two together and you will see the patterns emerge."

"Well, thanks," I sigh. "That clarifies a lot for me. Sorry for that interruption."

"Clarity is never an interruption. Before you ask, however, here is a brief synopsis: This is all about the three motive elements—noticing, resistance, and authenticity. These actions have brought you here and they will carry you through. As you no doubt know, karma means 'action'. Action leads to immersion in physical incarnation. But it also leads to freedom, when the time is right. You need not wrestle endlessly with all your karmic bonds from multiple lifetimes.

"This is the Apocalypse. All revelations and actions of awakening are greatly accelerated now. In this epoch, you are under the influence of a new kind of grace, *if* you would receive it. It is the *grace of freedom*. All you need do to take advantage of this, is to see the truth within you and around you. Truth is your authentic nature. That truth will make you free! The freedom of truth will provide the grace to *transform all your karma at once!*

"Once you recognize your ego's primary focus, accept it just as it is. Do not judge, condemn or resist it. Allow its life force to flow through your presence. It is truthfully an honorable part of your presence. See deeply into what it is. Appreciate it. Ask your guidance to clarify what you see. Ask, 'What is my ego's greatest defensiveness and resistance? Help me to be clear.' Allow the answer to come. It may not come immediately. Sit with your query again and again, until you receive an impulse. Repeat your deepening exercise until it produces the results you seek.

"Once you have a sense of where your ego is most strongly oriented, go again into the deep stillness within. This time enter with a new intention. That intention is *forgiveness*. Go into yourself, go into the wholeness of your body. Go with compassion and an open heart center. Address, in whatever manner is most sincere for you, that aspect of your being that is the little ego. Look straight into that self, straight into the resistance you have identified, and pour in the love of your heart. Feel the creation happening. *Project* creation into this place. Your portal is opening. Here and Now. Relax and appreciate what you have done. Extend healing and gratitude to the ego. Return slowly, deliberately, peacefully to this world."

Letter Thirty-Eight
Portal

"Now, it is not enough to manifest just a single, personal portal. You will, no doubt, have reasoned that by now. You next need to find and fuse other portals in order to open the greater passage. The first step then, after manifesting the personal portal, is to make it *impersonal.* Releasing your identity from it does this. It can be as simple and straightforward as setting an intention to do so. Just be clear and impersonal in the process. Not by chance, this is the same basic formula as freeing yourself from ego and self-identification with form. Extract your 'self' from the portal you have created. Leave it empty. This will invite in the Void. *The Void is the ultimate portal into Source."*

"Whoa. I like that. Will we have more on that later?"

"You guessed it—much more. And so, leave your portal empty. This is, at first, simply a state of readiness. Make it a *profound* readiness. Begin next your initiation of sharing. Offer your portal to the whole. Use the body model as a channel. See yourself with arms stretched wide, open heart, feeling the web of Life linking you with all others who are engaged in this work of awakening. Feel the Life flowing from this web into your body, through the heart and every chakra. Feel it projecting simultaneously back into the web from you, blessing and lifting all. Feel the opening of the portal iris, before your eyes, before your heart, before your soul.

"In these times, humanity is blessed with the power to *repay karma with joy!* Believe it or not, this is what I am asking you to do! Do not just believe, however. Rather *accept!* There is an enormous difference. Realize this: You must *choose* this blessing in order to activate it. Grace is extended to the very threshold of your awareness. You, the conscious awakening being, must open and allow it to cross your personal threshold! Blessings are never forced upon recipients. Blessings must be actively received. Always choose to be blessed. And you thereby are!"

"But karma is such a complex subject. I mean, think of it—all those actions from former lives, both positive and negative, that bind us to the so-called Wheel of Karma. How can we believe, or accept, that these bonds can be released all at once?"

"Releasing is releasing. When you know, within your own true being, the formula for letting go—for no longer holding on—then it is simple. It is *one* action to set all other actions free. The formula is 'focus and forgive'. The calculus of your focus does not matter. Forgive all! *Give for* all. Act for all and one. You speak of Oneness. You desire Oneness. Let *all* be Oneness then—in thought, word and deed. One elegantly clear action frees you from all karma.

"This is the pattern for finding and releasing your attachment to ego. Once you perform this consciously, with intention, the waves of grace will radiate out from that action into all your lifetimes, especially this one you're living right now. You will begin to immediately feel the forgiveness coming from you, into you. And you will begin to realize *freedom* from the inside out. The 'ego contract' is thus broken—from the center outward. The amount of time it takes depends on your own soul's destiny."

"Well, I must say, I have felt very different since I forgave myself in that past life. Nevertheless, my ego is still here. Just last evening it flared up in a most ridiculous performance. I was shocked, as were others around me."

"That's all right. This is part of your destiny right now. Your soul has agreed to remain within your ego contract—pride of mind—for a period of time, for a specific purpose. During that time you will finish writing this and the next book."

"Well, I can't really imagine being free of my ego. So, I guess it doesn't matter." I pause. "But thinking of it now, I feel almost left out, not to be partaking of that freedom. It doesn't seem quite fair, if you know what I mean. Why must I continue in my ego?"

"You make me laugh, dear friend. Not fair? Is that your ego arguing for its own demise?" You smile. The purpose for remaining in your ego is simple. It's to keep you grounded. This way our communication will be planted firmly in both time frames, in *both worlds*. Do not be alarmed. It's all for a good cause. Relax and enjoy having an ego a little while longer. I, for one, am enjoying it in you."

"This is all too much! I don't know what to say. I guess I see your point. My ego will certainly bring us down to Earth, if that's what we need."

"Precisely. But the major work has been wrought. You have demonstrated the pattern for release—for yourself and others. My continuing advice for all participating in this exercise is that you focus on the work of aligning with the greater vortex. Alignment in this case means emptying out yourself and everything you have ever created in all your lives on Earth. It is aligning your self, your being and your body into one synchronous whole. In so doing, we are opening the passageway between the universes. Now is the time for this."

"Excuse me, but what do you mean by *emptying out* what we have created?"

I sense you smiling again. "I thought you might ask me that. The great game we are playing here is the emptying out of the soul. The aspect of the soul that faces into duality carries much baggage from the past. I speak here, not of the oversoul, or the greater Ego, but of the localized conditional soul. This is where karma accumulates—as the soul breathes Life into its repeated forms on Earth. Allow me to explain.

"In the action of creating a form, each soul projects a breath of itself into the vehicle of incarnation. This great exhalation becomes the opportunity for karma to be attracted in the first place. To apply emptiness, the soul needs to breathe back the energy of awareness it has sent out, and empty its incarnate forms. From our incarnate perspective, the breathing is reversed. That is, we inhale as the soul breathes out; we exhale as the soul breathes in."

"Whoa. I'm getting lost here. What?"

"You do not need to understand my explanations with your mind."

"Well, I'm glad to hear that, because my mind is having some real difficulty with it."

"What's important here is the breathing. The soul's breathing is the means for clearing karma. Our forms take on esoteric emptiness as the soul breathes back its essence from our forms. This is what

we experience as *stillness*. By emptying the vessel of incarnation—
the little self—we prepare the way for deep presence to arise. The
Void is that presence. This is the *practice* of stillness—feeling the
soul's in-breath, and our personal out-breath. And it is a clue to
finding death before death finds you.

"Then a most exquisite paradox comes into play. The inner
emptiness finds resonance with the fullness of our energy bodies,
and resident in the universal wholeness around us; this is the fulfillment of our intercourse between form and formlessness."

"Please wait," I gasp. "I'm feeling particularly dense about this.
What does breathing and emptiness have to do with wholeness?
And what does this have to do with form and formlessness?"

"I can only suggest, for now, that you *feel* what I'm saying, rather than understand it; jump over the mind for this. Reach out
with your 'other' awareness—through the stillness. Breathe out to
your fellow humans. Use your energy body to find the wholeness in
you, and reach out with it into the wholeness of your species. Use
the breath to link your essence with that of other like souls. For
now, let it sink—through forgiveness—into your heart. Note the
relationship between lungs, throat and heart. You will eventually
know what I am saying.

"In linking with others, you may physically gather in actual
groups. But most importantly, you may imagine and intend non-
physical formations fusing, more upon more, becoming the wider
open portal. Of course, doing both would be best. At this moment
in history, you have the blessing and grace to go between the universes. Cross back and forth persistently through the portal, and
plant the seeds of transformation where they may grow. Create the
pathways for any to follow. Breathe this into being."

"Are you asking us to create a passage for others as well as ourselves then? Can we do this? What about people who will never
hear these words?"

"Very good questions. The answer is 'yes' to the first two.
There are those who will join you in the passage without creating
their own individual portal, and without releasing the ego contract.
Not many humans can actually accept the *grace of freedom* yet. Their
genetics will have to transmute first.

"Once the greater portal is open and active, all who can imagine the new universe may enter—regardless of their degree of awakening. Their passage will be more disorienting and turbulent, but they will not be turned away. There will be many who will discover the opportunity only after the Great Storm has passed. For this reason, the portal will remain open as long as is necessary to fulfill the individual destinies of humanity.

"As I have said, even for those who create their individual portals, there is a need to go beyond this, and gather together in a shared intention. Moving from one universe to another during the end of a Great Age is no conventional matter. A certain mass of individual effort must be marshaled, both in quantity and quality. There will be a wide variety of degrees of release and opening among the participants. This is natural. What is not usual is the very crossing between universes itself, especially on such a scale.

"Both universes will continue to exist in their own rights for millennia to come. Perhaps at the end of the next Great Year— 26,000 years approximately—the two universes will be aligned again to share the *vesica piscis* opening. That is the sacred geometry of the portal form we are generating. The *ovoid* shape conjures to imagery the formless *Void* underlying it all, at the Threshold of Source."

I take a deep breath as you pause. "You mentioned the *vesica piscis*. Could you talk about that a bit more?"

"I will. But first let me finish with your third question. There are many humans and vigilans alike who will never hear these *Letters*. They will nevertheless feel the energies moving within them. What we do here is to re-plant an ancient seed. These ideas are not new. They have been known throughout all ages, even well before *homo sapiens* evolved. They are eternal and archetypal. All souls will hear some message related to the Apocalypse. Our voice, to be sure, is not the only voice in this stormy wilderness. There are many teachers and guides coming forth in your time to fulfill a thousand prophecies.

"Each individual will take it in as they are able and process it within their own psyches, as their unique destiny dictates. Whatever messenger reaches them, the *true* message will come only from within, silently and beneath words. That message will direct them through the Storm, in the way appropriate. Our portal is one means that will offer a smoother transition to some, through the tranquil eye at the center of great turbulence.

"All human vehicles that cross into the new universe will genetically mutate into the new species, *homo evigilatus*. Those who remain with the old universe will know a slightly different process. Nevertheless, all souls in either universe are being given the opportunity to awaken, to find their passage or not."

"You said in the first book, that all humans would definitely awaken. Does what you're saying change your forecast now? Were you wrong? *Can* you be wrong?"

"I am indeed capable of being wrong. But in this case, I was not. True, I did not understand the nature of the two universes until we generated the last few letters of the first book. What I now understand and am able to affirm to you is that the *entire* species, while evolving out of its previous state into an awakened one, will move through this awakening in different stages.

"All humans in your world are in the throes of this in your current time. All will in fact awaken and make the 'enlightened' choice of which universe best fits their destiny. As we said before, some will choose to continue in a system that is built upon resistance and forgetfulness. They will continue in systems like your Earth, where egos are the primary tool for evolving the awareness. Others will enter the world that most vigilans inhabit. This system does not block remembrance of the soul realms. Thus it is called 'awakened'."

"OK. Here's another question that seems very challenging to me. Do vigilans exist only in the new universe? If they do, why didn't you see the two universes from the beginning?"

"The revelation that came to us as we unfolded the first book of *Letters*, was that we vigilans are also moving into the new universe. We were unaware until then that our time-transposition experiments were opening such a threshold. This is part of the evolution of our now-joint species.

"Vigilans will live in both universes to some degree. But in the old system, humans will transmute much more slowly. The ones who do awaken will become the advanced leaders, teachers and healers there. They will not be revealed as a new species for a much longer time, though they will suspect it among themselves soon after the Great Storm. Awakened beings have always walked among humans, just as extraterrestrials have. They have also always known how to disguise themselves and appear 'normal', if this was required.

"As *Conscious Evolution* proceeds in the old universe, the ego will continue its dominant role, but not for an inordinate time. Certain humans, who are awakening now, will continue to exist in both universes for a century or two, while the portal gradually closes. Some, like the members of our group, will maintain linkages between the worlds, primarily living in the new system. We will be as beacons, transmitting energy and support from the new system into the old. Over time, the souls who still prefer to evolve within a cloaked system will move to other planets in both the old and new universes, where they can proceed through schemes more suited to their souls' desire."

"Will there continue to be an awareness of the other universe among vigilans in your time?"

"I think not, in particular terms. We will know that it exists, but only a small minority will be able to correspond between the two, once the portal is closed. What I am sharing with you, is what we have been learning along with you over the course of the *Letters*. Our time has been altered, evolved, by intercourse with yours. This will continue. It is all good.

"What we were able to see and know was narrower at the beginning of the *Letters* than it is now. We are all growing by virtue of our relationship. You can witness that maturation within the pages of the first book itself. I feel I must remind you once again that vigilans are not omniscient as incarnate beings. We wonder and ponder at many of the mysteries of Life, right alongside you. We do not have all the answers, nor do we have all the questions!"

"OK. I keep forgetting that. So, can you tell me what the difference is between the universes? Why are there two of them now? Why did you and I cross over?"

"There are infinite universes in the Cosmos. When two systems are associated as ours are, they are referred to as 'parallel'; they have a special relationship to each other. Every incarnate form is manifested in both universes simultaneously. The forms in both systems are virtual duplicates; they feed information and experience back and forth through the one soul consciousness within them both.

"The transition between galactic ages produces periods of close proximity like this. Over time, however, the two incarnations begin to drift apart and evolve independently. The individuated souls then must make a decision about which universe to follow with their attention."

I squint. "Why would souls need parallel universes at all?"

"There are as many reasons as there are souls and universes. The simplest answer is that they afford greater exposure for *Conscious Evolution* to realize itself. Pause here for a moment to reflect on what this means in terms of the scope and depth of *Conscious Evolution*. Its reality is far beyond any of our imaginations. But beyond imagination, we can still *appreciate* the mystery.

"Parallel universes arise when a single system comes to a stage of its grand life where major evolutionary forces are pulling in different directions. While there are continuous spin-off sub-dimensions around us all the time, they normally remain interdependent and will soon flow back together like currents in a river."

"Hmm. So, the parallel universes are like enormous dimensions that *don't* flow back together."

"Yes, at least not for a very long time."

"I'm sure this subject could fill volumes," I surmise. "But I know you're about to say that's enough for now."

"Quite. There will be more, later. While it is important to know you're living in these two universes, the main emphasis of our letters will be the threads that link them. The two systems are powerfully reciprocal.

"During the Great Storm you are experiencing both at the same time. This is why you feel the divisions and clashes of ideologies so acutely now all over the world. The important thing to realize, is that you're making a simple choice between two paths—to awaken or not to awaken!"

"Well, I'm not so sure which choice I'm making," I hear my voice admit. "I'm not sure which universe I'm in."

"That's only natural for you right now. You are simultaneously living in both! Yet you think of them as only one. This is the plight of the human species at this time. You do not yet realize that your experiences and sensations are divided. Some are in the new world and some are still in the old."

"We're certainly divided these days; no doubt. That's an interesting idea. You're saying it's because we don't know we're really living a dual existence. What can be done to clarify things, to make us see what's really going on?" I plead.

"Indeed. What can be done? You and your fellow humans can *wake up*. It's simple, so simple—once you've done it," you chortle with a sympathetic smile. "It's only a choice away."

I cringe. "So simple? Only a 'choice'?"

"You are making that choice right now, all of you—each in her or his own way. Your very cells are choosing. They are learning to choose *for* you, and not be dominated by the mind. The mind is not the 'chooser', it turns out. It is only the seeker, and the explainer."

"All right. You keep advising me to go out of my mind. But surely my mind can be of some use in this 'choice'. Can't it help us see more clearly which door to walk through? Which portal?"

You take a noticeably deep breath. "Yes, we are using mind to articulate these letters. You yourself—and anyone reading this—are using the letters to clarify your choice, to see the two universes inside you. You are using thought to draw out the imagination, to in fact draw me into your reality. You are finding the opening as you write and read. Don't be fooled though, the discovery goes far beyond the mind."

I shrug and acquiesce. "Let's talk about portals again."

"A portal is much more than just an opening or a gateway. It is actually a *living being*. Its Life and yours, together, empower the passage. The word 'portal' derives from Indo-European, *pra*, and Sanskrit, *pri*, meaning 'to bring or carry over'. The French word, *porter*, still has this meaning.

"A true portal, such as the one we are manifesting, is the vital force that activates movement between worlds, spaces or dimensions; plus at the same time it constitutes the vessel itself. This is why you must take care to fabricate it out of your own living essence, out of the vessel that is your own physical-etheric body. The portal is made out of *you*, but it takes on a Life of its own by virtue of your pure *intention* to move beyond yourself. It is like the *tension* of a violin string, drawing you out of your old music into the new.

"The *vesica*, also known as a *mandorla*, is the essence of feminine mystery and power. The essential 'birth canal', it is the invocation into procreation and nativity; and likewise into death—a most sacred creative principle. The geometric shape is that of the merger of two circles—the almond or *yoni* shape made by the overlap of the circles' edges; the radius of each circle equals the width of the *vesica*. It has been called the pointed oval; the shape is approximately this: '()'. It symbolizes both the rebirth into Oneness, out of duality, and its opposite—the manifestation of form and incarnation *into* duality. It is clearly the bridge between.

"The *vesica piscis* is the *portal* between Oneness and duality. On the inside it links us with the Source, the formless Absolute. On the outside it bridges into the concrete manifestation of form and materiality. The *vesica* embraces it all, from utter simplicity to extreme complexity. It is the one, the two and the three. There is much written historically about this sacred geometric form.

"In Latin *vesica* means 'bladder', a vessel of animated fluids in the body. *Mandorla* derives from the Latin word for 'almond'. This latter word has been used religiously to describe auras and halos of saints, goddesses and gods. Such oval orbs have often symbolized vehicles of passage into subtler realms.

"For our purposes, the *vesica* embodies the living and life-giving qualities of the divine passage into *Conscious Evolution*, the bearer between worlds. The portal we construct here is nothing less than the living goddess of transubstantiation. This constitutes the underlying Oneness and wholeness of our bodies and our spiritual essence.

"The pointed oval with a circle inside it is another interesting elaboration on the vesica—the *eye*, symbolic of divine vision. Created from the partial overlap of two individuated circles, this image reveals the wholeness of the inner circle as well—the iris. And not accidentally, Iris was a messenger goddess, a channel of communication between heaven and Earth. The *vesica* eye is '*Oneness* looking us in the eye'. It is Oneness giving birth to itself through the means of united creative principles. Bear in mind here that we make no idle reference to the *eye* of the Great Storm."

"OK. Well. I'm glad I asked—I think!"

I feel you smiling again. "All that explanation was to impress upon you the sacred nature of our business. We are bringing together deep principles of Life through our actions. The portal we are constructing and opening must be constituted of a very fine substance. The degree of fineness in the sacred *vesica* contrasts with the coarseness of separation and animosity that has captivated many humans during the Great Storm. Allow me to reflect a bit on that, with some of my mentor's perspective. The confused of your time are victims of their own defensiveness. They are filled with fear such that they can no longer see or think rationally. These humans often succumb to the pronouncements of demagogues and conspiracy theorists that wish them nothing more than perpetual illusion.

"The demagogues, in themselves, are grossly misled, of course. They are mesmerized by the phenomenon of having others attracted to their egos. The more they incite their following, the more they believe what they preach, no matter how false. It is indeed the blind leading the blind, and slaves enslaving themselves. These infected beings constitute much of the human substance during the Great Storm. It is this substance we seek to pierce and pass through with our portal.

"Our portal, any portal, is most powerful at the very center— the eye of the Storm. It will draw upon the raw energies swirling around it in the vortex. The passage we are revealing will draw all the energies into itself without judgment or conditionality; it will transmute them into forces for safe conduct.

"The radiant gravity from this vortex will pull upon even the lost souls within the deluded swarm. These souls too will be brought under the influence of advancing consciousness, as much as this seems impossible for you to imagine. Their defensiveness and divisiveness are clear signs of that influence; powerful forces are in play all around them. Many within their number will be drawn, unsuspecting at first, into awakening by virtue of their suffering. Experiencing intense denial, fear and pain will alert them to unfolding dimensions inside themselves. In the end it is all good, in spite of the pain.

"This brings us, at last, to the other topic I must address. It is again the Void and its relationship to the portal. We cannot discuss the Void without looking into Source as well. The two are one, as I have alluded to before. No words are adequate to describe it, because descriptions are a function of mind awareness.

"From the world of form, our minds cannot reconcile the two and the one; we cannot truly comprehend, what is the deeper reality. It is buried in the inscrutable unknown. The ancients referred to it as 'The One About Whom Naught May Be Said'.

"Having said that phrase, however, we are in effect approaching the Absolute. We have said *something* about *no thing*. Paradox. We cannot describe or say *what* this 'no thing' is. Nevertheless, we *can* know it—intimately, in fact—and have firm assurance that it is the underpinning of all that is both form and formless. We can also imagine its grandeur.

"There is duality in all this—Source and Void, the portal and the passage. This duality is a projection, as I have pointed out repeatedly. The Source is the projector. We can only comprehend when we wind our way back into the projector itself.

"At the ends of ages, we are afforded vast opportunities to evolve and expand our awareness—to reach beyond limitation. This is why you feel so many disturbances in your day. Unfortunately, many ages have come and gone when opportunities were squandered."

"Sorry." My brow is wrinkling. "Can you please bring it down to Earth again? What do Source and Void have to do with the portals?"

"We are invoking the Void as the ultimate portal of consciousness. It is the only avenue there is into our true power. That would be Source itself. This is the end of the Great Age. It is a time for grand measures of all kinds—great transformations, great blessings and challenges, great cleavages; and, of course, the Great Storm. In order to generate the power we need for all these portals we are holding Source accountable for its promise, the vital promise within our DNA. We are calling out to Source to shine through the vortex, the Void, and infuse our passage with its mystery. The deepest sacredness must infuse us. We cannot activate our portals, to their ultimate mission, without the grandest alchemical magic."

"Whew!" I gasp. "Comprehending this magic is a bit beyond me right now."

"This is as it should be and must be, dear friend. Allow it and relax. Your mind does not have to digest this. In fact, if we had to rely on that vehicle, we would be wasting our time. Let your mind be troubled. Embrace the transformation with your knowing—your heart and body of wholeness. Comfort will arise from there.

"We will return now to specific suggestions for those who are participating in opening our portal. This will sound hopelessly fanciful to some readers. Nevertheless, I must tell you that you are moving in ever more etheric spheres. To the mind this is, of course, irrational and impossible. Let your mind think what it will; your mind will catch up later. Use rather your imaginative, awakening consciousness to know the truth of what you feel.

"Here then is our synoptic view. You are invoking an alchemical transmutation in yourselves through marrying the point of your awareness to the wholeness of your body. Marrying the point with the periphery—the center *and* the circle—opens the door into Oneness, and the vehicle for passage through the Storm. In drawing the *vesica*, recall, we place the center point upon the circumference.

"Visualize the opening created by the *vesica*. Allow yourselves to be as open as the portal you seek to create. Employ your imagination as a channel for communication with your soul. Learn to sense the voice of stillness. Follow it gently and humbly. Do not resist its presence in this birth process. And this is only the beginning.

"As the intensity rises, bear in mind that we are beneficiaries of the magnetism of Source. Each measure added is amplified by the presence of the assembled souls who are watching. We are human and vigilan together. We await you, reaching our arms back to you, welcoming you into the destiny you are revealing. You and we are one.

"There is room for every revelation in the Apocalypse."

Letter Thirty-Nine
Young Man

Am I dreaming? This is no place I've ever been before. Where am I? Why must I always find myself so confused? A cloud seems to lift from my vision. I look around. There's a long corridor, light streaming in from the far end. *Is this a tunnel?* I shudder for a moment. *Is this a 'near death experience'? No.* The image is clarifying. *It's not a tunnel.* I'm sitting at a table on a narrow street. There are shops and cafés, merchants. People are passing on the street. I feel like I've just arrived somewhere after a very long journey.

Out of the crowd, a figure appears. He is a young man, dark-skinned, handsome, wearing a white gown with a colorful sash. He smiles infectiously. I smile back. The man looks vaguely familiar.

"May I?" He motions to a small wooden chair on the opposite side of the table. I nod.

He sits down, still smiling. We stare at each other for a long time. I realize I am mesmerized. His eyes reach into mine and I recognize him at last. It is the Old Man. I laugh out loud and break free from the trance. His hands reach across the table and grip mine. He is still staring intently into my eyes. His smile has faded, replaced with a calm, yet serious expression.

"Thank you for coming," he offers in a firm, friendly voice.

"Where have I come? Where did I come from? Is this a dream?"

"In a way, yes. But it is a *real* dream. You are in my time again. How is Orange, by the way?"

"Wait. What's going on here? You look so young! O is fine. We've started a new book of *Letters*. Don't you know this? Don't you stay in touch with her?"

"I've only just turned 21. I have not yet regained full integration of previous times. The memories of that other life are beginning to return gradually. But you, my friend, were the first memory. I haven't reached back to her yet."

"I'm your first memory. I'm flattered. It's good to see you again, by the way, and so youthful. Though I still don't know where this is, or how it's happening."

He leans back and puts his hands on the edge of the table. "I would recommend that you think of this as a dream, a lucid one to be sure. That way I won't have to give you endless explanations about how it works. Basically, I created this dream space..."

"You mean a *sub-dimension?*" I look him in the eye.

"Yes, precisely. You understand that? I wouldn't have thought someone from your time would know about such things."

"O introduced me to them at the start of this book."

"Ah, I look forward to seeing her again."

"Why don't we just invite her to come here right now?" I suggest and look around at the people wandering past. They don't pay us any mind.

"Because I wish to speak to you alone first. We will take one step at a time. I just need to get my feet on the ground to start off. And *you* are the ground, friend."

"Well, all right. What is it that you want to get started with?"

His face gets serious again. "That's what I want to ask *you*."

"Eh?"

"I need you to bring me up to speed. Memories from other lives are still distorted for me. Crossing over into the physical planes always results in confusion."

"I thought you guys didn't have a 'veil' anymore, between levels of awareness."

"True. Not like humans did. Nevertheless, we have a lot of information to process through finite minds. A good portion of our first 30 years is spent sorting out connections with other lifetimes. It's all part of engaging with the incarnate world. That's what I'm asking for help with. I've just recently remembered who you and Orange are. But there are still big gaps in what I know."

I lean over the table toward the young man. "Let me get this straight. You want me to tell you about the *project*? About everything we've been doing together?"

"Not exactly. I wouldn't put that burden on you. I only need you to ground me, which is what we are doing right now in this conversation. Just speaking with you is drawing the patterns into my awareness. I don't need you to give me all the specifics, but it would help if you would talk to me. For instance, I understand we have this project together."

I exclaim, "Wait. This is too strange. It's actually *your* project, you know. You created it. Not me. But before we go any further, you have to explain some things. Just where are we? What time frame? What dimension, uh, universe?"

"I'm definitely in the future *you* have chosen. Though I see, in your time, you're still in the crossover zone."

"What's that? I'm afraid I'm getting confused. How *far* are you into my future?"

He shakes his head, as if clarifying his mind. "I'm referring to the Great Storm, the crossover zone. You're still there. I thought maybe you had already passed it."

"No, not at all. I'm still in the thick of it. And it's a real mess, if you want my opinion! But tell me when is *your* time. Where are you?"

"Oh, about 13,000 years in your future. I made quite a jump after our last encounter."

"Oh no. Not *another* future to deal with! Stop. There's already too much for me to process."

"It's not my intention to confuse you. Quite the contrary. I'm only asking you to help *my* confusion."

"I moan. How can I do that? I'm just a backward human. I think you need to talk to O."

"I will. But first I need you. I know the rough parameters of our project. I remember that much. And more is coming back to me by the day. I've been told by my guides to check in with *you*. I need a quick flash of insight about the scope of the whole business. I know that you are on the other end, the *far* end of a bridge we set up."

"Yeah. That's sure true. What else do you need to know from me then?" I try to relax.

He furrows his brow. "Believe me. I wish I knew! Maybe the best thing to do here is just start talking to me about what happened to you since the last time we met. And especially what you've been doing lately."

I shake my head in disbelief. "I thought *you* were the one who knew all about this. You're telling me you don't? So who's running the show?"

"We all are, my friend. We're making this all up as we go."

"Damn. That's what O used to say. But *you* made it up more than I did! I'm starting to lose my grasp of this whole thing."

"Please stop 'grasping'. And start talking!" he laughs.

"OK. I can't think of anything else to do. Where do I start? Let's see. We're building a portal between the universes—the old one and a new, more awakened one. O and Black took me back to Atlantis to relive a past life there."

"Black?"

"Never mind. In Atlantis I was a big-time bad guy. I had to resolve some karma in that life, in order to establish my portal."

"I see. It makes sense."

"It does?" I grimace a smile.

"And Atlantis was 13,000 years before your time. I'm seeing a pattern here. The portal notion is new to me. But if you need to open one, it stands to reason you'd have karmic issues to clear up, especially since you're moving into a more awakened universe."

I frown at him and shrug. "Well, besides, the portal has to be linked with others. We're making a grand passage for many souls, out of many portals."

The young man rubs his chin and ponders for a while. "I must say, this is an interesting development. I can only conjecture about why this would be necessary. The Great Storm must have been rougher than I realized."

"Say. Don't you have historical records? Can't you check this out?"

"Of course," he replies. "But 13,000 years is a long time ago. A lot of what happened back then is buried away in the archives. One would need a very good reason to go to all the trouble..."

I scowl. "Well, I think you have your reason now. How is it that you know about *me*, anyway? How did you know where to find me? God, thirteen thousand years in the future!"

"I had a dream, a very powerful dream."

"And I was in it? Was O there too?"

"Yes. I watched myself die, with the two of you nearby. Then I came back briefly from the other side and I was telling you things that sounded pretty wild—about our mission together. It had to do with embodying the merger of our two species. It had to do with using your bodies as some kind of instrument of Oneness."

"That all sounds a lot like what I've recently heard from O and Black." I add a clarification, "Black, by the way, is a member of O's group, her *mentor*, whatever that may mean."

The young man suddenly jerks back in his chair and stares straight up. There is an opening to the sky that runs the length of the street. His gaze is fixed there. Light is pouring down on him like a liquid, spilling over his face and chest, along his arms and hands. He sits frozen, vibrating like a feather in the wind. I too am frozen, staring at him. His face transforms before my eyes. It becomes the face of an old, old man. It is Sarites!

I am awestruck. *What magic is this?* His head drops and his eyes connect purposefully with mine—as Sarites. I am drawn in inexorably, drawn back down into Atlantis. So far beneath the sea—and years. 26,000 years. The ancient eyes bore into mine, challenging my resolve, my authenticity. He speaks in a ghostly voice. "Administrator. What have you done? Where have you gone? We are still waiting for your return."

The young face, turned ancient, stares intently upon me. At first, I take it as rebuke. But gazing on, another impression arises. He seems simply to be asking, not condemning. I cannot but respond to this plea in kind.

I speak, once again, with the voice of Levaticol. "Sarites, the eldest of the Elders. I will speak plainly and honestly to you. I had little use for you in our time. I thought of you as nothing but an impediment—an old, old man who needed to die and get out of my way, out of my swath of personal ambition."

The face is placid, absorbing my words. I begin again, sensing a voice from deep within me speaking. "You are right to call me back, and to ask where I am, what I have done. I will explain. I owe you that, at the very least. I have flown away, far beyond the bounds of many lifetimes. I have paid a great price for my indiscretions, a millennial price. Now I return to your presence, greatly humbled—not merely before you but before my very soul. Let us now renew our timeless bond, and realize who we really are. Look into my eyes and see who *I* really am."

The eyes of Sarites stare, unblinking. They then follow my head down, as I bow low. When I look at him again, the young man has returned. He sits very still, pondering. Suddenly, he knows why he has brought me here, why he must do this. His gaze is more powerful now. Fierce.

He speaks. "Thank you, friend. This is the ground I was seeking. It has been found. Vast and deep memories have returned. I know who we are! What we do here is not just an incarnate 'project'. We are not merely building a bridge between ages, or a portal between universes. Our work is to fuse our very souls—to make of our many individualities, one. Truly. No words can tell this story. We must *live* it to know. We must *know* it to return to where we really *are*. This world is only our image, sent forth to play in the light. And in the dark."

With that, the young man stands and bows to me, sweeping his hand gracefully in front of him. Tears are on his cheeks. He touches the backs of my hands with long, brown fingers, turns and walks into the street. Looking back over his shoulder, he calls, "Please wait. I shall return."

I'm sitting numbly, looking at the shapes of people moving past. 'What now?' I wonder. The movement blurs momentarily. Something has shifted in the sky and the buildings around me, in the coursing throng. The table remains as it was.

Who knows how much time has passed? I sit as requested. Then the figure of a man comes to me again out of the crowd. He comes wearing a similar gown. The sash is different. It has gold medallions along its edges, tinkling as he walks. He stands across the table from me, and motions to the empty chair. "May I?"

I nod passively. My mind is a stuttering confusion. He takes the seat. This is the same man who walked away minutes before. But now he is old, wrinkled by age. His hair is as white as his clothes. His maroon eyes meet mine and pierce. These are the same eyes I saw in the youth minutes before. How can this be?

"How?" he repeats my thought. "I needed to move through a lifetime in order to have the conversation we're about to have, dear brother of old."

"You look just like the Old Man I knew back in the year 1000. What's going on here? A few minutes ago, you left me sitting here. You were a young man. Now look at you," I manage. "Tell me, how long have I been sitting at this table?"

"Hah!" His laugh is as infectious as his smile. I begin to laugh with him. "Long enough, I'd say. Come with me now."

He rises with the energy of a much younger man and reaches over to lightly touch my elbow. "This way."

We walk halfway down the narrow street, then turn left into an alleyway. Steps lead down and around. Dark, stone walls follow us on both sides. In a short distance we break out into brilliant sunlight. A wide river spreads before us—dark green and full, flowing fast. Light vegetation edges it on this side. On the far shore is a solid verdant wall. Beyond the green I see desert, far off into the distance. Looking upstream, I see a series of bridges that span the water, and low buildings nestled in the trees on both sides. Where we stand is a platform just above the water's edge.

I take in a deep breath of the sweet, warm air. It fills me with joy and peace instantly. "Where are we?"

"On the banks of the River *Isa Ber* in western Africa. This my home. I've lived near here for many of my lifetimes on Earth. Of course, as I believe I told you long ago, you and I are communicating within a temporal sub-dimension—a dreamtime. You have been in this land before as well, I sense."

"Yes. I know this river," I murmur, "from 13,000 years ago. It had a different name then—the Niger."

"The names mean the same, 'Great River'. *Isa Ber* is Songhai."

"It doesn't really look much different. There are more trees, I guess. Isn't this near where O and I met you the first time, as OM?"

"Yes indeed."

"But I see desert out there now. It was a forest then."

"That's right. The desert returned again, in the greater climatic cycle. It is the will of nature. The forest will return again someday, I'm sure."

I continue, "When we met the first time, 12,000 years ago, your people were living in an inner space most of the time, and not on the surface of the Earth. Do you still do that?"

"Ah yes. I remember. It was a sub-dimension. Yes. We still live in these inner dimensions, but not exclusively. We now have much more commerce between the outer physical plane and the inner realms. You might say we live in both at once."

I think back to the earlier time, of my visit there with O. "And what of your work in the Threshold? Is that still going on?"

"Oh yes. We are tying that in with our surface lives much more now as well. We have merged and expanded. All things flow together in Source. It is the great in-breath and out-breath of Life in us."

I knit my brow. "At the end of your life, you said you'd have more influence out of the body. Has that been so? And after all this time, what has become of our 'project'? Is it still happening?"

"The clock does not run out on such a project, if you will permit me a little humor," he chuckles to himself.

I smile and touch his elbow. "Your jokes haven't improved much in all this time, I see!

He smiles his infectious smile back. "From my standpoint, it's not all that much time. I did not incarnate at all between that last life and this. Time is totally flexible in the soul realms, as you know. I have spent the soul-interval steeping myself in the deeper connections and realities of the project."

The river rustles softly below us. A fish jumps up and then, with a splash, returns to invisibility. I gaze out over the relentless, flowing water and then to the orange desert beyond. Old Man looks off into space for a moment, then resumes. "The overall project is a grand one, my son. Our part of it was rather contained in the early days. We knew only what we needed to know at the time. But in the larger scope, it will encompass *more* millennia before it reaches fruition. The deeper objective of it, I have discovered, is now to prepare for the next Great Storm, the one that is brewing 26,000 years in your future, at the end of the *next* Great Age."

"The next one? Oh please." I roll my eyes. "I can only take one Great Storm at a time."

Old Man laughs loudly and long at this. Wiping a tear from his eye, he continues, "Don't worry. You don't need to know the details of the greater project. But it does help to put it in perspective. What you are living through in your day—the lessons we all are learning from that—will help our species formulate its approach to the next transition. Your collective experience will be applied to the generation on Earth in those future days. What we record now, is preparation for that future time.

"The same sort of project was conceived, in its way, 26,000 years before you. The patterns and guidance for passage across the galactic plane were laid down by the previous civilizations, and preserved in the records of such people as the Maya, the Hopi, and the ancient Egyptians; not to mention the influence of Sumer, Atlantis, and the Avars of Hyperborea."

"Hyperborea?" I muse. "And just where is that?"

"Think of Siberia, Mongolia."

"OK. It does help to know the bigger picture, I'm sure. So, we're not doing this just for ourselves—for the human transition into vigilan? We will be helping out those far future beings who come after us? I like that idea."

Birdcalls catch my attention. Several egrets swoop nearby and float to rest in the reeds at the river's edge. After arriving together, they take up solitary positions. Alone and together, they are partners with the water—one inspiring presence.

"Tell me now. Why did you have to live a lifetime in order to have this conversation?"

"Because I needed to get this just right. I needed to understand the workings of the greater project, as I've just described it. That required research and inter-dimensional contacts, including some time transposition. I had to develop the skills to lead you through the experience we will soon have. It turned out that it required a full lifetime, as odd as that may appear to you. It also seems there is some mystery unfolding about our apparent ages. I seem to need to be an old man in relation to you. I don't know exactly why."

"That feels right to me too. Tell me more about our localized project then. What have you learned?"

"All right. This gets deep, so hold on. Perhaps you recall that I told you of several inter-nested triads we were composing—our three incarnations, the three species, the three states of projection."

"What do you mean by 'three states of projection'?" I ask.

"They are, in a phrase: formlessness, time and form."

"Yeah. I remember something about that." *Sort of,* I muse.

"Well, we have, all along, been incarnating in threes. We three—you, O and me—usually appear in three different time frames. There are rare lifetimes when we occur simultaneously, such as in your current one. *And* in Atlantis."

"That one was a doozy!"

He looks puzzled at my choice of words. Then with a quick look to the side and a long blink, he has retrieved the meaning. He chuckles. "Yes, a *doozy!* Well, here's another triad for you. One of the points on it is that long past civilization, Atlantis. Another point is here in my current life; and lastly, the third point is the vortex, or portal, you and O are creating."

"That makes *some* sense, I guess. But please refresh my memory about what all these triangles have to do with our project?"

"In the simplest statement, our project is a *projection*. It's all about cascading projections out of Source. Everything is a projection and a portal. They are interlinked phenomena. Portals enable projections; projections create portals."

I shake my head. "They do?"

"Take it simply as a metaphor. You don't have to understand it. The point is, it's the way manifestation works—in threes. That's the way all creation begins."

"OK. I remember something about this. Oneness generates duality. Duality and Oneness together make three-ness, or whatever. From there all the complexity manifests. Is that it?"

"Yes. These triangular dualities are the essence formula for manifestation, as we have discussed before. This so-called 'intelligent activity' is the *third ray* in the light of *Conscious Evolution*."

Old Man continues, "As you know, all experience is composed of *being* and *doing*. Projection is the doing, or secondary part; it is *not real*. Being is the *real* part. Portals are the mechanisms that enable the interchange; they're like catalysts. This is a long-winded way of saying our project isn't real."

"What?" I gasp impulsively.

"Just kidding. Of course that *is* true; no projection is real. But that's not my point. I'm only saying we need to look deeper to understand what the project *really* is. We need to look deeper to see who *we* really are."

"I've heard all this before. So, just what are we looking for in those depths?"

The old man sighs and his smile gleams. "That, my son, is the perfect question. I will not answer it yet though. Now that you have asked it, let the question steep like an infusion of fine tea. Let its fragrance rise in the morning air like an essential perfume.

"What I will say for now is that we are engaged in a dance between formlessness and form. It is the game of incarnation. Oneness is the gamekeeper. She decides who separates and who unites, when and where, and with whom. She directs all the action. She is alive, and we are her minions—her darlings, if you will. We do not dictate the rules or outcomes of the game; she does.

"Our minds join in the dance and the game, and it takes on a semblance of reality. Vigilans and humans alike are immersed in the illusion; and we must take it for real while we're here. For you humans, the intensity was much more acute. Everything is changing for you. Recall that your mind is a vehicle of *doing*, not of being. All that the mind has considered real must be renegotiated when faced with these eternal archetypes. And this has recently played out as the renegotiation of your *ego contract*."

"Recently?" I interrupt. "That was 26,000 years ago."

"That's only a matter of time!" Again he laughs at his own feeble joke. Then he puts on a face. "Seriously, it's as nothing. This is what I'm talking about. See through *all* the projected forms. Trace backward from the manifestation to the projection, to the Oneness. *This* is the passage you all seek in your tempestuous day.

"The more you cling to the illusion and fear the manifestations, the less you will be able to access the *grace of freedom*. Do not fear! Of course, being human, you *will* fear. Nevertheless, carry the *mantram* of fearlessness in your heart. That's just as good."

He pauses, considering. "In fact, it's even better. Being human, you have the opportunity to overcome fear. This produces awakening. Look into every fear and complaint, every disturbance, and see though to the other side. See that which is projecting out these forms of fear. See that which *cannot be seen*. Let seeing become knowing. Knowing *within* is power! It can be felt and realized at any moment.

"Transformation will only come to you when you accept your true power—that is, Source. With that acceptance, you will step back from the confusion, and from the illusion that you're caught in your disintegrating world. That disintegration is *not real*. That world is not real, and it never was!"

Letter Forty
Lens

"Is that a lion roaring out there, across the river?" I ask, staring intently into the far tree line.

"Yes. They come down to the shore often," Old Man answers casually. We are walking a narrow dirt path along the water's edge.

"That's amazing. There were no lions left when I lived here."

"Really?" He replies. "What a shame. That must have been a difficult time to be alive. In our age, the animals have all returned to their natural balance. Once humans woke up, all of nature followed suit and changed its own resonance."

"Aren't they dangerous, these lions?"

"Not if you know their ways. We can hear their desires at a long distance. That fellow over there is simply looking for his friends. He is wandering and sniffing to find them. His group is not far away."

The peace is profound here. The water flows swiftly out just a few meters. But it's almost silent, weaving gently through the grasses near the bank.

I query further. "Tell me, where does nature leave off and vigilan begin? How *natural* are you?"

"That's an interesting question. I'm not sure I've ever asked that of myself. I would say we do not feel separate from anything in nature. There is no boundary. And yet there is a threshold between our species and others. Similar thresholds run throughout our awareness and our world. These thresholds are never felt as barriers to the Life force in us. Rather, just the opposite. They are bridges. The underlying Oneness is predominant. Yet it coexists with, and integrates, differentiation.

"We feel nature within our bodies and beings. It is the same nature that is within the lion, within the grasses and water. Life energy flows through each species and crosses the thresholds among us at will. Part of that lion is my own energy, and his spirit is in me. We are each like pools in a meandering stream. Nature is our means of communion and sensation. Within its embrace, I know what that lion knows. It knows what I know. We each know in different, unique ways, but not separate ways."

My memories of Africa prompt another question. "I recall that the water in this river carried a deadly parasite, *shistosoma*. How do you relate to such a danger?"

"My dear colleague. You must remember, as well as I do, our conversation from the ancient past. We have no diseases here. There are no parasites that attack us. We found long ago, that nature would be beneficent if we chose for her to be. This is the awakening we have often spoken of. The microbe you mention still exists in these waters. But it is now *beneficial* to our health, not the reverse."

I shake my head. "It's just so hard for me to understand that. I'm glad to hear it. But I can't quite believe it."

"No problem. Just *allow* instead of believing."

"All right. I've heard that advice before too."

We have come to a small dock on the riverbank. There are a number of large canoes—*pirogues*—lined up, partially out of the water. The old man signals to two younger men sitting in the shade of a great tree. They rise and come near, exchanging comments in a language I don't recognize. My guess is that it's a descendant mix of Songhai and Hausa.

"Please. Come with me in the boat. We will take it out on the water. These friends of mine will paddle for us."

"Where are we going?" I wonder aloud, with a slight trepidation. "What other animals are out there in the river? Are there crocodiles? Hippos?"

"Yes indeed. They will do us no harm. Come."

I'm not convinced. But, after all, this is a dream. Right? I climb aboard and take a seat on an old wooden plank, fixed crosswise in the center of the canoe. The boat lurches uneasily from side to side as I try to steady myself. The two men push us out from shore and climb in, for and aft with long paddles, just as they would have done ages ago. The pirogue is long and narrow, made from some water-resistant wood. It could hold several more passengers.

We rock from side to side with the motion of the paddles. I'm a little nervous, but these men obviously know their business. I look at the water slipping alongside and wonder at its passage. This river has been flowing ceaselessly for millions of years. It is changeless and yet always changing.

An insight tells me I'm just like this river. I too am flowing, changeless and ever changing. I'm a living paradox! I feel the Life force flowing through me from the river, the air, the vigilans. I look at Old Man. I see he is already staring into my eyes. He is reading my soul, and my life, with all its fullness and emptiness, its joys and sorrows.

"Where are we going?" I inquire timidly.

"You asked me a question a while back. Would you like an answer now?"

"What question? Oh, I think I asked about our project. You said we needed to look deeper. I asked you what we should be looking for in those depths?"

"Yes," he says very slowly, deliberately, drawing out the word in slow motion. He glances out over the water. We have arrived in the middle of the wide river, a hundred meters from either shore. "The answer will come from within you, yourself. Look down into the water, into the deep. It is there inside you. Look down into the flowing waters within yourself."

The rushing current against the sides of the boat takes on a force I hadn't noticed before. The sound is loud. We begin turning laterally. I grip the gunnels with tight fists. The water swirls in a great ring. Deep dark ripples are encircling us. To my amazement, it's becoming a whirlpool, sweeping around on all sides. We are at the center. It spins faster, and the canoe is turning within it. The pool is pulling at me; its magnetism grows stronger. It sinks deeper in the center, where black water turns. I feel a powerful feminine energy in this darkness, a *fluid* deep.

Suddenly I'm helpless again, hypnotized. With a groan, I am leaning, now falling over the edge of the pirogue. What's happening? I cannot move; it's as if I'm paralyzed. My face descends in slow motion toward the surface. I'm out of the boat, in the air, then into the water. There's nothing I can do to stop it. But strangely, I have no fear. I do not resist. Something inside tells me to accept. OM watches on, calmly, from above in the boat.

The light of the sky obscures under the whorl and splashing water as I descend. I'm sinking. A dark mass brushes past me. *What was that?* Gasping, I let go of the air in my lungs. With no ability to resist, I breathe in the water. It fills my lungs, my mouth and nose. Yet again, I do not panic. I am breathing water! Slowly, thickly, I draw in deep breaths of the dark liquid, and sink farther down, and farther within myself. The vortex turns in me and around me.

"Listen. Watch with your body what is unfolding in the deep." The old one's voice is an echo in my head.

I want to call out to him, to get me out of this, to demand an explanation. But my voice is stifled by the heavy water in my lungs. Nevertheless, I'm still alive, breathing. Awake! *This darkness should not be new to me; I've gone into the Void before; I've fallen into the center of a black hole, for mercy's sake! Why should this be any more frightening?* This darkness is different though. I'm still very much in my body.

"You're inside yourself, my friend." There's that voice in my head, reading my thoughts.

Why am I here? I answer in like manner. *Why am I under water?*

"You're in dreamtime, remember. This is the answer to your question. It is the answer you are giving yourself."

But why can't you just give me the answer? I strain.

"Because you want this; your body wants to give you this."

My mind suddenly explodes with color. Abstract shapes fly past me on all sides. They are flung away, off me, like leaves in an autumn storm. Everything is a blur of motion. Light radiates from each form and penetrates my mind.

At first it is utter confusion. But slowly the photons begin to impart information. Light is coming into form! The energy itself is informing me, forming *in* my body. And now all is still, falling into a vibrant peace. The exploding light settles into a soft, liquid glow, embracing me, elevating me. Understanding begins to seep out of the peace—in passing. *A passage, a portal,* I note.

I now know that all my thoughts, my emotions, my personality, have been stripped away. I am in the center of myself—my body, physical and etheric. The colors and shapes were the accreted pieces of myself, gathered throughout all my lifetimes, being torn away as I descended to this center. Nevertheless, this is still a *physical* space.

Some of the shapes I just saw were the tissues, the cells and molecules hurtling past as I shrank down within them, beneath their size and dimension. Now I am utterly small, the tiniest physical portion of myself. This is 'core central' of my body. *I am* this *tiny!* I chuckle. *Who knew my sense of self could be this small?* I am beneath any measurable dimension. It would be easy to overlook this tininess of self entirely. In fact it *has* been overlooked by all human science.

To my surprise, I have not come down to a *point*. The center of my quest is not a form at all. It is a space, a field—the very tiniest, minuscule *field*. It shines with a fantasia light. I draw my awareness in closer. The field before me fluctuates, oscillating. It seems to come and go from existence. Inherently, I know this object is the *end* of me. It is the *limit;* smaller than this, there is no physical form of self. This is the quantum crossover into non-physicality.

My perspective shifts with each pulse of the field. When it is strongest, and more form-like, I feel I'm merging with it. When it pulses away into formlessness, I return to my 'self'. The more I watch, the more I *am* what I'm watching. My point of view slowly moves back and forth between the field and me, like sea grass in an underwater current. One pulse, I exist; the next, I do not. I know myself coming and going, both—in and out of the projected universe.

A strange realization comes. I know that as I shrank myself, I also compressed my perception of time. The pulse I'm registering in this field would take less than a nanosecond in my normal time. And yet it is slow motion to me here. I come and go in a smooth, flowing rhythm. The merging of mind and body is growing in me—body and universe, duality and Oneness.

I see the 'shine' of my being—whatever that is—moving in and projecting out through the field, then pulling back into nothing. This field is the final frontier, the last portal of my physical existence. And my sensations here are very different from mental awareness. In fact, this is a critical realization. My body and mind have been at odds until this moment. They have not been integrated—not at all. Now they are blending and acknowledging their inherent unity. In this embrace, the warring aspects of myself are at ease.

The Oneness continues drawing me into its field. My body-mind is, in fact, the aperture; it is the *vesica piscis*. I am the womb, the feminine opening into the abyss—*yoni*. Likewise, I am the form that it projects and receives—*lingam*. I understand what you have been saying.

This field of tininess is a new window on the great emptiness. Before, I have descended into it through a spiritual dimension—the Void, *Evam*. Now I am *physically* on its threshold, a whole different experience. It's visceral this time. Suddenly, I feel the water in my lungs again. So far above, but it's still there; *I* am still there. Each in-breath in that world takes a lifetime from this perspective. The complete breathing would take more time than I could even imagine. So vast, that illusion!

'I am' is in sheer ecstasy in all this. The wonder and bliss increase geometrically with each pulse into the nothingness. The pulse is projected up and out into the breathing above, in radiated waves. It is withdrawn again, alternately, into nothing. This is the pulse—duality out, Oneness in. Oneness is nothingness. Duality is 'everything-ness'. I'm passing in and out of my own life. *Is this death?* I muse. *How beautiful!* The 'self' is virtually gone. Then I'm back; then away again. But even while I'm gone, my awareness remains. However, it is the awareness of a being, far more expansive than I knew.

This awareness is the projector itself, an intuition alerts me. I am enfolded in its breast, its heart and blood, its eternal, conditionless love. No expectations or judgments. Those are forms. This love has no form, yet it projects all forms. Within the sensation I'm having there is no contradiction or distinction. I still sense, nevertheless, the magic of paradox here. All is one. All is nothing—*one* and *zero*. 'O' and '0' merge and part, merge and part.

After a timeless interval, I sense a voice from far away. It is the voice of someone familiar. Dreamily I decide it might be good to listen. Whispers unfold around me, and slowly pulse me back across the threshold.

"Come back, old friend. Come back. It is not your destiny to depart yet."

How silly! I think. *Of course I know my own destiny.* And then I really *do* know it. In a great rush, I realize what Old Man is saying. I must return from this bliss. With a shudder I separate myself in two again, enter the world of duality. I am physical again, looking down on the pulsing *vesica* from above. I remember. *I'm here to learn something more, something else about portals.*

What else could there be to know about portals? I try to shout, but underwater it comes out sounding like 'Wussel-tha-bunno-ptul?' I laugh, and recall my predicament.

Old Man's voice comes again. *"Know this. You are intended to be free and bound in one-and-the-same experience—that is your physical life. Accepting this is liberation to your spirit, and to your whole being. It is the gift of the formless to form, form to formless. Your blessing to be human, and mine to be vigilan, is to know the interplay of projection and Projector, of bounded-ness and boundlessness.*

"The portal you have just experienced, that you seek to create in the greater sphere—as a passage through the Storm—is your ultimate paradox. That Great Storm is the passage through you. It is your own living essence—projector and projection. You will pass into it, through the aperture, and find yourself. You will know who you really are. Pass through it and you will die!"

Die? I challenge, taken aback. *You're joking!*

"Not at all."

A new thought is dawning in me. *What? Wait. I thought you just said 'don't die'.*

"I said it is not your time to depart."

Are you telling me that if I use this portal-passage, I'll die? We'll all die? As the realization sinks in, I feel like shouting. I feel betrayed. Ego, apparently, has returned. *O never said anything about this. She said the species would die, not the individual. Why would anyone want to use this portal then? I thought it was supposed to be a safe passage?*

Chuckling, Old Man's deep, African voice continues, *"A moment ago you were ready to merge with the Void and give up your life. And now you're afraid to die? Humans!"*

I recall the feeling of bliss from a moment ago. Passing over wasn't bad at all. In fact, it was highly seductive. Gradually, I return to calmness. Then I say mockingly, *So, would you mind explaining about this 'portal of death' then?*

"Ah, human humor! Yes. I will explain. We are talking about transformation here, friend. Major transmutation—leaving one species behind, becoming another—this cannot happen without death. Did you think your species would die without its individuals going with it? I sense a smile. But don't worry. You won't feel a thing."

Is that vigilan *humor?* I retort. *All right. I do remember O talking about death in the first set of letters. But I guess I had forgotten. I wasn't applying it to myself. I guess I was starting to hope she was just speaking metaphorically.*

"Relax, friend. This is all happening just the way you yourself have planned it. Your soul has known it all along. Your destiny."

Well, I'm not sure that's much comfort, I scowl. *I don't always agree with what my soul wants.*

I gaze upon the beauty of the pulsing ovoid below me. It is indeed exquisite. I now see rainbow coruscations shimmering around it. I sigh. *OK. I think I'm ready. I'll die if I must! I guess it's not so bad in the great scheme. What about this portal?*

"The vesica piscis *is the centermost field of our incarnation,"* OM answers. *"It is our eternal birthplace—where we are always being born, without beginning and without end. This is eternal purity itself. And it is you!"*

I interrupt, projecting thoughts up from my tiny world. *I certainly got that sense just now. I was dying, leaving for sure, as I crossed that threshold. And it felt* so *good. Coming back was like a* birth. *I do understand it now, down here. But this place is 13,000 years in my future, at the bottom of a river, at the bottom limit of my physical body. It's so far removed and remote from the problems in my time, the time of the Great, Dark Storm. How can this be relevant in that world?*

"Trust me, it can. Yes, this does seem remote, just as I seem remote from you. But that is illusion—all those years are illusion, mere projections. In reali-

ty, we are together in one moment, you and I. No matter whether a million years separate us. The essence of 'who we are' is never far, never remote. It sits within every moment; it surrounds your illusory self with expansive reality, ready in an instant to become your presence. This knowing will be critical in your time of the Great Storm. Know it without thinking about it."

I react, *Well, I'll try. But how can I not think about it? You know, thinking is a big problem for humans. We get stuck in our minds all the time.*

The voice is quick to reply. *"Indeed. In fact for humans, the mind predominantly blocks awareness of who you are. You can learn to see through yourself, see through that mental sense of you. This is about learning to recognize the spaces between your thoughts, and within your thoughts. Use the subtler mind, or* manas. *Surely, you must be acquainted with that idea."*

Yes, I am. The spaces are always there in my thoughts, I know. Like holes in my head. I can't resist a joke.

OM continues, punning, *"Hah. And the space is also 'holy'. Seriously, it is all around, in vast dimensions—holistic. Imagine this: A small cloud is above you in the sky. That cloud is like a thought; the greater sky is the field of your holistic awareness. That is the relationship between who you really are and what your mind is."*

Well, I can't see the sky from here. But I know what you mean.

"The relationship between your mind and your appreciation of who you really are is the portal; it is the vesica. And it is your living presence."

I'm getting confused again. The vesica is my 'presence'? The relationship is the portal?

"Is that not what you just experienced, my friend? We are all channels; it is our nature. The portal you seek to open is within yourself. I'm certain O has said that to you. It is manifested in the vesica field. But the essence of it really is the opening of your deep appreciation, and grounding that in your understanding. You are moving out of your mind and into the appreciated universe.

"We are each, one aperture for the projector. This is to say we are lenses, focusing the light of creation into infinite images. There is a grand prismatic effect to all this. By this means we are co-creators of the Cosmos. This is our most intimate destiny in the Now. We are bringers of light into form! Collectively projected, we are the full spectrum of colors of the divine rainbow. Some have called our light bodies, 'rainbow bodies' for this reason.

"Now, here is the new twist on this ancient reality. In passing through the 'portal', we are reversing the projection. This reversal is what evolution is demanding of humanity in your time. It is a reversal of intention in the very depths of your body and soul. The intention is to move away from separation and into union—awareness of Oneness! This is what lies behind the evolutionary step away from ego. It is a shift from within the projection and within the projector itself. I know you are troubled with comprehending how your species can change. It seems impossible to you."

Yes, *I must admit. It still does.*

"In reality this is not about you as a person or even as a species. It is that the projector itself is shifting its direction. Conscious Evolution is what is changing."

I ask, *Is the projector God then?*

"Do not labor for explanations. God or Source cannot be explained to the mind. O and I have given you many explanations. It's true. But there comes a time when your awareness must reach maturity, and stop demanding that the mind be your only means of understanding. It is a childish thing from where I stand.

"I intend no condescension here. I know that you and your kind are ready for maturity. Your consciousness no longer needs to grasp the explanation of things, with all the comparisons and form constructions. The answer to your last question is then, 'Yes and no'. Embrace the projector as an intuitive realization. It is not a thing, a form, a soul, a God. And yet it is all of these. Let the embrace surpass your need for explanation. Let the power of formlessness be sufficient."

I *hear you. I feel what you just said. Wanting endless explanations is suddenly so cumbersome. I think I'm almost ready for that maturity. I hope so.*

"You are. Still, I will offer an explanation in mental terms—a summation of what you have come here to know. The vesica *aperture within each of us, within each living creature, is a lens of our own creation, out of our own 'stuff' and being. But now, as we speak of a passage through the Storm and through the portal, we are speaking of reversing the current. We are returning to the projector,* de-projecting, *if you will.*

"In so doing, we must ride the light beam in reverse through the lens. This means we must redefine time within ourselves to allow the return to timelessness, to Oneness. We are adjusting the pulse—the fire—to draw us in, not to push

us out. The vesica has been called the Lens of Creation, the Seed of Life, in some traditions. You may now comprehend what is the essence of the portal project, and indeed the entire transposition project. It is a return to Oneness, out of duality."

No more words, please. I've heard enough. I turn back and see the aperture moving away below me. I am zooming out, up through the quarks, atoms and molecules. Finally, flesh and body. Water is in my lungs as I rise back to the surface of the river. This is suddenly not comfortable at all. I force the liquid out in vomiting surges, coughing and choking. My head breaks the surface in time to see a great crocodile swimming away. My God, I'm in danger! In seconds, the men in the canoe have hauled me back aboard. I'm gasping air, spitting water, blood in my eyes.

"Welcome back, friend." OM is smiling down at me, as I squirm on the floor of the canoe. "This part is a bit rough, I admit. But you'll be fine in a minute. Let's go back to the shore and have a nice meal. How about a fish dinner?"

"Wait," I sputter, trying to rise to my knees. "What was that crocodile about? Why didn't it have *me* for dinner?"

"Oh, you mean old Tijani? He was just helping us out a little. He's an old friend of mine in these waters. He was contributing some serpent energy to the whole equation. You know, *kundalini* and all. I think he did rather well in giving you the water breath. It was his influence that brought us out here in the first place. As I was saying, the animals are much more a part of our awareness now. It's the *intuitive* linkage—back to *instinct*. We are in tune with them and they with us. Our destinies cross paths often in the most beneficial ways. It's not just Life force that flows amongst us, but consciousness as well."

"All right," I sigh. "Whatever you say. Thanks. I don't want any more explanations just now."

I manage to prop myself up, still dripping, against the gunnels and close my eyes. The paddlers have already turned us back toward shore.

Letter Forty-One
The Bridge and the Stars

The dream is over. But I know it was more than a dream. It was as real as anything. I lie in bed, staring at the clock. 4 am. Everything is still. There's a police siren, faint in the distance—a ubiquitous sign of humanity. *Where is it going? Who's in trouble now? What about me? Am I in trouble? Why not just admit it.* I have no idea what's really going on. I'm in a constant state of confusion with these letters. Mostly I *know* they're for real, and yet at other times—like right now—I have grave doubts.

I look into my mind—a decidedly dangerous thing to do at this hour—and brood. I sense darkness there, and fear. It's a deep, bottomless fear. The more I look into it, the deeper it gets. It is endless. My mind manufactures this fear from the beginning. Then it manufactures all the vain attempts to escape from that same fear, to avoid facing it. It's all an incestuous tangle of mind-games.

My thoughts stir . The world is such a contentious mess these days. We seem to be sliding into ever-wider separation. There are so many divisive factions, between religions, between nations, within nations. Humanity seems on the verge of being ungovernable. No one wants to be told what to do. Yet many allow themselves to be told what to think. *Am I like them? Is my mind telling* me *what to think?*

Of course, government is the scapegoat right now. It can't do anything right. It can't find solutions to problems that keep morphing into twisted new parodies of themselves. Who's in charge—the banks, corporations, religions? Is it the super-wealthy elite, or some secret shadow government lurking behind it all? Maybe it's *aliens*, as some have proclaimed. *Is there any way out of this doubt? Is there any way to know the truth?* My mind reels on.

The clock has reached 4:30. I have spent half an hour twisting and contorting under the covers. *And what about the dream of Old Man, the river and the vesica? What relevance can that possibly have in this world, this dark night around my house, with its police sirens vanishing into the emptiness. Am I awake or am I dreaming? Does it even matter?*

Gradually, I return to sleep, and escape my questions for a time. I dream a tangle of things—people from my past in frustrating situations, places that are not real places, problems that are not real. They are all manufactured in my mind, for its own purposes. *What is this? Is there any meaning behind such dreams?* I drift awake again, slowly returning to my perennial fear—the emptiness. Sleep weaves in and out of this labyrinth, and finally, up into day. And I call it a night's rest.

Morning. I wander out from my house, into sunlight. It's a beautiful day, but I'm not appreciating it. I drive groggily to my favorite coffee house hoping caffeine will awaken me. I look numbly at the world in front of my windshield. Buildings and trees, people on the sidewalks, slide past—present for a few seconds, then gone into invisibility. *Were they real one moment, unreal the next?*

Am I real? Am I here? I've been told there is a 'projector' inside it all—way down below, underneath this sunny day, below the street façades, behind all the questioning and doubting within myself. *Is that projector the* real *reality? Or is this world the reality, and the projector just a figment of its imagination? Can anything have meaning, given what I'm feeling?*

A deeper part of me sends up a signal. *These are just thoughts. And thoughts are not real. Don't we all agree?* I continue arguing in my head, as I get the inevitable coffee—double espresso—and take it to a small table on the street—my favorite table. I'm grateful it's empty. Ah, gratitude. I get a flash of positive feeling. The warm sun on my arms and hands, the chair I'm sitting on, the cup I'm holding. It all seems so real. *How could this be just a projection? No. It can't. And yet, maybe it is.*

I reach into my pocket and take out the silver marble—our sphere of communion. It gleams in the sunlight, radiant. *Why don't I remember this more often?*

"Because you're human, my friend. May I join you?"

I know this voice. The mind chatter stops, and I look up. It's you. You're here again, standing in front of me. I rise, disoriented.

"O, what a delight. You never stop surprising me. You? Here in public? What is this? Can others see you?"

"No. But I thought I'd dress for this time anyway." You spread your arms and do a half-turn, inviting me to look you over. You're wearing a 21st-century dress of pale orange with subtle patterns woven in; a copper belt ties the waist against your slim figure.

"You look elegant. I love the way you've done your hair. That's new."

"Yes. I wanted to look my best for you."

I blush. "Well, that's very nice of you. Please sit. Can I get you a cuppa' ... What do you drink, anyway?"

"I already have a drink," you state, smiling. A cup appears suddenly in your hand. It's steaming with some warm liquid. You set it on the table, but remain standing.

"A little magic?" I react.

"Just a little." Your smile persists. Demurely, you add a faint wink.

I'm still holding the marble in my fingers. I lift it gleefully up, looking through it at you. In that moment I realize it's the color of your eyes! *It is your eye on my world!* "Look, O. Here's the sphere we manifested."

You grin. "It's beautiful. What a good partner you are."

I feel like a child, mumbling, "So what brings you to my time? God, it's good to see you!" I reach to hug you. Your arms fold around me warmly, with just the right pressure of fingers on my back. I feel your electricity again.

"How could I stay away? We have a project to tend to, right?" You let go of me and we sit down, facing.

"Sure. Sure," I mutter, frowning. I'm suddenly remembering my night's musings—and everything that's happened recently. Questions come heaving up. With effort, I hold them back. "Tell me again how it is that other people can't see you here? I mean we're on a public street. People are passing us right now."

"They are in your normal dimension. We are in a sub-dimension, as I believe I told you before. It's just like dreamtime."

I raise an eyebrow. "Hey. Have you been in touch with the old man?"

"Of course. He wouldn't leave me out of the loop. He seems to be doing just fine in his new life. He came to me in a sub-dimension, just like this. You recall, they use those inner spaces all the time in his world, like we use different rooms in a house."

"Yeah. It's a great idea. I wish I could create them myself."

"Well you *can*, you know. In fact you often do, without noticing it. The *subdi's*—sub-dimensions—flow and weave into your so-called normal time unannounced. If you pay attention you can detect the thresholds. It's only a matter of making conscious what's already there."

"Really? I can? What do you mean?"

"Let's see. Every time you sit down to write these letters—in a light trance—is one example of creating a *subdi*. Whenever you daydream or feel alone in a crowd, you're doing the same. Sub-dimensions can be very transparent and light, or completely encapsulated and off in their own sphere. For humans they can also be very dark and isolated—like your experience of fear last night."

"Hmm. You noticed that." I frown. But I don't want to talk about it yet. I continue asking about sub-dimensions. "Can we interact with others from those states? What accounts for that?"

"Some *subdi's* are very close to the consensus flow, and you can easily slip back and forth. It depends on the nature of one's creation. There are infinite possibilities."

"OK. That makes sense," I pause, wondering. "Sorry if I'm distracting you from the purpose of your visit with these questions. I'm sure you have more important things to talk about."

"You know by now that nothing between us is off-purpose. Whatever we say to each other is the reason we are together! We are in each other's destiny. That close." You stare into me, straight through my eyes, and touch the backs of my hands with your long, delicate fingers. I cringe with a sensation. *Oh no! Not right now, not in public. Please.*

"Oh, all right." You lift your hands away and laugh, glancing away, then back. I'm always with you, love. You know that, don't you?"

"My God, O. I can't handle this. I mean... thank you. But I've got a troubled mind today." I feign a grimace and look down.

"That's part of the reason I'm here, dear one. Tell me about it."

"Don't you already know? I can never tell how much you know about me. I'm such a sucker for you." My eyes fall and look away. "You're a very elusive spirit in my life. Yet, so close. But how do I even know you're real? How do I know I'm not hallucinating, and just making you up?"

"How do you know?" You smile and lean back, crossing your arms under your small, comely breasts. In a flash, I remember the adventure we had in your bedroom. The image excites me, and I'm caught up in it for a moment.

"There you are—creating a *subdi!* Do you see it?"

I laugh. "Ah, yes. I see it all right. What a vivid memory!"

"Sub-dimensions are often made of memories."

"Yes. I can imagine so. But I'd rather not go there right now."

"You'd rather not think about it?" Your eyes widen brightly.

"Please. I'm trying to focus."

"My friend, you know I'm just playing with you. It's important for us to be light, *and* to be in love. It's good for our soul! It's about bridging our times and our hearts. You know that."

"Yes. I feel it, I guess. Thank you."

"Now tell me what's troubling you." You uncross your arms and lay down your hands, up and open on the table. Sunlight streams over your shoulders onto them.

I turn my eyes to the sky. Clouds are drifting over. "Well, where do I start? Old Man took me 13,000 years into the future and dumped me into a river. Rather against my will, I'd say."

"Not against your *will,* but against your ego, for sure."

I wrinkle my brow. " Anyway, I sank to the bottom; then I went even deeper into my body. I was breathing water, for Pete's sake!"

I'm at last staring into your eyes. "Then I saw the *ultimate portal.* Old Man told me we have to die to enter it. What's that about? And, of course, as you recall, you and B took me 13,000 years into the past and—come to think of it—the same thing happened there. Only I drowned that time! I've got all these loose ends inside me right now. I've had a rough night of dark thoughts. I feel very fearful and *fragmented!*"

I take a long breath. "That's it. I feel like I'm in pieces all over the place—all over *time,* in fact. That sounds pretty psycho to me."

"Yes. It does to me too."

I frown and look you in the eye. "Gee, thanks. I thought you were here to *help.*"

"I am. I'm agreeing with your personal assessment. But don't worry. That's only a starting point. You humans need to feel the psychosis of your times. You're *all* crazy, you know!"

"Huh? Now that you mention it, I've been thinking that myself. Everyone I know has characteristics that seem really insane to me. Like we're all missing some very important piece of sanity in ourselves; we don't really know right from wrong sometimes."

Your eyes follow mine, but you say nothing. I continue, "Mostly, we don't even take time to notice it. Everyone I know, even my best friends believe pretty weird things about reality. I am including myself in this insanity, of course. Like, we think it's just normal, and there's nothing we can do about it. What's worse is we're all isolated by it, even the sanest of us. Our beliefs don't seem to unite us the way we want them to."

"That is a very sane assessment, friend. Beliefs *do* isolate you. They separate you from what you seek, because they're *substitutes* for what is real. Once you accept a belief in place of 'what is', you build a barrier around your mind, against reality. This is a constant mental condition for humans. It is insane indeed! Nevertheless, recognizing it is a good thing. Sometimes beliefs are necessary. But they can be seen as the transparencies they are.

"Simple noticing is often enough. Once you encounter the surface of reality, you can go further into it. You do this by stopping the resistance. You can just pause for a second and let resistance melt away." Your eyes are suddenly intense. "Right now. Take a moment and do that. Just *be* with your being."

I follow your advice, and stop my thoughts for a second or two. It's as though my mind is melting into a peaceful space. I recognize that space as the Now. It's always there in my best meditations. *Stillness.* I smile. *It works!*

You resume, "In that space, it's easier to know who you really are, what really *is,* and what action is appropriate to take. In a word, you can choose to be *authentic.* All resistance disappears. That's the beginning of sanity. And it's the beginning of unity with others."

"Yeah, the 'three suggestions'. I've often found them really helpful. I do see the need for them. But I still have so many questions. Just what am I to do with the memories of my experience in Atlantis and in the River *Isa Ber?*"

"That is just what we will explore next. Take my hands, please."

I know what this means. I look again into the sky, resigned. I see the clouds are getting thicker and darker above us, somehow reflecting my apprehension. Hesitantly, I open my palms and push them a little forward across the table. I glance around to see if anyone is watching. No one pays us any mind. We two are clearly in our own *subdi.*

"Just relax and follow me. We will create a *secondary* subdimension now. Observe how I do it."

You close your eyes and take a deep breath. As I watch, you seem to flicker in space. It's like a projection has been distorted by mist. I see a faint impression of your aura. It vibrates in waves, from the periphery toward the center. There is a secondary set of waves moving down from your head to your heart, and up to your heart from below as well. Slowly the daylight fades.

You and I are now standing on a city street. It's nighttime. There's a crisp starry sky above. We're still holding hands. The table and chairs, everything else is gone. The stars twinkle brightly overhead. The night is clear and very still, no breeze. In a rush I recognize where we are. We're in Seattle, my old hometown. *How can the stars be so bright here in the city?* I wonder.

I know this street well. You pull on my right hand and we begin to walk. It's late at night with no traffic around. Not even police sirens, I notice. We turn a corner and I see a familiar site. It's the Eastlake Bridge on the edge of Lake Union. Something's different about it though. There are shops nearby that were closed years ago. All the parked cars are decades old. It dawns on me that this is not the present time. You've taken me into the past. Intuition is unfolding in my mind. This is one of *my memories;* I suddenly know the event that's about to unfold.

"You were twenty-three in this scene, I believe."

"Yes. I remember well. There I am." It's so strange to see. I watch my younger self leave the little houseboat down on the lake, where my girl friend lived. I had recently met her in a class at the university. The young man walks up the ramp and the winding trail to the street. Ignoring our presence, this figure proceeds right past us out onto the bridge. We slowly follow him. In the middle of the bridge he stops and looks down. The walkway is a metal grating. He can see through it down into the water. But to his astonishment, looking straight down, he finds himself staring at the sky, brilliant with stars! It is a perfect mirror reflection of the sky above. The air is so still that the surface is like glass.

I remember how disoriented I had become, staring down and then up, and not really knowing which was which; it was like an optical illusion, hypnotic. I watch as the young me loses his balance, grabbing at the iron railing. He realizes he must hang on or else fall down from dizziness.

I see the expression on his face and remember even more fully how I felt at the time. This was a cosmic event in my imagination. An attractive young woman had just made love to me—but not quite.

As it turned out, I was anything but disappointed. The notion was strange and wonderful to me—lying naked, intertwined, totally conscious of each other, yet motionless. Our bodies and sensations were held in reverent stillness. I have always remembered that experience as vividly as I remember the bridge, the water and the stars. For some reason though, I never thought of them as parts of the same event over the years. They had become separate memories in my mind.

I explain, "Beth and I had just made love—sort of. It was different."

"What do you mean by that?" you ask, smiling discretely.

I answer, a little embarrassed, "Well, we were holding each other—clothes off—all evening. You know what I mean. But that's as far as it went. And this was in the years of the 'sexual revolution' no less!"

You look at me with great tenderness. "No less."

As I ponder, the youthful image before me changes. Seamlessly, I flow into his body and his place. I now stand at the railing, gazing paradoxically *down* at the black sky. Thousands of stars reach up at me, and move away at the same time. Parallax. It is just as mesmerizing now as it was all those years ago, even more so. You are standing slightly behind me. I whisper over my shoulder, with awe in my voice. "O, would you mind telling me what this means. Why am I reliving this?"

"It's beautiful. Is it not?"

"Yes, of course. I'm thrilled to see this again. It was a once-in-a-lifetime event! It has never been duplicated since. But why are you and I here?"

"It was a seminal event for you."

"Yes," I whisper and stare down into the Cosmos. Tears are streaming down my cheeks now. Emotion is overflowing my senses.

"I have witnessed your memory. I know what is happening. This, my friend, is the *orgasm* you did not experience with your lover. It is your *union* with Earth and Sky, with light and night, with fire and water. Let your mind play with this, and you will know why we are here."

I turn to her, sobbing out of sheer ecstasy. *This is all so overwhelming and intimate.* But there is clarity as well. I am on the bridge of my destiny, suspended between two mirrored infinities. *How synchronistic that this is Lake Union!* All of my pasts and futures are arrayed below, and above me in these stars. They too are suspended. They are parts of me. We are alike, projections on this sable canvas.

The emptiness now rises up and swamps my feelings. I'm helpless, hopeless, without recourse to safe passage. I am *insane!* All the stars in my sea and my sky are afloat, in the same boat, on the same bridge. I am pierced with an inescapable anguish, seized by sudden doubt and fear, in a place where that should not be. *What is this ache in my heart?* I taste the same fear I felt in my bed last night. It hangs in the air. I stare into it with all my might.

At last you speak. "My friend, I will help you now. I can feel your pain. I know this to be the pain that all humans are capable of feeling, that most humans will do anything to *avoid* feeling. I applaud your courage to allow it. Let this pain now be your guide."

Bewildered, I let go. In allowing, I discover the pain is not insurmountable, though it is sharp. It softens and transforms within my sensibilities, but it's no less profound. It is echoing the ache of the Earth. There is an infinity within it. I see that, strangely, the *anxiety* is an essential part of the *ecstasy*. Without this, humanity itself would never have come into being.

To my additional astonishment, I begin to *relish* feeling it. It surrounds me and penetrates me, fills me to overflowing. The pain takes on a face. It is not anonymous! And then it transforms further. It turns into the face of the woman I just made love to in the houseboat. She smiles at me from her soul, beyond the kin of pain. Embracing her own ecstasy, she laughs at this pain.

And now I realize. She was *not human!* She was a divine gift—an angelan. She was an angel, planted in my experience for this night's very purpose. That purpose is only now coming to fruition. As I watch, this angel's face takes full womanly form. Her beautiful, naked body descends into view like a curtain of mist. She gracefully lifts her hands up beside her head. Then she slides them deliberately across her face, like scissors; finally, she brings them back to the sides of her face. It is a most beguiling and mystical *mudra.* Her smile, her motion, intoxicates me. It is a blessing from heaven. Now I can fully accept this blessing.

Beth had disappeared from my life soon after that night. I think we had walked a trail near the lake just one last time, late at night, talking of weighty subjects. Perhaps we spoke about the slowly waking consciousness in the world. That was the last time I ever saw or heard from her. She simply vanished. She had given me some excuse, like traveling to California to visit a relative—never to return. No forwarding address. None of our friends knew her whereabouts either. She had forever after remained a mystery, a hole in my mind, and indeed in my heart. That was many, many years ago.

"A beautiful memory."

"O, you're reading my thoughts!"

"I am not. This is not about *thought* at all," you say firmly. "The 'aurora in your aura', my friend, is like an open book. I can't help but appreciate the experience."

Your words bring me back to you, and back to the bridge. Tears are still streaming down my cheeks. "This is truly special, O. Thank you so much for bringing me to relive this. How could I have forgotten such a beautiful feeling?"

"Because you had not fully felt it until this moment! That memory of the past is totally here now. So, without further ado, allow me to bring your attention to the stars again."

I turn my gaze, first up, then down. It seems I am *floating* in the center of a huge star field. It wraps above and below, and would continue to the horizon if I could see that far. The sides of the bay are thick, dark frames to the celestial vision. But instead of rendering solidity, these frames just exaggerate the visual depth, below and above. Suddenly I cannot say which is up or down. I feel weightless. *Yes, now the memory returns. This is what I felt at the time.* I recall grabbing the railing, not just to keep from falling. But to keep from floating away!

"Take a good deep look at those stars, friend. Tell me what you see."

"Oh no! Not Atlantis again! Somehow it's right in that star. Do we have to go through this *again?*"

"Keep looking."

I turn my eyes to another star. It's a life scene from a far-away land. But I know it is me in that body, in another lifetime. Another star. I see myself as a soldier, bleeding and dying on a great, anonymous battlefield, lying in the mud among fallen horses. Another star. I see myself as a monk in Tibet, reverently fingering prayer beads in a dark chamber. Then there is another, as a dying soldier. Monk and soldier images alternate, one after another. At last all these star-scenes begin to group together in a circle, into a mandala of images. They form a huge orbit in both the sky and water around me.

I am watching the death scenes of each of those lives—all in one vision. Then I see the birth scenes of each lifetime as well. Other lives, not soldiers or monks, join into the circle. It is a great, glowing wreath of birth and death—all mine. This is reflecting what I saw it in the crypt in Atlantis with Allamorath. But now it has become more vivid and complete.

Your voice is somber, ceremonial. "The Buddhists and Hindus called this the Wheel of Karma. It is the wheel of duality—cause and effect. This visual form of it is about projection and return, in all your lives. Each lifetime is a karmic wheel in itself, moving into form and back out again. Your spirit—the apportioned Life energy that is your individual nature—is bound to these wheels by the laws of duality and action. For every action, there is an equal and opposite reaction."

The panoply fleshes out with images from other significant parts of all those lives. The details fill in more and more as I watch. All the feelings that went with the images now press upon me. All my lives on Earth are now appearing in this grand wreath. All the details and feelings and lessons of those lives are there to behold. It's the 'lifetime-review' of every life I've ever had. *This is impossible! How can my awareness hold so much information?*

"This is far beyond your mind's capacity to contain," you whisper.

"Are you sure you're not reading my mind?" I manage a quip.

"I'm sure. This is way out of mind's league. Be alert to what I said. You are experiencing first-hand the 'other' awareness that I spoke of in the first letters. It is that which transcends the mind, via the heart. Just be aware of that."

"Yes, indeed. You're right. That's the only way I could be seeing and feeling all this. And I'm *still* seeing it. You can see it too?"

"Yes. It's quite a picture show. You know, these are *my* lives as well. Now perhaps you could tell me what it all means?"

I stop, then sigh. "Me? I was hoping *you* would do that. I should have known."

"I *will* tell you one thing. You are about to reconcile a profound imbalance in your personality. This is why we're here, my brother. All your sub-personalities are being brought together for this. This is why you sank into the river and why you met your *vesica*. You must rejoin your soul through these lives and bring them into Oneness with your spirit. This is the *passage* of which we speak!"

"Yes. I sense it. Yes!" The wreath of lifetimes begins to slowly roll. In the motion, there is a message. The images are arranged in an order that tells me how all these lives fit together—far deeper than mere chronology. It is an intricate pattern, arranged by my soul, *our* soul. I can see the lifetime you are living now, in 500, among these stars. I see future lives, beyond yours as well. This is the catalogue of our soul's entire experience on Earth.

"O, I see these *are* your lifetimes too! We are one soul! I guess I didn't really believe it until now."

You hold silence reverently. Now the stars around the wreath draw closer. The whole night sphere is shrinking, pulling everything together around us on the bridge. It occurs to me now that the shapes of color that flew off me in my descending vision were pieces of all my life experiences. But they do not want to be discarded; they want to be joined again, *bound*—this time, with conscious intent. They want to be part of the elegant equation with boundlessness. They can only do this if I accept them into my awareness as blessings, each and every one—the good, bad and ugly.

I lurch suddenly. My heart is open, seemingly split wide. It is broken into a thousand million pieces. And these pieces too rise up and merge into my presence. They join the dance of boundless joy. *I can't wait any longer.* This is excruciating. I shout, "Cut to the chase. I accept! I accept!"

Then a shot rings out through my mind, and all else of me. I hear. I see. I know. This is the *repaying of karma with joy* that you talked about. Or was it Old Man? Or was it B? I can't seem to remember. We are *one*—the soul matrix, the whole group. All of us. I know that my acceptance, in full consciousness, is the repayment. And it is totally joyful. Only pure bliss could exceed this joy. Only Oneness could exceed this freedom.

"There is yet one more step—beyond acceptance," you whisper.

"Truly?" My voice is virtual silence now. "What else?"

"Forgiveness. The projection can only return to its Source through *giving* up your life—for Life! You must accept and forgive yourself, in each and every moment of action in all these lives. This is literally a *death* in you. And, my dearest heart and self-same soul, I must join you in this. We are one projection, you and I. Together, we must return through the lens."

Now around us, above and below, in the sky and in its perfect reflection in the underworld, the great wheel begins to turn. I am frozen in place by its motion. It is the excruciatingly wonderful, *movement within stillness*. I see two great circles take form and begin to separate from within—a wheel within a wheel; one is gold, one is silver. The silver orbit is made from my lives as soldiers and 'hardened' selves. The gold is that of monks and 'softened' selves. All the scenes fuse into these thin metallic tubes of light. In their turning, the two rings pull away from each other sideways. Slowly. Then they stop.

The gold and silver rings are overlapping to form a *vesica!* And you and I are in its center, aglow with its pulsing Life force! Once again it overtakes my presence. I am at one with its infinite depth. *We* are at one. It has transplanted its field into our being. It tells me that there is, in reality, only one *vesica piscis* in all the Cosmos; it is the singularity that unifies and reveals Oneness for all creation.

My experience is simultaneously here, in this vision above Lake Union, and likewise at the tiniest threshold of physicality—the essence of birth and death—in the waters of the *Isa Ber.* Around us, all the births and deaths and karma of lifetimes, fused in the rings, are resonating, projecting themselves in and out of our Earth evolu-

tion. Some hundred births and lives and deaths are resolving themselves within us in this timeless moment. You pour your own spirit
of forgiveness into mine. And, as one soul, we offer it into the *vesica.*

"Stop now!" Your voice cracks the space. "This is where you
must and *will* go, my love, when it is your time. But not yet! For
now, take the full measure of appreciation from the display, from
our joining and our revelation. Take all these lives and all this understanding into yourself and return to the one life you are living
now, on Earth, on the edge of the Storm."

Like a stroke of lightning, the *vesica* field snaps directly into my
heart. There it sears into my flesh—a molten star, a crystalline lens
of being, and of *not* being. Shakespeare's question mutates. "To be
and not to be." Quickly this implosion is followed by the collapse of
the silver and gold rings. They plunge into my body through the
crown and root chakras. I feel filled by their power and electricity,
surging in every atom of me. With no warning or preparation, I
suddenly explode with energy! White light gushes in all directions
out, erupting from the central lens. My body, shaken and roused,
convulses and spins into a fetal ball. I collapse.

Darkness. Lightning sparks sizzle through me and around me.
They finally fall to quiescence. I'm lying, face down on the metal
grating of the bridge. All is still. The night and its revelation are a
frozen firmament. I lie here this way, in silence, for a long time.

"O?" at last I murmur.

"I'm here. I've been waiting," your whispering voice caresses.
"Let me heal your wounds."

"My what?" I croak, still lying prone. "Wounds?"

"Yes. You've cut yourself on the metal."

Blood is trickling down my cheek, and onto my hands. You
wave your fingers over the cuts. They are sutured instantly. Erased.

Slowly I rise up on my elbows, my eyes blurry. I manage a feeble smile and mumble, "These sub-dimensions can be pretty realis-
tic, eh?"

You grin and continue moving your hands purposefully around my aura. I study your beautiful face while you're working your healing miracle. Those silver eyes are focused like none I've ever seen this close. There is an awesome power in them. And I'm struck, knitting my brow. *Those are* my *eyes!* I grin.

"Now, I did read *that* thought! You can't have my eyes just yet. I still need them," you smile and sigh deliberately. "Ah, my friend, we are here as distinct individuals for a reason, you know."

"I know indeed. I think it is so that I can love you, and learn to love my own *self*." I lay contentedly at you feet.

Your eyes, your hands on my face bring me full circle to you. I *know* you. There is no one else I could ever know this way. You bend down and kiss me, slowly, deeply. I feel totally touched by your body and your essence. A sense of fullness, completion, buoys me inside.

Revived, I wrestle myself to a sitting position and look at you, then around at the city street. Everything is magically silent. Lights blink gently on the distant shore. But nearby, all is dark and asleep.

"There! Better now?" You are kneeling beside me, lightly stroking the top of my head. You laugh suddenly and pull me to my feet. The laughter wells up out of the wide silence. Your eyes are on mine, sparkling. "You are so young, human soul. You are so full of freshness and innocence. And dare I say, *naïveté*. You totally beguile me. I am in love with the soul of humanity. You are a wonder of evolution!"

Letter Forty-Two
Naïveté

The dark street suddenly vanishes and we are back at the table and the sunny morning. I blink and look around, covering my eyes against the glare. Nothing has changed. The same woman, who was walking past our table when we left, is still doing so. The passage of time in the 'Lake Union' *subdi*, it seems, was nil. That makes sense, I guess, since it was mostly just memory.

Sitting across from me, you continue your commentary as though nothing has changed.

"Humanity has huge problems, don't get me wrong. But your collective soul is strong. It is pure. All souls are pure, of course. But for your species, with the destiny to lift itself out of darkness and unconsciousness, the soul purity becomes illumined. That's what beguiles me about all of you."

"I thought we *failed* to do that! You've always said we *didn't* become conscious."

"True, but you did lift yourselves up. That self-lifting quality is the most important gift of humanity. Your ultimate success was your transmutation into my kind. And many humans found ways of being compassionate and altruistic, even while ego dominated their personalities. This has always touched vigilans. And it was this side of humanity that was worth saving and instilling into the next species. All that goodness that kept shining through was what we kept. *Conscious Evolution* tossed out the rest."

"You said we were naïve. I have to agree, up to a point. We bumble through our lives, with all kinds of inflexible opinions and limitations, without a sense of where we're really going. But I can't see that we're so *innocent*. When I look at my world I see dark, clever schemes of control and manipulation of people, to keep them 'dumbed-down', crazy, and distracted away from confronting the power elite. There are vast systems of cruelty and abuse among humans. I see governments and corporations willing to destroy their natural home planet, just for some temporary, personal gain. These schemes seem very calculated and scary."

"But they *are* naïve. The ego congenitally lacks the requisite for real *mastery*. This is the case whether you are a peasant or a king. Ego awareness, remember, is only the first step toward awakened consciousness. These organizations you speak of, who believe they have power over the masses of humanity, are in for a great surprise. Their world is passing into history. They have no idea how fragile and shallow their supremacy is.

"I say 'innocent', because even the most sophisticated manipulators are only fooling *themselves*, ignorant of the *vesica piscis* that pulses within, uniting them to the whole. They are but children in the Cosmos, playing in the projection as though it were real, as though they actually knew the full extent of reality. They play at manipulating shadows on the wall, while knowing nothing of the projector behind them. Their world is built on very false assumptions. They suppose that people can be dominated endlessly. They also assume that objects of desire will actually satisfy their longing.

"That longing *is* real! But it cannot be satisfied by the world of form. Unconsciously, they long to know the *true* power within themselves, to know who they *really* are. Every living being instinctively desires this. Instinct satisfies that desire among animals and plants, through innate openness. But access to instinctual fulfillment is closed to humans by virtue of their ascendant intellect."

I look around us toward people at other tables, working on their computers and cell phones. Doing business remotely, intellectually—apart.

"The separative ego mistakenly believes that control will amass power. But power does not reside in forms, nor can it be under one's 'control'. Control is an illusion of time and mind. The mastery of forms only comes when the *mystery of forms* is revealed within oneself, and when one is awakened to the essence of *mystery* itself. The mystery of forms is that all materiality is *immaterial*, all form is a projection from formlessness. Emptiness is the foundation for all expression. Insubstantial reality is the essence of all substance. Not to realize this basic truth makes you *naïve*.

"Your naïveté is actually what saves you though. It renders you ultimately blameless. It is simple ignorance—an artifact of unconsciousness and the Veil of Forgetfulness, a product of the Earth evolutionary experiment. It is naïveté, in the end, that avails you the *grace of freedom* for transforming karma.

"All the discomfort and disaster that accompanies being human is necessary to the experiment. You managed, over the centuries, to build up your civilizations, with no certainty of the soul, or afterlife, or even Source. Humanity's ready enthrallment to religions and captivating belief systems testifies to this uncertainty. Look into yourself right now and see if that fear isn't still there—the fear that all this spirit-based wonderment might just be so much wishful thinking."

I sigh, "You won't get an argument from me on that."

"Nevertheless, you always, simultaneously, have the open heart through which truth and reality may flow. Your body picks up these things, even when your mind does not. And even your minds are now allowing more of the flow, as your species slides into the Great Storm. Look into your etheric body right now and see the opening there. It is in your heart *and* at the subatomic threshold—the *vesica*. Because it truly has existed within you from the very beginning, inevitably it would open to you when the time was right.

"Through trial and error, rising and falling, your bi-polar nature—both benighted and enlightened—managed to pierce the Veil. The fact is, that you achieved this largely under your own steam; at times you saw beyond the separateness. This is an amazing accomplishment in evolution!"

"Yes, but it resulted in so much misunderstanding and mischief," I argue. My eyes look beyond you at the others and wonder what they're thinking and talking about. "All the politicized religions and megalomaniacs of human history used it to glorify themselves and build in more separateness. What starts as pure always ends up corrupted."

"Yes indeed. That was inevitable, given the rules of this planet, under the 'unconsciousness' protocol. To see it as mistaken or malevolent, however, is shortsighted and blocks appreciation of the greater picture. Also, to insist that you have been completely manipulated and victimized by outside forces is far too narrow. From the larger view, it was all destined to be as it is. Even if you had succeeded in destroying yourselves and the planet, destiny was always at work. It was unfolding its *own* authenticity.

"In order for your consciousness to move forward, that is, to create and pass through the cosmic portal, you must accept the authenticity of *all* that is, and of *what is.* Accepting this is the catalyst for wholeness and thence, Oneness. And Oneness is the vehicle of passage.

"Soon the revelations will mount into a crescendo, the likes of which the Earth has not seen for 26 millennia. The passage is opening. It is in you and in many others everywhere around the planet. The Earth is rising up effulgent. It is a terrible sight for darkened eyes to behold. They shall be blinded by their own vision. The Storm is upon you, dearest humans. Rejoice in the cleansing it brings. If you fear it, it will devour you. If you look upon it with deepest appreciation—within your heart and *lens of creation*—it will shine you into the new Earth. You choose! This is the Apocalypse! This is the Revelation!"

A cloud that was covering the sun suddenly passes, letting a golden brightness engulf us. "That sounds very difficult. I can't imagine many people understanding how to do it. How can ordinary men and women come to this awareness? Does it mean that some will be left behind? I thought you said that no one would be left behind."

"I said that all will awaken. The mutation is not based on any action you take, or your particular worthiness as an individual. It is not about how good you are or how much knowledge you have, or which teaching you follow. The change occurs first in your body and your heart. The mind comes along only after that. It is a genetic shift, in response to the environment of the times. All beings alive on Earth in your day are part of that environment.

"No one on the physical Earth is left out of the opportunity and evolutionary step. But I also pointed out, you will recall, that each soul has free will and power to choose its own path. Awakening is the power of choice. Your soul makes the choice. At the time of the Storm, each human awakens to his or her own choice point. This point bestows an evolutionary mutation no matter which universe one chooses, no matter whether the particular soul chooses to continue under the Veil or not. Vigilan souls chose the world where the Veil was lifted."

"But you said the Veil was synonymous with being unawakened. How can *awakened* souls choose to be *un-awakened*? Why would they want to?"

"Yes. I said that. Explanations can sometimes be misleading," she smiles. "All souls are 'awakened' *a priori*. It is a given. But they choose to enter forgetfulness in order to be part of the human Earth plane experience. The destinies of all souls on this planet proceeded, happily or unhappily, along this path for millennia. But the wheels turned, the greater cycle for awakening arrived. It was destined to be. And humanity forced the issue, of course, with its aggravated ego. To manifest any large-scale awakening on a planet like this, evolution itself needs to become *conscious*. This process is a *contextual* shift, and can leave no soul behind."

Your beautiful shining eyes are wide, holding a much greater vision than mine. I want to see what they see. "What if a soul chooses not to follow the program? What happens to that individual?"

You are ready with an answer. "For souls who prefer not to be in an awakened system, there is a transition out of the new Earth. There are many such souls. Their physical bodies must, nevertheless, undergo the mutation, or die. As you can guess—and witness around you in your present world—there is much distress and turmoil as a result. Some individuals are pulled rapidly out of incarnation; some remain under duress, impacted by the general awakening around and within them, but refusing to consciously participate. Others are drawn into the vortex of evolution and turned inside out by the forces at play.

"For all physical beings who remain, there is a transmutation. The genetic shift may be repressed within the body and become recessive, but only temporarily. The mutated genes lie in wait for such a time that the soul is ready. These mutated vehicles—of souls who choose to delay their activation—are identical to those who *do* choose the awakened system; it is only a matter of 'timing'."

"I think you're splitting hairs. It still sounds like some people are *left behind* in this shift."

"Not so," you respond, shaking your head. Your hair catches little beams of light. "On this distinction lies the whole reason behind our message and the *Letters*. The portals we build will not open to those who choose *not* to accept them. The passage through the Storm will be very, very different for those who do not choose to find a portal that resonates with them. But they will pass through the Storm no matter what."

"So, some will be left out of awakening then. It's all the same, as far as I can see."

"Not 'left out'. *Delayed*. And this is by free will and destiny. Their vehicles will undergo the change just like everyone else. Their awareness of that fact will come later."

I shrug, not conceding the point. *The results are the same.* Above us, the sun is no longer so bright. Clouds are continuing to drift in. A man walks by with a small dog on a leash. I stare after him, sipping my drink.

"Say, I have a question about animals and the rest of life on the planet. You said that all beings are part of the environmental shift. Does that mean that *everything* awakens? Animals, plants, minerals?"

"Yes. But each soul makes its own independent choices. An awakened zebra or crocodile is not the same as an awakened person. A flowering plant is different from a flowering human. The souls of animals, on the vigilan Earth, have chosen to continue within their animal natures. The vast majority are not yet experienced enough for the separative, intellectual stage known as 'human'. Nor are they ready to jump from instinctive guidance systems into intuitive ones.

"Nevertheless, animals, plants and minerals in my world exhibit a great deal more awareness and communion with us than they did with you. And we appreciate their capabilities and presence much more than the average human did. I believe you saw some of this when you visited OM in his dreamtime. Was there not a helpful crocodile in the river?"

"Yes. Though I didn't get a chance to inquire into that. I was just glad not to be eaten."

"The animal was attuned to your experience. In essence what he did was to link you with his own instinctual presence. Animals can do that for you now, in your human times, if you allow yourself to be sensitive to it. Many humans are doing just that. There is much still to be discovered in the instinctual realms of consciousness."

I nod appreciatively. "Animals link us with our instincts. I like that."

A large cloud blocks the sun again and its shadow turns the street dark. My mind follows the shade and takes on a darker brooding. You look on at me compassionately. My emotional fear memory rises up from last night.

I groan, "As you're aware, I'm struggling these days with a kind of craziness. It comes and goes rather unpredictably. Everything is fine and 'normal' one minute. Then the next, I feel a battle raging inside me. I often feel very vulnerable for no particular reason. Can you tell me what's going on?"

"Of course. You're feeling the presence of the Great Storm within you. This is where it all happens. What you see of it in the outer world is simply the after effects. The *passage* through the Storm is likewise *within* you. When you have these vulnerable feelings, use them to be more aware. Use them as reminders of the awakening that is coming."

"I'll tell you, I feel a long way from awakened when I have these attacks."

"Understood. But they can still trigger your recognition that a deeper awareness awaits you. Say to your mind, 'This too shall pass'."

I center myself and imagine the passing of these emotions. It does help. *But perhaps it's just because of your presence with me now.* I whine, "But I thought by now, I wouldn't still be feeling like this. It makes me feel cynical and hopeful at the same time. It's like I have two minds inside me."

"This is nothing new. Of course you have two minds—one in the head, the other in the heart. The mind in your heart is the true consciousness some have called the *higher* mind. Interesting, is it not, that this is *lower* in your body? The truth is often upside-down inside you."

"That makes sense in a crazy way. I know I may sound like a broken record, but it's very disturbing to feel so divided inside. I can't stop myself from asking you about it."

"So, go ahead. Ask. You know you're not alone in this." You look around at the others, with a nod. Then, with eyes pouring essence into mine, "What's troubling you most?"

"Well, I'm afraid it's just going to be more of the same. Maybe I just need to vent. I hear so many different opinions about what's happening in my world. Many people seem so convinced about their perspectives. When I listen to them, they make sense for a while. Then I listen to someone else, saying something very different, even opposite, and I see the sense in that too. But they don't jibe. As a result, I just get depressed and confused. I feel lost and cut off."

"You are simply coming face-to-face with your reality. You *are* cut off. You are sensing that there is a great gulf between your head and your heart. I can only advise you to feel it thoroughly. But I can tell there's something else. What is the underlying cause of your feelings? What's *really* bothering you?"

"Well, I guess it's that I keep shifting inside myself—first one way, then the other. I don't know where the solid ground is. I don't seem to know myself, where *I* am."

You lean forward. Your silver eyes pierce into me. "Go deeper."

"All right," I ponder aloud. "I'm separated from my essence, like you said. I know there's truth inside me somewhere. But it alludes me at those times when I'm crazy."

Like an unseen breeze, I feel the collective presence of the other customers. A thought sweeps in with it. "Here's an example of what I'm talking about. Stefan has set up some book interviews for me. Because of that, I went back to look at what you've been saying, very critically. Since I'm the one doing the writing, it's also what *I'm* saying. But I don't have your command of the subject. What can I say about it, really? Part of me feels like I don't know enough to make any sense during an interview. This part of me doesn't want to have to defend the books or be responsible for them. I'm very reluctant to be out in the public eye."

"Yes. I understand now. There is, in fact, a deep division within you. Your reaction to the divisiveness in your society is actually evidence that you have that same separation within yourself. But again, you're not alone. All humanity is feeling those same forces of separateness arising in their minds and emotions. This is what I'm talking about when I say the Storm is within you. That is what you're feeling above all else right now. That is increasing your sensitivity. Bear in mind, also, that contrasts and polarities point the way to greater clarity. In your *divisiveness*, you are opening the way for *decisiveness*. Your choices and your path through the Storm become very clear through this dynamic."

"It doesn't seem all that clear to *me*. I feel like I'm going to explode sometimes, and *im*plode at others."

"All right. Those are not times of clarity perhaps. But if you will stop and observe your body's sensations and your heart's feelings, you will know the way that is right for you. Your ego is not giving up without a fight, my friend. It is putting up major resistance. This will continue throughout the writing of these books, I must remind you. We need your ego for our purposes. I understand that it makes things difficult for you. I will help as much as I can. But you will just have to make the best of your insanity for a while yet. Every human must.

"Don't take it personally. Take it like a soul! The resistance in you, of course, wants you to feel it as a personal assault. The liberation that is coming to you requires that the battle burn itself into exhaustion. The more acute the battle, the sooner it will be over, the sooner will the darkness reveal the light. You have our empathy and love. And you carry within you your own pure heart and presence. You will feel the Oneness soon. Persevere!"

The dark clouds have swallowed the sun completely now. Suddenly a swarm of crows sweeps past overhead on a gust of wind, making much noise. *It's going to rain.* You stare up, listening. Then you reach over the table and grab my hand.

"Here is a signal for us. Look at that sky, there's a storm approaching. Are you finished with your coffee?"

"Yeah. I guess so."

"Come with me." You rise, pulling my hand. I stumble and feel the ground give way under my feet.

Letter Forty-Three
The Great Storm

We are standing on a precipice, high above an ocean beach. The sky is roiling with black clouds. Fierce winds whip at us, stinging my face with a sharp mist. Steep mountains rise behind us, disappearing in the overcast. I can't imagine how we got here. There's no path up or down from this forsaken perch. I look around, alarmed. But you are still clutching my hand.

"O, where have you brought me this time? Why are you gripping my hand so tightly?"

"I wouldn't want you to fall. Even though this is another sub-dimension, you would not enjoy the experience. And this is no ordinary *subdi.*"

"So, where are we?"

"We are at the Ends of the Earth."

"What? What kind of thing is that? That's a place?"

"It is indeed. It is a *physical metaphor* for your times. In this dimension we can see the extent of the Storm that rages throughout your planet, even now. Look there, down against the rocks in the surf."

Strangely, I see two figures standing in huge, crashing waves on the rocks. They are somehow maintaining there, in spite of the tumult. Wave after wave pounds the ledge. The figures stumble back, but regain their foothold and stand again, bracing for the next onslaught.

"O, who is that? Why are they standing there? They're getting pounded. They'll be swept away. Or torn apart."

"You think so? Many would agree with your assessment. These two are the avatars of your age. They represent all humanity, facing the Great Storm."

"Avatars? What do you mean? Who are they? Why don't they save themselves?"

"That's not what avatars do. They are here for *you*, and not for themselves personally. Their destiny is to be right where they are. Avatars only come when humanity is all but lost, when you are in the most dire straits. This isn't the first time in your history when avatars have come. Humanity created many such situations over the ages. But this is the first time in 26,000 years that they have come together as *two*—for the entire species."

"I don't get it. This is crazy. Destiny or not, people don't behave like that!"

"In this *subdi* they do. All behavior here is metaphorical, representing events and individuals in the general dimension. These twin figures are embodied in your world as we speak, living prominent lives, at the center of great turbulence. One is female; one is male. You would readily know their names if I spoke them to you."

"Well then, why don't you do that? Tell me who they are!"

"It is not the way of avatars, to be known widely in their own times as they truly are. They must remain anonymous. It is what they represent that's important. Like so many icons in your world today, they are bridges. They represent two worlds, two universes. They bridge two sides of creation. In duality, they embody the Oneness of which many so glibly speak."

The noise is fierce. I lean close to your ear to make myself heard. "I've been meaning to get back to that question. You said quite a while ago that '*Oneness* doesn't manifest'. What did you mean by that?"

You lean toward me in response, raising your voice. "I will explain in good time. For now, I request you to hold that question in your heart. Let it steep and mature into a question worthy of the answer you will receive."

"All right. I've waited this long." I trail off, looking quizzically at you, watching the duo below buffeted by the waves. Now there is rain in the wind. It lashes at us and we're soon drenched.

"Well, O. This is getting rather uncomfortable. Are we staying long?"

"One thing you have to say about this. It sure has taken your mind off your personal troubles. Right?"

"Correct. But couldn't we watch from a dry place somewhere? How long do we have to stay?"

"Not much longer. Watch the figures below." You are now shouting to be heard above the gale.

The female suddenly walks to the edge and dives down into the water. She is pulled quickly out into the foaming surge. She disappears from view. The man moves back against the rocks, holding fast. Now I see the woman swimming out from shore, rising and falling with the enormous waves. Her shape is tiny in the enormity of the ocean. Sheets of rain pound down upon Earth and sea.

I yell at the top of my lungs. "O, this is insane. What the hell is going on?"

"Hell, indeed! Insanity indeed! Look more closely."

I stare into the raging swirl below. There, on both sides of the man, I can now make out other shapes of people. *How could I have missed them before?* There are dozens on each side. *I took them to be rocky crags,* I guess. They seem to be struggling, fighting with one another, pulling and pushing. Their voices are wafting through the wind in faint bursts. They're screaming at the lone man on the ledge, who continues to be struck by mighty waves. And what of the woman? Where is she now? Some of the people on the rocks are looking out toward her, screaming in hostile voices.

My attention is totally absorbed in the drama beneath us. Oddly, I now have no concern for the cold rain in my face. I feel you holding both my arms from behind as I lean into the wind, trying to see the woman in the surf. There she is at last, fifty meters from shore. She is no longer swimming, but is treading water on the swells. And around her I see dark shapes moving. Fins!

"Sharks!" I cry. "Stop this, O! I can't stand it."

But you are silent, face against the wind, eyes fixed on the woman in grave danger. I look away back to the man. The crowd that has closed in on him is now haranguing him. They are pulling and tearing, beating on him with their fists. Their angry shouts ride up through the mist and tumult.

"O, can't we *do* something? What can we do?"

"You tell me. You're the human being. What would you do if you *could* do something?"

"I'd help them. I'd put a stop to this whole thing. You said these two are avatars? Why would humanity treat avatars like this?"

"It is very important that *you* tell me why. The answer must come from a human heart."

My mind is frenzied. I shake my head and try to understand what you're getting at. *What is it you want me to say or do?* I reach back inside my body, feeling for my heart, in spite of the maelstrom outside. I feel an expansion in my chest, a warmth. An answer.

My voice is calm and firm. It rises above the storm. "Humanity wants to destroy the avatars, because we feel hopeless. We are torn, divided within ourselves, and just want to tear away and reject everything. And insanely, at the same time we demand something to cling to. But it is not there. What is offered we reject; what we desire is no longer offered; it was *never* really there.

"The forces of rejection and clinging are like bile in our hearts. Burning lies. We feel there is no one who can save us or help us or lead us. We are helpless and cynical. Yet we want to banish anyone who is stronger and wiser. We *want* to be insane, to actually retreat into unconsciousness. We, collectively, have created the insanity I've been feeling. We've seen a glimpse of awakening, and it has frightened us to the core. We are mad with fear.

"That fear is the only thing we can feel behind our glib, modern façades. It has gripped us by the throat, by the gut, and will not let go. We will kill anyone who does not accept this fear and denial. The fear is our savior! Fear is our God! The avatars have proclaimed that we do not have to fear. We cannot abide this. 'Lies, lies,' we scream. What do *they* know of our God! We know better. We know that fear is all there is. The fear of God! We must clutch to it for our very lives!"

This voice has erupted out of me from the heart of fear in humanity. I know within myself that it does not speak for everyone though. *It does not speak for me.* And yet it is the voice of the times, the voice that shouts the loudest. It is the voice of ego, division and separation, desperate to preserve itself. *What will humanity do with this wayward voice?*

On the ledge below, the throng from both sides has pulled the man to the ground. He rises up again. Some of the mob are now trying to defend the man, arguing with the others. Waves crash over them all. There is great tumult and thrashing. Waves come again, smashing into the struggling group. Some are washed away with the waves, screaming and cursing loudly. Sharks, near the shore, are quick to respond. The man, the avatar, does not struggle. He simply holds his ground in the midst.

After one great wave, he is separated from the writhing mass. He leans forward toward the sea, looking out at his partner, just as another wave strikes. He is forced back against the rocks, but stands firm. His strength is astounding; his courage inspiring. Around him I see many great birds, ravens, black as the storm—at one with the storm. They hover, defying the whipping wind. There is a mystery about them, I sense. They are harbingers. But for good or ill? I cannot tell.

I look back out to sea. Incredibly, the woman is still alive, afloat amidst the circling sharks. They have closed into a tighter circle. There must be at least a dozen of them. She does not move or try to defend. She is waiting for something. She is at peace, come what may. Her poise is radiant, even across this distance; her presence is grace itself. I am in awe. *So, this is an avatar!* The pounding storm is as nothing to me now. I am outside it. I surround it with my being, my *human* being! I realize here that this whole scenario is inside me, in my mind. I must place it in my heart as well. You've always said the Storm is within.

Your words come to me again, this time from a still, small place, untouched by the storm or the struggle. *Tell me now, brother. What would you do to help these avatars?*

This time I do not hesitate. The answer does not come from my mind. My mind has shrunk back into a tiny corner of itself, consumed by its own fear-filled nature. This time my heart speaks. My soul acts. Down upon the rolling water a point of light briefly gleams. Then, from above, a blinding flash of lightning connects to the point on the water. A mighty explosion of thunder peals across the blackness above. Then the lightning strikes several more times. Again the gleam of light appears on the waves. It is halfway between the woman and the man. This time it does not fade, but holds and begins to grow slowly outward from its center.

The rain and wind have suddenly ceased with the last of the thunder. Below and out to sea there descends a calm. Gradually, one by one, the raging waves fall lower and the surface mellows. I look upon the woman in the water. Something has shifted. The fins of the sharks have changed.

They are dolphins! Could I have been mistaken all along? The dolphins are swimming the circles now, leaping and dancing with the surf. They seem to be arriving from all directions. Hundreds of them ring the woman, splashing and playing in joy. The circle of light has enlarged to reach them all at last. There is an air of jubilation. I am overjoyed to see this.

Now I look over to the man. The circle of light has also reached the shore. It slides up to where he is standing erect, still, in the center of the ledge. He has been watching the ocean, the woman and the dolphins. The struggling people around him have pulled aside. They shrink back and are falling to the ground; some are on their knees, bowing, and others seem to be praying, with hands clasped or arms outstretched. Some are prostrate or have curled into fetal balls. *I can swear I hear the 'gnashing of teeth'.*

The male avatar spreads out his arms, wide. Two great eagles swoop down from the cliffs, parting the flock of ravens. The eagles are each the size of the man himself. They fly together past his outstretched hands, brushing them as they head out over the water. They dive low to the surface, speeding toward the center of the circle of light. In a flash they have pierced the water with their mighty claws and are pulling out a huge, shining fish from the deep, one bird at each end. This fish is the source of light on the water. Now they release it and the fish turns in the air, gleaming like diamond.

The scene slides into slow motion. The eagles hover. The giant fish, a *vesica* shape, is aloft and free, transforming into a pure golden oval. The woman floats amidst the dolphins. The man stands, arms outstretched on the land, ravens at hand. You and I watch from high above. The light radiates out in gentle, fierce waves from the gilded fish.

Now your voice is close by. "You have done this, my human friend. Congratulations. There is indeed hope for your species. If *you* could do it, so can others, many others. There is a keen opportunity for the calming of the seas. And this, at the very height of the Great Storm."

"I did *what* exactly?"

"It is your heart's desire that has manifested here just now."

As we continue to watch the epoch scene, the woman in the rolling surf, begins to swim toward shore. As she arrives below the *vesica,* the water around her falls still in a wide circle. The dolphins swim into this ring of stillness. They continue to circle her, leaping into the air in celebration. She swims on toward the beach. The *vesica* hovers above, following her and calming the waters. She brushes several of the dolphins affectionately with her hands before climbing up the rocky precipice. At last she draws the brilliant *vesica* ashore and rejoins the man who has been watching attentively.

Now there is a shift within the fallen crowd on the rocky ledge. A woman rises and walks tentatively out; then a man, then several other people come forward. They halt and form a half-circle behind the avatars, standing resolute. The avatars are no longer alone. There are a few, at last, who recognize them as they are.

My mind's eye glimpses into another vision, another sub-dimension. In it the numbers of those gathered with the avatars begin to grow. At first, it's just a few dozen. Then there are hundreds of humans all around, ready to finally appreciate this opportunity. Then there are tens of thousands, and finally many, many more. There are groupings, small and large, networks, gatherings, congresses. Vigilans! That vision fades, and my gaze returns below.

The two, now together, turn their united gaze back out over the churning sea. Their friends tighten the circle. We watch transfixed—removed, yet in the heart of it all. Out from shore, new waves are rising, re-forming, swelling ever higher into the sky. Storm clouds sweep in again on mighty winds.

Gradually, my gaze penetrates the waves, one after another, and I see in them the shapes of people, rising with the water. Great multitudes are rolling and tumbling like waves on the sea. Their forms surge upon one another, flow together and apart—each ripple an individual soul. These, I sense, are the many nations of the world. They engage and separate, confront and dissolve—war and peace. Within these swells, the masses are infused, alternately, with hope, with despair. Their cries of anguish, prayer and joy are like a solemn chorus in the gale. All souls on Earth are caught up in this chant. The swirl is endless, without resolve. At the threshold of it all stand the avatars—in place, in light and destiny.

Lightning, again and again. Thousands of fire-bolts now descend. Energy is pounding relentlessly down. Thunder racks the fabric of the air, the ground and the planet. The clouds of the Storm part in a rush at last, with a wrenching of the Earth. There are the stars. They gleam like never before in brightness. Space has never been so dark or so bright. Out of the night sky, meteors and comets are raining down upon the sea. Their numbers are uncountable.

Gigantic plumes of fire, streams of phosphor, are frightful to behold. The waters part; they steam with cataclysmic force, rising up with billions of souls in flux. Higher, higher, wider they rise into the sky, up to meet the falling flame of stars. Incredibly, the oceans continue to rise. Up and up they flow to heaven! Within minutes the entire ocean, and all its living force, has departed and dispersed upon the sky, beyond the sky. Below, the world is empty, void. The bottom of the sea is bare and splitting open, hard and smoking.

Great mountains of the sea are dry and thrust up, visible, like never before. The Earth opens more. Gargantuan fissures appear and strike themselves around the globe, shattering all into a vast network of rifts. We can see the entire Earth from this promontory. The rifts begin to part along their seams, exposing yet another light. It is the light itself of Body Earth, the molten fire of the planet's heart.

I suck in a deep breath and look around at you. Your eyes are fixed on me, pouring your energy of vision into mine. I know that this is no ordinary sight I see. This vision looks into the very soul of the Great Storm. I am privileged beyond my means to see this sight.

It is horrible and exhilarating. The Life of Death itself. No words can be sufficient in this space.

The lava boils, far below in lakes of fermentation. Something's coming, brewing, something fierce, up out of those effulgent lakes. It is rising far beyond the imagination of man. We are but a whisper of a memory upon these airs. We are burned to nothing in these fires. Liquid rock, orange and bright, gushes upward from the core. The mighty molten waves are on their way, onto all the Earth. I cover my face against the ghastly blast of light and heat. It swallows up the whole, the spectacle of all we've seen—of nations, oceans, creatures, you and me. The fire is at once complete. All is fire! Only the flaming tongues of the fiercest angels could taste and breathe this atmosphere.

Stillness, bright! Silence, everlasting! Cleansing flood from the *hearth* of the Earth! Life has risen out and shot beyond the tumult. It has left this tiny globe of rock. Life has come and gone, utterly! The Cosmos holds its breath. An eternity—a full *Pralaya*—is in that lull, that truce. But now there is a turning. I feel it coming in us all. The greater Life has checked its presence and reset itself for what will follow.

The glowing lava, covering the globe, is stirring. It swirls in response to Life returning. It begins to dance with the heavens. It feels the divine invitation of return. Slowly water is coming. It begins to pour down from the sky. It crashes to the fires below. Now the rains fall in earnest. All is sudden steam and mist, a global haze. This, in turn, condenses again to water, falling, drenching everywhere. The hydrologic cycles roll and writhe.

Oceans are falling back into themselves. All the skies are summoned, descending onto Earth. They have been purged, washed down through airy deluge. Heavens cleansed are coming home. Falling, falling, endless rain from endless skies! This seems to last a lifetime.

Off the land it runs, obeying gravity, the magnetic heart of God. It gathers all its substance, holy, pure, into ocean's sepulcher. As water flows, the lakes of fire are closing, sealing back the hephaestian lair. The cracks and seams are sutured over once again with blackest basalt.

Slowly, the ocean floor is covered everywhere; the level of the sea is coming back. It is a tide like no other, rising. Yard by yard it lifts itself, replenished, full and thirsty, coming up the slopes. At last the ocean reaches to the shore—just as it was before.

During this whole event, the images of the avatars and the *vesica piscis* have remained firm. They have contained and guided, assuring that the transformations be fulfilled. These two together are the transcendent channel for our greatest blessing. I know now their influence is much greater than we have seen. In my inner vision I feel the DNA of all the planet has been cleansed. Nothing is as it was before. All is burned and healed, and thus restored.

Finally, out of its stillness, the *vesica* descends upon them, embracing them. It stretches and pulls upon itself, pulls apart. Miraculously, it divides in two, hovering like parentheses above the man and woman. The cloven portions move down on either side, transformed into golden bows. Two silver arrows jut up between the twins, thrust from out of the very ground. The light they emit temporarily blinds me.

The twin avatars take up these arcs of *vesica*—golden bows—in their hands and hold them forward. The radiant, bright arrows are strung. The figures look and fix on each other's eyes. They pause, waiting on the full attention of the Cosmos. Then they turn toward the mountains above. Raising their arms in unison, they shoot the arrows straight toward the impenetrable escarpment. They fly. A radiant force within them produces a lilting song of the muses. It is raw with power. Trails of astral sparks follow in their wake.

Just as the arrows are about to strike the cliff, an unbelievable and marvelous thing happens. The mountains open up before them. Solid rock turns to powder and hovers in the air. It then yields into a vast and empty chasm. As fast as the singing missiles move, so does the stone give way. A huge, deep valley is carved, faster than an instant, as they pass. On they go. They create one great, long channel across the Earth. Our vision follows them as they go.

The arrows, powered from within, move past the mountains, out over a broad, fertile plain. At last the holy wands begin to sink. They finally fall to Earth at the base of a high and verdant hill. On that hill is an enormous, ancient tree. Its branches spread tall and wide. The tree is surrounded by an iridescent aura of golden light. Our magical missiles now enter the Earth. And there they disappear. In their place, we see a fountain of water spring up.

Sitting at the base of the Great Tree, we see a small child. I need not say, the child is no ordinary child. It is born of archangels. Its beauty is astounding to both eyes and heart. This, I hear, is the new true species to be born on Earth, beyond our times—in the *next* Great Age. We gaze upon the far future legacy of our own genetic trace. It is a vision that will inspire the world for eons to come.

This tree is the *Tree of Life*, we hear within. And at its feet lies the Spring of the Child, the veritable *Fountain of Youth*. This great arboreal presence has stood forever here, beyond the Ends of the Earth, waiting in pristine silence for this destiny, this day when its fountain would be born.

The water flowing from the fountain now forms a river. It passes before the feet of the fair youth, who smiles serenely into its waters. The stream turns down into the valley below and begins a course across the plain, a journey to the sea. It flows for countless thousand miles, back toward the avatars, and toward where we stand. It courses through the mountain valley through the channel made ready by the singing arrows.

At long last the river pours over the ocean rocks in a gold and silver fluorescence, splashing at the feet of the man and woman standing on the ledge. They reach down in tandem and dip their hands in the sweet water; they drink. This water from the Tree of Life cascades over mammoth rocks and ledges and down, ultimately, to the ocean itself. *"Okeanos, in Greek, means 'great river',"* I hear you whisper in my mind. I think of the *Isa Ber*. You continue, *"And so, the rivers merge and meet in joyous reunion, shining with an inner light and Life that only water may give."*

You and I stand in reverent silence, observing the finale to this spectacle. Over several minutes these sights and sounds gradually dissolve into stillness. The twin avatars begin to walk along the stream, in the direction of the angelic child, in the distant land. Their group follows solemnly, yet with perfect joy. Its ranks begin to grow as they go. Soon thousands are in the retinue. I know not what will come to pass when they meet the child. Surely, the world will be blessed. I am numb, still transfixed and motionless. While I gaze, the very space begins to shake and split, vibrating me out and away.

And then, astoundingly, we're back at the sidewalk table. Rain is hitting my face and arms. You're pulling at my hand, as before. The rain has come quickly. The crows still call furiously. We stumble toward the door of the shop, interrupted yet entirely in the moment. I breathe heavily, reverently. This rain seems, just now, to have come from another world.

Letter Forty-Four
Knowing the Oneself

People are scurrying all around us to get out of the rain. Coffee cups and plates are left behind. The napkins are drenched. We make our way into an alcove. I look at you with a serious expression, then we shrug and laugh. It's a way of putting some distance from the bizarre events we've just witnessed. We hug, standing only half out of the storm.

"Let's get in your car." You smile quaintly. "I'd like to see how your vehicle works."

I look at you—a small, delicate woman with a childish grin. "You, dear Orange, seem like the *innocent* one, all of a sudden. Yes. Let's go."

We rush to the car and scramble in, slamming the doors against the pounding stream.

"Ah, at last," I sigh. "Back to something familiar. That last trip was awesome, O. But very bizarre! I don't know what to think or believe. What is all this adding up to? There are so many things I want to ask you that I can't put them into words. I'm drowning with questions."

"That makes me happy! That is exactly the reaction I was hoping for."

I look out at the downpour. The sound is heavy on the roof. "Well, drowning or not, I have to start asking. What was I looking at in that last *subdi*? How real was it? What was the symbolism? How does it connect with *my* real world?"

"You still believe there is a *real* world?"

"I have to believe something, don't I?"

"Yes. I'm only making fun. You *do* in fact have to believe something—that is, if you choose to be on Earth in a body. A fundamental kind of belief creates all the illusion and projection we live in. That is the *root thought* about our collective incarnate world—the 'consensus reality'. In my time, we still experience this root projection as well. But at the same time, we can see through it to the underlying truth. We can *believe and know* simultaneously—seeing with both the outer and inner eyes.

"To answer your first question, the Ends of the Earth is a physical metaphor, as I said. It does not directly depict the world you're in. This is obvious. Yet it tells a story that lies in each human heart, in the dense physical body of your times. Every element of it has its correspondence in the meaning and revelations of your day."

"Are there really *avatars* in my time?" I ask. "Or is that just a metaphor too?"

"Yes, there are. They're real human beings, just like yourself, on Earth now. There are two of them—twins of the soul. They are *not* perfected beings; nor are they angels. They have, however, accepted an elevated mission in this life. It is their charge to embody the energy of transformation—for all—within themselves. They are representatives and channels of the inspirational force that shines into and beyond the Great Storm. It behooves you to recognize what these individuals stand for, in your own hearts."

I lean forward pensively, and put the keys in the ignition. But I decide not to start the car yet. "Can you tell me who they are?"

"I have told you—in your heart! I will not say it in words. True recognition demands that you find them and hear their voices for yourself."

"All right. I get it. So, what will they accomplish? What is most important for us to know about their mission?"

"You know that, at critical times in your species' history, there have been individuals who stood out in leadership and inspiration. Their memories, and the goodness they generated, are carried down through the ages to you even now. But often, in their own times, they were misunderstood and rejected by the masses and by the authorities of humanity. Avatars are rarely seen at first for who they are. The word *avatar* comes from Sanskrit, meaning 'to cross over and descend'. Thus they embody an other-worldliness that is difficult for existing systems to accept.

"Those souls who take on such missions, come to assist during the most severe transitions. They only appear when the people are in greatest distress, when there is a pent-up demand rising to the heavens. The heavens always answer that prayer. Some avatars have been great, advanced beings. For instance, the Buddha was recognized as an avatar of the Hindu god, Vishnu. Christ, Krishna, Lao-Tse, Moses and Mohammed were all avatars for their ages. Some avatars were just simple humans with no particular claim to divine hierarchy. Such is the case with the twin avatars of your time."

"But if this is the time of the Great Storm, why don't we rate a *god incarnate,* like a Buddha or a Christ? Surely the need is great enough."

"Yes, the need is great. However, it is such an acute and focused need that these particular souls are the ones best fit for the task. The essential mission is to form a psychical bridge between the old species and the new. To make up for whatever might be lacking in divine authority, these two individuals have come forth together, as one force.

"In the twinship, there is yet another powerful bridging function: Two pillars of stability; two visions of destiny—feminine and masculine, embracing all the consciousness of your species, inside the *vesica piscis.* Together, these twin visionaries are calling upon all humans to open their hearts, their own portals, into the next species—away from ego into the *grace of freedom.*"

Watching your face as you talk always puts me in a kind of trance. I feel a wave of appreciation, just being in the same space with you. I lean back against the door of the car and ask, "What do you mean exactly by 'twins'?"

"Well you might ask. I will give you some specific information here then. Twinship may appear a bit obtuse. Simply allow it to stream through your awareness for now. It matters little whether your mind grasps it. I am speaking symbolically, for your heart to hear.

"The *vesica piscis,* you have witnessed, is formed from the intersection of two circles; the geometry is such that the width of the *vesica* is just the radius of each circle. This correspondence embodies the principle of *identity* between the two. It reveals that the two are actually one—sacred *intercourse.*

"Twin souls, so-called, are actually *one* soul that has divided into two parts upon the Earth plane. This is a natural function of Oneness expressing into duality. You and I are such a formation. All souls divide this way in some fashion as they enter the world, particularly at the level of the root *vesica,* the microcosmic field you encountered with OM. Some have called this a *twin flame;* flames can easily assume the *vesica* shape, by the way. Also look into the *macrocosm* to see a similar duality. A majority of stars in the galaxy are contained within binary systems. And the expression of twinship is seen in human mysticism all through the ages.

"As we observed at the Ends of the Earth, the parentheses embody the presence of the *vesica.* The divine portal mystically divides itself during twin incarnations. All that is experienced over all their lifetimes by the two halves—that is, between one *parenthesis* and the other—is embraced and synthesized by them both."

I relax in my seat, soothed by your voice and the patter of rain all around us. "Tell me more about these parentheses."

"There are many expressions of this symbolism in your culture. A parenthetical phrase in literature contains qualifications related to its main text. Parentheses in mathematics are called *binary commutators*—'the communion of two factors'. In chemistry they are used to denote two or more elements within a single compound."

"OK. I get it," I break in, realizing you could go on. "This *is* obtuse, and probably more information than I needed. But I think I'm following you. How often do these parentheses—soul 'halves'— meet while in incarnation?"

"Normally, not often. The point of the whole experience is to be differentiated and physically *separated.* Twin souls spend the vast majority of their lives in very different places, different circumstances from their counterparts. But they are always bracketing an integral worldview. When they do eventually begin to encounter each other on Earth, as you and I are, it signifies that the time of re-integration is approaching—the time of re-forming the *vesica* is at hand."

"We are re-integrating, you and I?" I ask with interest.

"Not in either of our lifetimes, no—but soon enough from the oversoul's perspective. The reason you and I have taken on this mission is that we are beginning to close the parentheses again. It suits us, therefore, to be transmitting and receiving these letters."

"That makes sense. So, the twin avatars are twin souls?"

"They are indeed," you affirm.

"Where are they along this path of re-integration?"

"They had already come back together in their most recent lifetime, as one integrated incarnation. They chose this new assignment based upon that awareness. They agreed to separate again, one more time, for this high calling. Since they know intimately all that is involved in reuniting, they are in a unique position to offer humanity a symbolic portal for transmuting itself, and 're-membering' what has been forgotten through separation."

"All right. This is deep." I shake my head. "So, they're here to help move us into Oneness?"

"Into an awareness of our *underlying* Oneness, yes."

I turn the ignition key, prompted by a sudden impulse. "Shall we go?" The engine thrums to life. Your eyebrows lift as you listen and nod. I chuckle and continue along my list of questions. "I'm getting more and more curious about this 'underlying Oneness' you keep mentioning. So, what else do we need to do, beyond just knowing about these avatars?"

You appear intent on feeling the rhythm of the motor, bending forward toward the sound. "I have read in the chronicles that your engines made such noise—a curious resonance. So, about the avatars, I would say *resonate* with them, in your hearts and bodies. Stand with them in essence. You do not need to *believe in* them, or revere them as divinities. They are not that. They do not seek overt recognition of their deeper, spiritual status—neither in your minds nor in your media. They do not seek accolades or devoted followers; they have very little ego at play within them. And yet, in their individualities, they are well known to most humans in the world of your time.

"What they seek to promote is realization of the greater opportunity opening to you all—the destiny of your species. This is a heart and body function. The mind is at a loss to truly comprehend the profundity of the blessing you are being offered. Many humans, being locked in their minds, are choosing to reject the offer, unfortunately.

"A word to the wise: One would do well *not* to stand in their way. To reject the *essence destiny* of your species is to invoke the god of resistance and denial. It is to refute the authenticity of your very being. Such action will not deliver you from the Storm. Rather, it invites the Storm upon you—with all its rage, fear and dark illusions, rising as a tempest to devour your sanity. This is the madness of your times, rampant.

"There are many who are profoundly resistant. They can't believe what they see right before their eyes. They have cut themselves off from *natural trust.* Fear has displaced their ability to discern truth. This is, of course, also a manifestation of their greater destiny. It is all part of the apocalyptic drama. All actors must play their roles.

"The outpouring of apocalyptic rage is the voice of fear you tapped into in the other dimension. This is some of what you're feeling in yourself, my friend, when you have your 'insane' moments. In these moments, you are resonating with the losing souls—those who *choose to lose* within themselves—in resonance with the dark side of destiny. Ego, dying and writhing, makes this choice for them. Thus *resistance* reaches its apotheosis. On the other side of the Storm, I hasten to add, these souls too shall be released. All is one behind the projection."

"That voice if fear was very loud," I mutter. "And yet it feels *weak* at the same time."

"It is the last gasp—at the Ends of the Earth," you reply. "The weakness testifies to its inauthenticity. It is cut off from true power, and is attempting to make up for it with bravado."

The rain is thunderous on the roof—threatening, yet hypnotic. Water streams down the windows. We are enclosed in a bubble. All the world is outside, nearly invisible. I ponder, *I'm trying to absorb your words, but at times they're like this rain on the windows—splashing and running off.*

"It all seems so sad that anyone would choose that path," I muse, staring out though the drizzle.

"They believe it's the right choice," you answer. "They believe what their fear tells them, and what the fear of others tells them."

I turn my attention to the car and set out to move. You watch all the motions closely as I back out of the parking space. *You really are curious about this,* I chuckle. "So be it. Let me go in another direction. The biggest question I can think of right now is how can the personal adventures that I'm having in these letters be relevant to anyone else? The places you and the old man have taken me— Atlantis, the River *Isa Ber*, Lake Union. I can't yet see these being much help to anyone but me—or perhaps not *even* me."

"You're wrong," you rejoin. "These stories, though personal, are universal to your species, particular to each soul, in symbolic and inspirational form. They demonstrate the importance of knowing *oneself* in order to know the *One Self.* Recognizing that there are antecedents to your current life and that karmic effects do still influence you right now, is a key to knowing the code of who you are."

"Are you saying that people should be studying their past lives then?"

"Not so much literally. The real conscious being in you is none of these incarnations, nor is it even in your karma, *per se.* Your real being is the *presence* behind these projections of awareness. The real you, exists only now. It can be helpful to know about incarnational patterns in your life system. But you do not need to know the specifics of each past life to find these patterns. Use them to lead you to your presence. They are playing themselves out all around you in your persona of today. Nevertheless, if it is your choice to explore past lives, I recommend you look for clues to your destiny—here and now—in them. Do not get lost in details of the past.

"Lifetimes are discrete projections out from Source. Karma is the *web of action* that builds up amongst these projections, and binds them together. It is also the system that alerts you to needed *course corrections.* The patterns you will see in its web can then be keys to releasing their hold on you. In them, you can realize your wholeness, your identity with the deeper Oneness and truth. That truth will make you free. Use past life memories to uncover reality, not to compound the illusion."

"OK. But you didn't show me any *patterns* in Atlantis. You showed me just one life."

"We showed you the doorway, the *Akasha*. You walked through it, and what you revealed to yourself was indeed an overarching *pattern*. The 'ego contract' was just that, the summation of all your ego experiences. Therefore, it was most efficient to go straight for it. Others may find this technique useful. But if not, sorting through the larger pattern of lives can serve the same purpose. It just takes a little longer.

"Your Atlantean lifetime was a synopsis of your greater ego pattern. Revisiting it was an opportunity for you to see what you had become, and to see that you needed no further development along that line. Each individual who chooses to open the portal within must do so through one-pointed self-examination and discovery. Each person's approach will be individualized and unique to them. However, the larger effect will be at one with the whole human race. Uniqueness is Oneness."

My mind is suddenly racing. "I was such a dastardly character in that life though. How is that a *synopsis* of all my lives? Have I always been that bad?"

"The essence of that pattern was not *evil*. The administrator generated much harm, to be sure. But the real lesson in it for you is the mental separation you achieved by being him. This pride of mind is the thread that runs through all your incarnations. You saw, in your visit to Atlantis, that you need no further pursuit of that sort. All the mentally challenged lives you've lived since then are evidence of that fact, clues to the direction of your awakening.

"Now, there is another approach that readers may follow. It is another shortcut to wisdom and freedom; it will work for those who do not wish to explore past lives. Under the divine grace being extended to you in this epoch, there are many opportunities. To hasten your steps, you may go to your inner guides, angels, saints, or simply to your own soul, to assist you in finding *who you really are* and, thus, what the greater pattern is. These illumined beings can either tell you directly what your ego pattern is, or they can assist you to uncover it for yourself. In your case, Black and I acted as your guides to reveal the life you needed to revisit."

"You are my *saints?*" I chuckle. "I'll buy that. How would someone go about doing this on their own?"

"There are many sources of guidance available in your time—practicing professionals, books, teachings, even religious groups that can facilitate such inquiry. I can only recommend finding an approach that resonates with you, the individual. Feel that resonance in your heart. Remember, the objective is to uncover the *pattern* that is binding you to ego domination, and that, once found, can reveal the Oneness beneath. In that emptiness, your portal will be formed."

I've been driving slowly toward an intersection. I stop for the light. Your eyes flash between my foot on the brake pedal and the traffic light. The fixture sways in the wind and rain. Windshield wipers slap back and forth.

You continue, "Another approach is to just put on the brakes in your mind. Enter deep incubation or meditation and move down into the Void as you have done many times now. The forms appearing there are the most ephemeral and primordial. Any awakening being can access the space of *Akasha* and open deep, profound connections into the Cosmos. This, at last, can provide the revelations you need to move ahead and to encounter one's past-life pattern."

"So, what you're saying is that my story can give impetus to others. But each person will have unique ways of applying it to themselves."

"Yes." You nod.

"It all seems so mysterious." I pause, feeling a twinge of doubt. "Dare I say 'unpredictable'?"

The light turns green and, on impulse, I swing the car around the corner, proceeding slowly down a winding road. I don't really know where I'm headed.

Letter Forty-Five
Oneness Does Not Manifest

"You must admit, friend, you are learning to love the unknown. Are you not?"

"I hadn't exactly thought of it that way. But I guess you're right. I do kind of like not knowing what's coming next—at least sometimes. So, I'm learning to love the *unknown*? Are others learning that from these letters too?"

"You know, the *Letters* are revealing much about your potential future, but there is so much more in the vigilan world than can ever be described in a book, or a series of books. Thus, your future remains largely a mystery. This is only right. Though we are telling you that great things are in store for you, the future is still unknown.

"And yes, others are indeed learning the same thing from their encounters with these messages. The unknown is the *Source*. As you or anyone else reads this, you are embracing what the mind cannot know. You are embracing the greatest blessing of all. Yes, we are building portals. But the kinds of portals you need for the Storm cannot be built through predictable means. 'Unpredictability' is an advantage in this work. What has come to be *predictable* for you, can often be an obstacle to awakening. Learn to rely on the unknown. It is the greatest of gift-givers. For our task, we must stretch the imagination and the credibility of the human mind. The imagination is critical here. It is a device for communication and communion. And more than that, it is a means for *divination*."

"I like the sound of that. Just what does that mean?"

"You write these letters for me—*divining* the future—through your imagination. It is hardly a perfect vehicle for transmission, one might argue. And you spend much time editing and revising—as if this demonstrates some weakness in the transmission. Nevertheless, imperfection *can be* perfection in the karmic mirror. All is upside-down and inside-out in these realms. Imagination is an excellent vehicle for sidestepping the mental ego, while still using the faculties of mind. When ego tries to enter the imagination, it is quickly swamped by its own bravado. Ego isn't satisfied with imagining. It wants controllable thought-forms, it wants an identity-bond with them. Imagination bridges us into the formless, the realm of mystery. It releases you from form-identity.

"Now, there is a deep, esoteric function of the imagination related to divination. It is working through certain teachers and public figures of your time, even though most of them know little of this function. This is an ancient art, developed and practiced by the original shamans of Hyperborea. It is making predictions of future events in order to *prevent* their manifestation."

"Really? You mean like predicting World War III to keep it from happening?" I muse. "How would that work?"

"It works through a mirroring effect. You know, like Alice and the looking glass. The secret behind it is quite simple. The prognostication reflects and reveals what is being kept 'secret', or intentionally hidden. It is a means for undermining the forces of darkness by injecting illumination. Beyond that, the mirror is also a means of merging both light and dark.

"I know you're hearing many dire predictions in your time—of disasters, wars, meltdowns, and various catastrophic events, forecasts of doomsday. These, believe it or not, aid greatly in averting the events they anticipate, at least in the 'awakening' timeline of the *new universe*. Some of the teachers who make such predictions are aware of the magic of this ancient, long-forgotten technique; others are unwitting instruments of a deeper influence on their minds; they speak what they sincerely believe is about to befall humanity. They speak of their fears and worst-case visions."

I've been driving rather aimlessly, not knowing a destination. Suddenly, we've come to a small park on a creek. I pull off into the parking area, splashing through puddles where the rainwater is collecting. I angle the car toward the stream.

"Did you pick this location, O?"

You smile and pat my hand on the steering wheel. I turn off the engine, as you respond. "I've observed your transportation technology long enough. Thank you."

I smile. "I'm realizing that my feelings of craziness have to do with all those doomsday predictions, conspiracy theories, and the fears of eminent collapse of civilization. I hear these things from political pundits and spiritual types alike. My mind feels all twisted up and wrung out by it. I can't seem to get away from it. Some people seem to have just thrown up their hands and given up. Maybe that's what I've done in a some ways."

"I wouldn't say you've given up exactly." You lay your hand back down on mine. I feel a small jolt of fluid electricity. The rain is still falling steadily on the windshield. But through it we can see the creek and an old stone bridge nearby. Your voice is melodic and firm. "You're recalibrating, like many are. Recalibration of awareness has an unpredictable quality that can lead to instability. That's what I'd say you're experiencing."

"I think you're right." I pause to reflect. "It's like my wireless phone has to keep reconnecting to the signal. That's what I feel like—I'm constantly resetting my channel all the time. I can't quite get a lock on the beacon. That's making me crazy."

"That's just what it's designed to do—from the deep, inner Source." You look earnestly over to me. "Everyone in your time needs re-balancing and repositioning in light of your awakening and the events of the Great Storm. You all need to experience some 'craziness' along the way, both individually and as a species. This, believe it or not, is quite natural, given your situation. With each episode of recalibration, you ratchet up to a wider comprehension, to a new plateau. You're stretching the envelope, outgrowing old understandings."

"So, the predictions and feelings of doom and gloom are natural? And they're not all bad? How can we know which ones are good and which aren't?"

"They're all good. They all trigger a conscious response in you, *if* you are on the road to awakening. And you are *all* on that road, at differing speeds—all of humanity. Do not worry for the future, dear friend. As the Christ presence said 'tomorrow will look after itself'. Look to the Now as your center of balance.

"The more unbalanced you feel—in time—the faster you're traveling beyond time, the faster you're regenerating your portal. This portal is your *cocoon of chrysalis*. The caterpillar's flesh and structure must utterly dissolve before the butterfly can form. The more you dissolve, the closer you are to stability. Formlessness is the ultimate stability. If you can just keep noticing *what is,* and *all* that is, you will be fine. You will always come back to equilibrium. I cannot promise that you will always feel comfortable, however. You won't!"

"Gee, thanks." I look over at your gleaming eyes. "At least you're honest."

"At least. Hold for a moment. Something is streaming in. Here's a quick exercise that will be helpful to your sensibilities. Feel your heart—that presence in the center of your chest. Sense its vibration and radiation. Then feel the presence of Now all around you, in the space everywhere. Next, feel it linking with your heart presence. These two presences are one; there is no separation. And they are formless. Here you have your Source of peace and balance—all that is. Do this when you feel worried or unstable, or 'insane'."

"Thanks. That feels good, very restorative. But are you advising us to notice 'all that is'. Can we really do that? It sounds like a tall order. I'm lucky if I can notice two or three things at once."

"Do not try to do it with your mind. Noticing is an inner—*other*—function. For that, you need only be in the moment, at peace. The Now provides all the awareness you require. And 'all that is' is synonymous with 'what is'. All experience is in the moment. It cannot be anywhere else. *What* then equals *all!* This is indeed one of the deep, esoteric mysteries. The formless nature embraces all forms. If you resonate with your formlessness, then you resonate with all forms.

"Do not struggle with feelings of inadequacy or incompleteness when facing any situation. The situation—however it appears—is *within* the deeper you. And it is your *environmental self* as well. Your true awareness provides all you need for comprehension and response. I know this is difficult for humans, especially when the environment appears threatening or volatile in a given time frame. Just notice what is before you. And take small steps into realizing the greater embrace—the embrace of grace."

While you pause, the silence feels alive around me. I soak it in. "You make it sound so simple. I just wish it were. Why is there so much mystery to all this? Why can't we just know what we all want to know, when we want it?"

"Because you are in a system that *requires* awakening. To bring this about, you must first realize that you need to wake up, that you're dreaming. You are *not* awake yet. The dream is all you know right now, so it appears very convincing. Your mind is certain that it *is* awake. Do not trust your mind!

"And to 'know what you want to know', you first would need to know you *want*. There is no consensus on that for humans, nor within any given individual. There are many divergent desires at play in the field of your evolution. This, you experience as divisiveness, indecision, reaction, rebellion, mistrust, and so on. Before you could have the wishful consensus you were just imagining, you would first need to find resonance within yourselves. That is one reason for my urging you to 'look within'. There, you can truly resonate and *con-sense* with the souls of others.

"As for why there is so much mystery, it is because mystery is *reality*—particularly in reference to the mind. Viewed from within any incarnate perspective—vigilan included—reality is pure mystery. It is the *great unknown*, the Source of everything; and yet it is no thing. And here's another clue, the unknown is *Oneness*."

"The unknown is Oneness? How is that?"

"Think about it. All things 'unknown' are formless. They are beyond the threshold of the known—in that sphere where all is possible, and where all *is*. The unknown is infinitely abundant, without limitation or boundary. It is Oneness. Even what we call 'known' is a continuously metamorphosing projection out of formlessness. The unknown embraces and suffuses all that is known with its own singular—unique—essence."

"OK, I get it. And I think this may be a good time to ask that question again. What do you say?"

"Yes. I've been waiting for it to come up. And you've been very patient. Go ahead. Restate the question from where your awareness is right now."

A burst of rain surges down. "All right. You said early on, that 'Oneness does not manifest'. That shocked me. It sounds controversial and even hopeless in a way—especially, when you think so many new age teachers are preaching the opposite. Some of them are saying we're about to move into a dimension of Oneness, and leave duality behind altogether. Their hope is that through unity we can solve all the problems of the world. Haven't you yourself said that we need to see ourselves as *one?*"

"I'm not contradicting your teachers in essence. Humanity is indeed moving into a realm of connection with pure essence. This is a state of *openness to Oneness.* Vigilans experience this continuously. But we are not about to abandon the world of duality. In fact, your very understanding of Oneness is based on duality; it is a reflection in the mirror. And duality/Oneness is yet another duality. Oneness, as humans understand it, is a *form.* It is a representation and symbol for the Absolute.

"The Absolute does not manifest. It never does. It cannot. It is the Projector. Imagine an image of a projector; say in one of your movie theaters, projecting itself onto a screen. This would be theoretically feasible, would it not?"

"Yeah, I guess."

"But even if it did this, it would still be nothing but a projection. It would not be the *real* source of images. The Projector metaphor we've used many times is the Absolute, the indefinable state of formlessness and true Oneness. It can and does project a representation of itself onto the screen of your experience. It projects an *image* of Oneness. You may interact with it, engage it, be inspired, even awakened by it. But that image still remains only a representation and a metaphor."

The rain is beginning to slow. Strange, how the rain ending always makes me feel a bit melancholy. The patter of rain is so peaceful, unifying—like a state of Oneness. *I don't want that gentle sound to stop.* But it does; and the world of multiplicity abruptly returns.

The last droplets are trickling down the window beside you. You smile softly. "What do you think people mean when they use the word 'Oneness'?" Then you answer your own question. "I think what they mean is an inner bond of essences, uninterrupted by separate, differentiated desires. They are, in effect, saying that one overarching *will* dictates the awareness and behavior of all creatures.

This is valid, of course, in the formless realm. But I ask you, is this what you truly want in the world of form?"

You lean forward and look through the windshield, covered with tiny droplets. Out there are the woods, the bridge and the gray, overcast sky. A light breeze rustles the leaves. You look down at the rippling stream, the rocks and splashes, as if absorbing all the elements into a singular vision.

"Humans also had other views about the matter. John Lennon might have said, 'Oneness is a concept by which we measure our pain'. It is a concept that mirrors all the hopes and dreams of your species—utopia, nirvana, or universality. But you only know of it by reference to the pain, struggles and separateness of duality existence. You measure it because you *don't* have it, not in the physical world. You don't have it here, because it would not fit.

"I submit to you that Oneness is *not* what we want in the physical world. We want and need differentiation and diversity, the wide array of perspectives and opinions, the give and take of expression and realization. If we did not have duality, we would have no contrast, no distinction between our consciousness and what we make ourselves *conscious of.* If Oneness were uninterrupted, we would not be able to move within the stillness. Duality gives us the power to move and explore, to know and embrace the unknown, the great ever-compelling mystery of Life. Duality—and 'many-ness'—is what makes us *alive* on this Earth—able to realize and appreciate the underlying Life of Oneness.

"Certainly Oneness, as a reference point and concept, is eternally important to us. Literally, it *imports* to us the mystery of being connected to Source, the Absolute. It is the bridging form for that. It is the one thing we can say regarding *That About Whom Naught May Be Said.*

"Conceptual Oneness is our *sense* of belonging to one species, one nature, one Cosmos. In all the differentiation we observe on this planet, we innately know there must be a context for it all." You inhale slowly, deeply, as if holding all these concepts inside your breath.

After a long moment, you resume, "We are ever moving toward unity. But we will never achieve it. Not totally. Not here. As your human poet-politician, Vaklav Havel wrote, 'Search out those who seek the truth. Run away from those who have found it!' The same may be said of Oneness. It is an ideal, a motivator toward perfection."

After another respectful silence, you continue. "But if we achieved perfection on Earth, all would be finished—a 'done deal'. It would be stasis, leaving no room for further development and exploration. If Oneness could manifest on Earth it would rob us of our intimate intercourse with the unknown. We all are in love with the process of exploring mysteries. That is why we come to Earth. That is why we love our *dual* nature.

"Now, those who preach the movement into a state of Oneness are *not* misleading you. They are holding the torch high for evolution into awakened consciousness. What they may not realize is that their goal will never be achieved on Earth. But as you know, it's the journey that counts, not the destination. Yes, come together. Find mutuality, compassion and trust amongst yourselves. Seek ever to build common goodness and equality, based on the underlying Oneness of Source. But do not defeat your ambitions by generating unrealizable expectations. *Formlessness* cannot be *form* in your world.

"Look around you at that world. See beyond the strife and conflict, beyond the fear and manipulation. Look at the victory you have all achieved. Look at the unity you have already evolved into, the wholeness your species has. It is all around you.

"Acknowledge the wonders of your own creation. In most of your world today the highways and the skies are safe from pirates, your landscapes are teaming with agricultural abundance, the ideal of democracy is inspiring people everywhere. Sharing and 'humanitarian' acts are even quite common among you, in spite of the ego's contrary tendencies.

"Women and men are freer to express themselves and to re-create themselves than ever before in your history. The feminine archetype is reborn triumphant and rising strong. This force is serene and seductive, interwoven throughout all cultures—even in the most repressive. This feminization is *wholeness* on the move. Why would you want to stop it in its tracks with sudden Oneness?"

"What a funny thought! But aren't wholeness and Oneness the same thing?"

"Yes, you're right. But I refer to their *movement*, and the principles directing their destiny. To institute Oneness—and halt duality—by divine fiat would force immobility upon the whole. It would shut off the flow of evolution through diversity.

"*Conscious Evolution* is nevertheless ever mindful of its underlying Oneness. This is the motive force driving the interplay of atoms and molecules, nations and philosophies, species and families. You are in the midst of its creative energy and manifestation. All the great unity movements of your history are important. But not in the way you have conceived. Their importance lies not in their achievements. They typically fail! Their value lies in the motivation within, the ideal that pulls them onward into the unknown. It is indeed the value of realizing there is truly only *one being* of consciousness, even though that being manifests itself in multiplicity.

"Some would have you feel disappointed at the lack of unity in your politics, your species and nations. I would urge you to see the movement *toward* unity as a great blessing. Accept that blessing. Do not denigrate it with dismay. Do not despair that you never see it, arm-in-arm across the masses of workers and managers, warriors and pacifists, rich and poor. These are just the elements of the shared, differentiated world you possess, *as one*. And it is the same in our world. For us, the separative and dominating ego is gone. But the values of diversity, uniqueness and duality-in-Oneness remain."

Between the parking lot and the water, there is a strip of grass. A small rabbit has appeared there and is nibbling something, looking nervously around. *Does it feel the Oneness? If so, why is it afraid?*

You follow my gaze. "I sense your question. The rabbit exists within the field of shared instinct. She feels the fear because of that connection. It is necessary to her manifestation. The instinct provides both elements of consciousness for her—the fear of exposure in duality, and the destiny inherent in Source. For animals functioning on pure instinct, there is no separation. It is quite different for the human animal, however."

"OK. I'm almost finished with my questions about Oneness."

"I doubt that." You tilt your head, smiling, and raise an eye-brow.

"So instinctual animals are working with both sides of the equa-tion as one. Humans have it divided. What then is the relationship between Oneness, duality and three-ness, or whatever you call it? You said before, that manifestation comes in threes, right?"

"Yes. Let's call it 'triality'. The third aspect of the projected world might also be called 'relationship'. It is the space *within* duali-ty, between the polarities. In terms of perception, there is the con-scious being, there is the object of consciousness, and then there is the *link* of awareness between. This *or* that becomes this *and* that. *Three* is an expression of *one*, shone through the aperture of *two*."

"Whoa. You lost me there." My confusion is abrupt, and yet I immediately sense you are about to wipe it away.

"Unity integrates. Duality divides. Triality re-joins what has been divided. Imagine that Oneness is the Projector; duality is the lens; and triality is the screen. All three are necessary to manifest the image. That is the root of it all—these three functions, or images, move us out into the world of form. That is why imagination and imaging are our instruments of choice for communication. It is closest to the heart of our project, our projection."

You take my right hand between your two hands. They're warm to the touch. You look me in the eye, playfully, and direct my gaze down at our three hands. There is an electric glow around them now, radiating out in flowing waves. The waves form petals, like a flower, and then come together in a bubble of light. The globe im-mediately bursts, and the light dissolves. You laugh happily at your little creation.

"Imagination is the initial impulse of manifestation. The projec-tion is the image appearing, that is, manifesting. Through the se-quence of three levels, all the infinity of dimensions is generated. This is why we may sense Oneness while immersed in the world of form—if we know the code. We merely look backward through the lens, and into the mirror."

"How do we do that?"

"That which manifests as multiplicity reveals its Source in simplicity and singularity. Look at the many to see the one. Look at the *space*, not the objects. Look within. We are one, because we are many. We are the one Life that is living itself out through trillions upon trillions of forms, over all the eons of time. This is Oneness living through many-ness. That is a key. The projection guarantees the Projector. If you hold this awareness in your heart—not mind—when you look at the diversity, you will see the underlying unity. It cannot be otherwise.

"All that appears to be real in your experience is a necessary illusion—that is, if there is to be any manifestation at all. Take comfort in this. Illusion, on this side of the Veil, guarantees reality. That is why, if we want to have any world to experience, we require the illusion, the projection. And in the end—as well as in the beginning—it is why Oneness *cannot* manifest."

I shake my head. "How does this fit with what you've said about separateness being the core problem of the ego? It sounds hopeless if Oneness can't ever manifest. I thought you had gotten over that in your society."

"The impulse to separate is built into duality. But it can be rendered transparent. Vigilans see through the form and resonate with the formlessness beneath it. At the same time, we also experience the differentiation we need for incarnate life. The human ego used separateness under the influence of the Veil of Forgetfulness. This was a destructive combination in the end. It closed off your deeper vision of reality. Without the Veil, however, in our world, separation is merely a matter of distinguishing; it opens our realization to opportunity, integrity and equality."

A childish question comes to me. "O, why is this important? Why do we need to know about it?"

"Because Oneness is the vehicle of passage through the portal. To build it and to access it, you will need all the keys and codes of your being, from all the accumulated experience of your times on Earth. This is the time of the great *revelation* within your being— your personal and species' Apocalypse. It is your time to move beyond all the previous limitations, time to lift the Veil. And *it is time to reveal all the secrets!*

"Your species will all move with the flow of the times. But many are entering the Storm with little awareness of who they really are. This will be painful and disorienting for them. What we are doing—the portal builders of your time and mine—is facilitating the passage; we are opening a more benign way through this mutational process. Recall that we spoke of the *vesica* as a bridge to Oneness. It is the bridging lens of duality, interfacing with Oneness. It is the essential aperture into which we have placed our conscious imagination to reach you in these letters. Likewise, it will be your means to reach us, and indeed to *become* us in the new universe."

"Oneness does not manifest, you say." I'm still puzzled. "But isn't a 'vehicle' a manifestation? You talk of formlessness, but this sounds like a *form* to me. It sounds like a contradiction."

"It sounds like a *paradox,*" you respond calmly, perfectly still.

You look intently at me. It is as though your two, shining eyes have become one in my imagination. There is a new, fresh feeling in your gaze. It penetrates my own eyes, like an invisible beam of being. It has substance, though I cannot see it. I know it's joining our minds, our consciousness, one-soul-in-two-bodies. And now again, I sense you are beginning to leave me. Your image, sitting so concretely in the front seat of my car, is turning into thin air, into invisibility. I blink and you are gone.

The sun breaks out of the clouds and beams down against the steamy window where you were, just a moment before. I gasp involuntarily, sadly. *I don't want you gone. I want you here.* I feel you know what I'm thinking. I hear an almost-voice in my mind. It seems to say, 'Come along.'

I sit transfixed for several minutes, looking out at the sunshine on the stream and the grassy bank. It's only natural for me to get out of the car now. I close the door quietly behind me with a click, and walk to the riverbank. Sunlight streams through the misty air and leafy tree branches, down upon the water. Birds are calling from the trees on the other bank. The creek is gurgling at my feet. Without hesitation I slip out of my sandals and step into the cool water. I wade out a few steps, up to my ankles, and stop.

Letter Forty-Six
Glimpse of Awakening

The water around my feet suddenly feels different. It's swirling and alive, massaging my skin. The stones underfoot have changed. There's a whole different energy in them. The sunlight is higher in the sky. Looking up and around, my jaw drops. *I'm not here anymore! I mean, I'm not where I was!*

The stream is smaller. The trees are now willows and cedars instead of maples. *Am I hallucinating? Going crazy for real? And my car is gone!* A wave of apprehension surges over me. But then I hear the simple melody of a musical instrument. Behind me a wide, grassy field stretches out beyond the creek. There are mountains in the distance. This place is familiar. Now a man in flowing emerald robes steps down from the opposite bank into the water. I know him; he's holding a flute. It's *Green*—from the future!

"That was quick," he says in a matter-of-fact voice, gesturing with his wooden instrument. He wades out toward me. "You're getting good at this transposing."

At last I recognize what's happened. I'm the one who's just traveled. I'm back in the year 500, at the stream where Green lives, near O's house. I'm dumbfounded. *How did this happen?*

My host answers aloud, "We invited you. Didn't you hear us?"

"That was your voice I heard in my head?" I mutter. "Well, I'll be..."

"Yes, *be*. Be at peace, friend." G reaches out his hands in greeting, and touches mine. "Welcome to my home." He stretches wide his arms, indicating his residence in the trees, and makes a slow turn toward the bank. We wade across the stream. My feet are firmly on the bottom this time—unlike my first visit here. I feel the sand with my toes, the tug of the knee-deep water against my legs as I walk.

"Thank you," I finally manage to reply. We climb the grassy embankment and enter the opening under a giant willow. The ground is covered with soft duff, apparently woven; it is a firm surface. The space under the trees is large and intriguing—a vigilan habitation, infused with wild nature. I can't stop looking around, turning several circles. The textures and colors are rich; the details, entrancing, the aroma pleasing. But more than anything, there is a *feeling* in the air. Magic is here.

"This is where I live. Do you find it agreeable?"

"Very much so. It has a wonderful essence to it. I feel like Pan is going to step out of the branches any minute."

The tall man only smiles mysteriously in response.

"The ground, uh, floor, is so comfortable to my feet. This is *luxurious*. Who would have thought!" I trail off, mumbling.

Willow branches create walls and partitions around us where they meet the grassy edge. And yet they're open and light, moving gently with the breeze. Great gnarly roots form what appear to be furniture—bench and table shapes. A low fire burns in a stone bowl in the center. It casts flickering light about the space. The massive tree trunk has small openings and alcoves, where objects have been placed; they gleam out like fairy treasures.

Above us there is a high, cavernous vault. It's an awesome site. I swing my head up and down, to soak up the details. The smell is fresh and natural, like sage. Flowering plants and vines are spaced around, growing out of the floor and up in the nooks and crotches of the tree. Birds twitter in the branches high above. Everything seems to be alive.

"So, where is O?" I stammer, a little nervous that this is your 'husband'.

"She has business elsewhere right now. We'll see her soon." He is pleasant enough, but elusive; his inscrutable smile doesn't waver. "She asked me to greet you and make you comfortable."

He looks down at me from above—at least a foot taller than I. Now I take note of his robes; they're impressive in a way I hadn't realized before. There are *real leaves* sewn into the fabric. It's an artistic tangle of shapes and textures, shades of verdure; there are jewels in the fabric as well. The cut of the floor-length garment is regal, with a wide, erect collar around the neck. G's rich brown face, framed in cascading black hair, adds even more elegance to his demeanor. I feel totally underdressed in my kaki shorts and sport shirt.

My host recognizes this discomfort and chuckles softly. "Come. I'll show you the rest of my place."

He motions me to follow him. We pass through one of the openings in the willow curtain, and at once are enveloped in a new environment. The magic has changed, but it is no less enchanting. This space is under yet another tree—a cedar. The smell is powerful and infusing. The light is filtered with a dark auburn hue, streaming down through the heavy canopy above. I inhale deeply. This 'room' is quiet and empty except for a kind of altar in the center. The altar is composed of three illuminated quartz pillars about two feet high. They lean together at the top.

"Say, how do you keep out the rain?"

The tall man smiles. "We have our ways."

The serenity here absorbs my senses. I am ushered into a deep, transcendent space of mind. Through the overwhelming silence, I hear the faint play of water outside. G gazes down at me. "A moment ago you said, 'Who would have *thought?*' I assume that, as a human, you are often caught up in *thinking?* Am I right?"

"That's an understatement!" I assert.

"And you have wondered how you could ever do without it?"

"Yeah. Thought seems to be around us all the time. It seems to be inescapable and, in fact, *indispensable.* To be honest, I still don't see how anyone can be truly conscious without thinking."

Green's face takes on a beneficent look. "Let me draw some currents together for you—here beside the *stream.*" He gestures in the direction of the sound outside and pauses, as if to allow inspiration to flow in. Now he continues, "There is a word we use in my time that has its roots in yours. The word is 'streaming'. My understanding is that it was related to your computer networks."

"Yes. I'm quite familiar with it. 'Streaming' is the transmission of live data. We use that term to describe how computers, via the Internet, communicate in *real-time.* Information flows directly from sender to receiver in a continuous... well... stream."

"Hmm," G chuckles. "That's a curious term—'real time'. As if time were *real.* But I understand. In the vigilan vocabulary 'stream-

ing' still means something like that. For us it connotes 'live processing of awareness'—in the moment. It is in fact bringing the *real*
into the unreal. The formlessness becomes form, timelessness
bridges into time."

I ponder what he's said; we both fall silent. His soft eyes bore
into mine. *Streaming? Yes.* At last I respond, "I get it. I really do get
it! *Streaming* is to conscious awareness as *thinking* is to the intellectual
mind."

"You do *get* it, my friend. In fact 'getting it' *is* streaming. Streaming is Source, speaking within us—alive and in the moment. Using
other words, it is 'the *peace* that passes understanding'. That peace
flows around, and *passes* through understanding, infusing it with
presence. It delivers knowing directly to our senses, and thus *fulfills*
understanding." He smiles and pats my back lightly. I feel a splash
of energy in his touch. In the same motion, smoothly, he moves me
ahead. "This way, please."

Next, we enter a smaller space. G's head nearly touches the
branches above. I don't recognize the type of tree, but it's wiry and
twisted. The leaves are deciduous, small and yellow. I'm startled at a
furtive movement near the edge. I turn.

As my eyes focus, I glimpse a fox darting away through the
grass perimeter. Above, a raven is perched, unmoved. It looks on
with piercing, black eyes. Along another branch, nearby, a thin
green serpent winds itself out of sight. I'm a bit disturbed at the
sight of it, I realize. G smiles at this and reaches in amongst the
branches behind him. *What's he reaching for?* I'm a little apprehensive.
But instead of a snake, he pulls out a folded bundle of cloth. It's
composed of many shades of green, similar to his own robe.

"Here. You may feel more comfortable in this," he says sympathetically.

Unfurling the cloth, he reveals a long garment. He holds it up
for me to slip my arms into. I nod and smile, a little sheepishly, and
thank him. It fits well; I'm surprised. Even the arms are the right
length. I stroke the material with my fingers and look down appreciatively. It's a masterpiece of composition and weaving.

I sense a new energy suddenly. It's as though the cloak I'm wearing is somehow *wearing me!* It's become part of me, radiating an essence that scintillates and empowers my own essence and awareness. I look up into G's impassive eyes. I can see into him in a new way. His eyes are the same deep maroon color of Old Man's eyes, I realize. There's a gentle, ancient soul behind them, ready to help me take whatever my next steps might be.

"I have other spaces in my dwelling, of course. But I think you've seen enough for now. Come back to the cedar with me. There's something O asked me to show you there."

Back though the leafy partition, I look at the space with new vision. I see globes of light, four of them, hovering in the room now. They're high above, glowing soft and warm. Small sparks drop lazily from them. All around the perimeter of the circle, illuminated columns have appeared; these cylinders have points of light spiraling up inside. They're ghostly. It's as if they are not quite in this dimension.

An explanation pops into my head unbidden. *Streaming!* They are indeed 'dimension-straddling' features; their purpose is to help bring essences across boundaries—like portals. I'm intrigued and begin to count them. Strangely though, when I try, each time I lose track of the counting. *Are there ten or twelve? Or nine? I simply can't tell.* Baffled in the end, I accept them as the countenance of mystery.

"Please sit down." Green interrupts my absorption and motions to some cushions that have appeared near the crystal altar. I bow and slide down to sitting. He follows suit on the opposite side. We sit facing each other in silence. Uncharacteristically, I'm content to wait for whatever he wants to show me. This patience, too, seems imbued from the fabric I wear. A profound peace is here, all around and inside.

Green stares intently into the crystals for several minutes. He finally, slowly, lifts his eyes and arms. His hands are open before him—one up, the other down. With a slight twitch if his fingers, a plane of light erupts on top of the crystals. It's a flat circle of chartreuse light, glowing, transparent like a hologram. It wavers and fluctuates, continually renewing its hold on this dimension.

"Follow the light," G whispers. That's all.

I look into the shining disk. It sparkles with many colors, like rainbow spirals. A figure gradually materializes on the surface—a holographic miniature. It's a transparent image of a woman in black robes. Long white hair falls over her shoulders. *It's B!* In my hypnotic state, this does not surprise me. She bows, but does not speak. Neither do I. She stands and faces me, arms out like Green.

I'm suddenly dizzy and light-headed. But my gaze is fixed on B. Smoothly, another image appears beside her, arms outstretched toward her. Incredibly it's *me!* I'm watching a tiny figure of myself on the gleaming dish. The more I look, the more I'm drawn into the image. *Is this a dimension-within-a-dimension? Is that what all* subdi's *are?* As I wonder about it, I see myself both here and there, just as before. And then there is no separation. I'm just standing in front of Black, on the disk.

My palms are also up and down. I lay one hand in hers, and she reciprocates with the other. The electricity flows at once. We seem to be completing a circuit, up from the disk, through our bodies and hands. I stare into her dark eyes. She smiles and we begin to slowly whirl. The disk below us whirls in the opposite direction. The room above blurs. I'm losing control. I stop resisting. Down we go, into the abyss once more.

The sensation of falling is much stronger this time. It feels like we've jumped off the cliff above the stormy sea of the avatars. There is no cliff or ocean, but there are shapes, walls and caverns, rushing past as we plummet. A harsh screaming sound assaults my ears. The air is speeding around us; we're both falling and spinning. I smell smoke. It's frightening. I hold my breath and close my eyes for a moment. The fear increases with this, so I open them again, searching for B's face. I stare into her eyes fiercely. The falling continues, but the fear relaxes and slowly abates. She is placid, composed, and I'm absorbing that from her.

"B, can you hear me?" I shout above the whipping wind. "What's happening?"

She continues to stare, and says nothing. But she tightens her grip on my hands. I feel a message inwardly. *Look through the projection,* it says. My eyes are still fixed on hers. She begins to grow more transparent. At first I see nothing behind her. *But no, there is something else—shapes, objects.* There's a great beam of light surging up through them. *How could I have missed it?* On it's edges I see many forms coming and going, whirling up, and then drawn back into the beam, dissolving. At first they are simple—buildings, people, animals, places.

All at once the shapes become more complex—large groups of things, events. I see the seething ocean of human bodies I witnessed at the Ends of the Earth. They rise and fall along the periphery of the light shaft, spinning like a slow-motion tornado. Now the vision plunges into the past. It seems to be receding farther and farther into the past, as we fall. Smoke streams up from the fires of friction everywhere.

I see ancient civilizations, great cities and monuments. They rise and fall in mere seconds. Finally we come to a smooth halt. There are the Giza pyramids and the Sphinx. But they are not the way I've ever seen them. They're alight with vibrant colors, radiating energy waves into the sky and land.

"B, what am I looking at?"

At last I hear her voice, low and firm. "We are visiting elements of the origin of humanity's form. We are proceeding toward the source of that form. Watch, and learn what you can about yourself."

I stare at the scene in the beam. It does not dissolve as the others have. The Sphinx looks new, like it was just built. Its face is freshly carved and has the smile of the Mona Lisa. There is a faint triangle of light formed by the two eyes and the smile; it points down. The eyes are smiling, like the lips. Now I see the Mona Lisa.

What does this mean to me? I'm shaking with anticipation.

The triangle glows more vibrantly. And then there is another glowing triad. It is the pyramid itself, standing behind the Sphinx—one triangle points to the Earth, one to the heavens. Both of them are now glowing brightly, dominating my vision. *What does it mean?* I ask again. A streaming tells me the smaller, lower triangle is a 'V'; the upper is an 'A'—the first and last letters of '*vesica*'. The triangles now join into a diamond *rhombus* shape. It turns slowly into three dimensions, becoming a tetrahedron. And then the turning accelerates into a spin.

Soon the tetrahedron is whirling so fast, it has blurred into a rounded form—a three-dimensional *vesica piscis*. *That shape again!* But what I see is not static. It morphs rapidly into other shapes. First it is an egg, then a glassy waveform. Next it flows into an hourglass, then the rhombus again; this elongates and transforms into an obelisk. Slowly a *vesica* forms around it in a shimmering, multi-dimensional apparition. Finally, the obelisk dissolves back into the simple *vesica*. It hovers, transparent like a lens. The great, flowing beam of history is passing through this lens and diffusing out in a multitude of smaller rays. It projects over the land and water, over the whole Earth.

Without warning, our holographic bodies are picked up and swept into the vortex, and the lens. As I look upon the parade of historical events and people churning inside the beam, I am in awe. From this universal lens, all the Cosmos can be seen, reflected and magnified endlessly. It is a miraculous looking glass.

This is far beyond my mental comprehension. It's so vast my mind seems to disintegrate. To see this and know this, I cannot use a human mind. I am beyond myself. My mind seems to be too small to grasp the grandeur. *But no, that's not it. It's just the reverse. My mind is not small enough! It's not simple enough.*

I keep going with the vision. The Mona Lisa face appears, along with the Sphinx. They're within us—the lens—now. The mystery remains. These two icons seem to represent the heart of mystery for our civilization. They're smiling out at the world because they know something important. They seem to say this is a game, an elaborate mystery game. Our whole task as humans, and as vigilans, is to comprehend and to play this *game!*

I hear laughter. Cosmic laughter from Source echoes through the images. *What is the Mona Lisa smiling about? What is the riddle of the Sphinx?* 'Play, my child,' comes an answer. 'Play with the smile. It is the root of your blessings. It is how you are born and how you die. Play the game of freedom! Grow with this blessing.'

I hear my ego calling from a great distance. It demands to know why these bizarre things are happening to it, to me. I turn my attention and listen. My ego refuses to accept the simplicity, the mystery. It reminds me of all the troubles, disasters and cruelty in the world.

How can this be just a game, just a riddle? But here, within the bubble lens beneath my mind, the ego is powerless, naked. I look out to it, amused. I feel compassion for it. A simple seed-link streams in. I know it will reveal its content to me at another time. *The game is afoot. I will understand it later.*

In the twinkling of an eye everything changes. I'm back in the cedar room, standing in miniature on the disk. Green and Black are with me there as well—in a triangle. The vision has vanished. Our hands are joined. I still smell the smoke from below, mixed now with the scent of cedar.

I speak hesitantly, "I know this is a strange question, B. But I feel I must ask it. Am I a *vigilan?* Have I transformed?"

B looks over to Green, smiling. He speaks, "Yes, for this projection. That is now true. When you return to your own time, you will again be human, however."

B continues with her explanation. "It is time now for you to see through our eyes for a while. We wish you to know the blessing being given to humanity. It is an opening into everything your hearts can ever desire. You may now know, as we know. *Accept your blessing!* This is the ultimate message from our species to yours. Lift the ego veil and look with clear eyes upon the wonder of true freedom. If you humans only knew the blessing being offered, you would be dancing—not fighting—in the streets."

I gasp. *It's true!* The feeling is exhilarating, light and free. It's like a giant, invisible claw has let go of me! I'm still in a physical form, and yet, I feel as free as a god! Everything is so, so beautiful, so peaceful. I'm ebullient, expansive and joyful—almost into bliss. The word that comes to mind is 'enormous'. I feel enormous and transparent. *This is how it is to be free of ego!* I have nothing to defend or protect, nothing to hide or feel shame about. No regrets.

I realize this is my opportunity to really look at the differences between human and vigilan. I see, finally, from both sides now. My fears are gone. Though my desires are still with me, they are clean and clear; they're keyed to the sensibilities of those around me, and more—with the entire species, and all other species. I can literally feel the Oneness vibrating down low, inside my sensations. I can feel what others are feeling. All I need do is look, allow and accept. Appreciation is hanging in the air, in every breath I take.

"B, I'm finally getting it! I know who you really are, all of you. I'm dazzled by the presence and peace you all have. I can't wipe this smile off my face." We three are still standing with hands clasped around the miniature circle. I feel a sparkling energy coursing through me from these two wonderful beings."

"Welcome to your destiny, brother."

The strongest feeling I have is, again, appreciation—just as you've always said. It is continuous and unending. It welcomes me to each moment of perception, and I in turn welcome it. The reciprocity of this equation is boundlessly creative, regenerating and amplifying itself in steady measure. There is an expansive spiral to it; hence the feeling of enormity. And underlying it all, especially comparing it to my *human* being, there is an almost excruciating sense of peace. I know this peace as vital, the power center of my new being. I am using it to see through all forms, from the state of formlessness. *How will I feel when I have to give this up again?*

Vigilans live in an unending flow of truth. They cannot hide from it; they cannot hide themselves from it, as humans do. Sadly, I realize we humans are living the last of our collective *lies*. We are blindly clinging to a sunken ship. We have ridden our horse into its grave. And even then, we do not yet see. Our fear of the unknown continually *contracts* us into separation, compounded upon separation. This is the very definition of 'ego contract'—ego *contraction!*

Instead of realizing the appreciation, alive in the atmosphere of each out-breath, we humans choose to suck in and hold to our separatism. Holding our collective breath, out of fear and defense, we prefer to retreat away from the glory of true being. This is why the world of my time is so turbulent, violent and dishonest. We are denying our blessing. We are being supremely dishonest to our deep nature. So, we play the cosmic *game* in shame and disappointment.

In my vigilan consciousness now, I look back with greater compassion. I realize that humanity *must* do what it's doing. We must live through this to its bitter end—the Ends of the Earth. We must exhaust the demon of our illusion, the longstanding contract with ego.

We are not in fact *separate*, yet we *are* particular. We have been confused. That's all it is. We have dreamt that differentiation means separation, danger and dread. We have invented all the fear in the world out of this. We've spread it far and wide across the land, onto all creatures and forms—animals, plants, and minerals. We have perpetrated a curse upon ourselves and upon nature, based on ignorance—the Veil of Forgetfulness.

An inspiration flashes into my mind. *Being human is nothing more than a belief!* Yes, it's a *root* belief, and that's very strong. But any belief can be changed, given enough inner acceptance. It is just a matter of looking behind the projection and redefining ourselves. It's a matter of being *authentic. Could humanity do that? It's a tall order. But, yes. Emphatically, yes!*

"All right. I see it, B. I feel it and know now what's happening. But I'm left with a question. What can I do about it? What can we all do about it? I understand how it feels to be really free. I feel our transmutation coming from deep inside myself. That's fine for me, but what can I take back to my fellow humans? They're all struggling so hard to change and evolve. And yet the forces of resistance are strong. Those forces are rigidly entrenched and in control. It seems hopeless to try to do anything against them. I don't want to return from this glimpse of awakening empty-handed."

Black looks back to Green. He answers, "It is hopeless to *try*. Yea. It is hopeless to be *against* the old form. That form *is* you. Do not negate yourself, your vehicle. Instead, evolve! Believe it or not, the hope that you feel right now is a type of resistance, aimed from within limitation. So also, is your desire to *change* the world. This takes you away from Source."

"But can we not apply hope to this change? Why not hope?"

"Because it takes you backwards into the old projection. It seeks salvation *within* that old form. You must enter the *new* projection, the new form! You must *grow* beyond the old. Let *Conscious Evolution* change the world *through* you, within you."

"All right. But I still need something to take back with me."

Green answers, echoing what you always say, "Take *acceptance*. Activate your appreciation in this moment. There is no other moment to hope for. *Change* can only come in this moment. Hope implies and generates distance from your objective, from the moment. Do not *try*. Do not *hope*. Rather, allow and accept."

I'm looking into the man's deep maroon eyes. His presence feels very familiar in this moment. His face begins to shift. The skin takes on wrinkles; it is aging before my eyes. I'm reminded of my experience with Young Man. His black hair turns white. The face grows thinner, gaunt. His eyes, however, remain the same. *Beyond this time and place, I am looking at the old man!* He bows his head and raises it again, smiling triumphantly. I see the Cosmos radiating out behind him.

Green's voice speaks from the aged face. "I am who you have always known, my son. This is where we begin, where we are returning. Yes, the old man is part of the path of my soul."

I shake my head. *What am I seeing?* Green's face slides back up through the background image of his essence. I realize I've just met his soul. *Old Man* is his soul. Amazing!

"Does O know this?" I blurt out.

"She does now."

"Well, I'll be damned!" I sigh. "Uh, that's just an expression."

Green chuckles, "You may in fact be *damned*. But you don't have to stay that way. Truly, we all want humanity to realize this. You are not damned, except by yourselves. You are blessed. We wish you to accept it."

I draw in a deep, long breath. I feel the ever-present field of appreciation entering me. Within its embrace, I must now return to my overarching concern. "I want to ask you all for your help. Would you please help us, G, Black, OM? There must be something we can do besides just sitting and waiting for the so-called transmutation. That seems so indefinite, and rather like a cop out."

Black speaks again. "We understand. There *is* something you can do besides wait. You can look *through* the façade of the projection. For this, you must know *yourself* first. This is of paramount importance. Look into your own being deeply. Explore yourself to the very root and foundation. You, all humans, must go back and remember your roots. Without this awareness, you cannot grow to flowering. Do this in heart and body, more than mind."

Green picks up, "This means cultivating intuitive awareness. Learn to see your ego for what it is. *Accept it* for what it is. Do not fight it or try to kill it out. Paradoxically, bring your awareness into the ego and let it shine there. Let it burn out through the illusion of the little self. Let the ego know itself to be illusion. Let it decide for itself—in the light of consciousness—to release you."

"Yes," B continues. "It is all quite paradoxical. Allow paradox. It is spirit's blood in your veins. Ego will release you, once it has the light of awareness within itself. This you can facilitate, hand-in-hand with *Conscious Evolution*. Your time is indeed at hand, each and every one of you.

"You cannot make the transformation happen of your own volition, no. Such an effort would be of the mind and persona. This is impossibility. The genetic mutation is enabled through bodily and etheric forces, not mental. Nevertheless, you may influence the approach of awakening through your heart. You may invoke it's arousal through openness within.

"You are not left without avenues of action. You may certainly participate in the transition events of your epoch. But refrain from thinking you can *make* it happen. You cannot *control* this. Give up the desire to control anything. *Control is resistance.* Rather, reach within, to your real power. Resonance with Source is the true means for directing your life, and especially your behavior during the Great Storm. *Act from resonance, not resistance.*"

I interrupt, "OK. But what are we to do with the greatest resistance of all—the ego?"

Black answers, "Listen carefully. Listen from beyond ego and mind. Here is my suggestion. When you return, do not empower your separative nature. Open your awareness to the flow and flexibility of the moment. Find it at the root of all movement within you—in the stillness beyond thought. Allow all change to come from there. Find the full measure of stillness in you. Do this only once. If you do it *truly* one time, it will be complete.

"From there, look out at that illusory pattern we call ego. Look at it from the inside out, as I said before, from beneath it. Watch it like you would watch a small child. Nurture it, care for it, *empower* it. Do this with love and conscious intention. Allow your Life force to inhabit this fragile, defensive being. Embrace it from the inside out. Embody it consciously and appreciate it fully. Heal it fully.

B takes a deep breath. "Then allow the expansion of appreciation to grow up and out through this newly conscious vehicle, the *persona nova*. It is the *awakened* ego, host of the living soul. Do this in your purest imagination, not your intellect. Allow the image of this transformation to be born in you."

G nods and interjects, "Such, friend, is the mystery fulfilled. So let it be."

Black resumes, "Now, there is something else you may do when you return. It will not come easily, I'm afraid. Come to know your ego, and the egos of others—like never before. Watch continuously, but do this without creating thought forms, without judgments. Allow the watchfulness to loosen the grip of separatism in you. You do not have to continue in the old ways—under the yoke of an outworn, inferior vehicle. Release the vehicle of separation, and take up the vehicle of Oneness.

The fierce woman gestures with her hands, cupping them together and staring into the space there, as if holding a crystal ball. "Awareness of the ego and its patterns, is a most powerful starting point. See the subtle, intimate way it is woven into your innermost thoughts and feelings. It is there everywhere. You need not look far. Your willingness to look is your invitation for evolution to arise within you, and within your institutions, societies, and species. If you can but *notice*—as Orange likes to say—when it is both active and passive in you, you will see how transparent it really is."

Her fiery eyes glance away for a moment. The penetrating gaze transfers into the eyes of Green; his look pierces into me. "We have studied you humans, thoroughly now. And what we see most prominently is the shallowness of your defenses. We would have you see the same thing."

"Shallowness?" I react, with a squint.

"Indeed. Your separatism has no depth." Green is holding my gaze fiercely. "In fact it *denies* depth of consciousness. This is its primary focus—and its fundamental weakness. All the problems of your world, all the obstacles to your desired transformation, lie at the feet of this shallowness in you. It is not just the aggressive, domineering, arrogant ego, but also the victimized, withdrawn and complaining sense of self, that denies depth and Source.

"Any form of resistance you feel about yourself or your environment needs to be examined and appreciated for what it is. It needs to be filled with light—from within. This you can easily do from where you are now. This is the beginning of the change you seek. This is the understanding you may take back with you."

I see what he's saying. And yet there's still a smoldering concern in my mind. "I see it clearly right now, just as you do, friends. But I'm afraid that, in my human form, I will lose this awareness, and revert back to fear and doubt, and the hopelessness. Is there something I can do to ensure that I'll remember this?"

Black answers, raising her hand as if to make space. "Your body portal is open, nearly ready to employ. This can be your guide and assurance when you return into the Storm. The process of opening, once begun, will not be reversed. Pause now your questioning. Go and revisit your portal; do this in your imagination. Go now, while we wait."

I'm surprised at this command, but I understand. Immediately I sink within myself, plunging down the beam of light to the edge of the Void. There before me is the field of portals. My transparent body form is floating with the others, its point of light glowing brighter than ever. I stare and wonder. *You said this was the seed, O. I have planted it, but I must wait for an invitation to enter the portal. What does the invitation look like? Will I know it when it arrives?*

Is my mind playing tricks? The point suddenly changes shape. It wobbles and vibrates, opens. It takes on the *vesica* shape. Could this be the invitation? I approach closer, and examine the opening. It is silent, but radiant, like living glass, like the greater lens I witnessed in the beam.

Just as before, I'm drawn in, with a burst of light. Everything is twisting and turning, falling, imploding. *I'm inside!* Down. Down.

I'm in the Void again. The sensation is unmistakable, profound. Empty and full; all and nothing. Limitless energy tears my being apart and reassembles it into another space. I am at the Oneness. It is at me. I am Source.

Then all is blank, as usual. I experience nothing until I'm back. I'm floating before my body again, feeling the bliss that accompanies the return from the Void. Awe surrounds me. I know the portal is working. That at least! But, alas, I know also it is not my time to cross into the new universe. Not quite yet. I must return to the old one, and for a reason. That reason knows itself within me. I do not need to voice it here. It is another seed-link.

I pop out and back to the cedar room, holding the hands of my companions again. We have resumed our normal size. Light from the etheric disk is shining on our faces from below in a ghostly way. *What is real?* There is an inner process revealing itself here. *But what is it exactly? Am I really a vigilan? Or is it just the power of the robes I wear? Does it flow through the hands of my friends? Does it really matter?*

Now in my mind, the two seed-links are joining and opening out for me. They are beginning to explain the so-called 'game of my life'. The flat plane of this disk on the altar represents a *plateau*. It is my current station and personal assignment. I cannot rise higher until this mission is complete.

My destiny is to fully inhabit this plateau until all my loose energies catch up to me. My body has summoned them from the patterns of the past, from Atlantis, from all the scattered pieces of my soul lying in far away places. I must allow them their time to gather. During this period of accumulation, I will continue to know myself better, to see through the illusion, and to renegotiate my ego contract. *I will continue to act as a translator for the Letters of O.*

It dawns on me that this plateau is a cause for the frustrations I've been feeling lately in my world. *I've wanted to rise and shift prematurely. But it's not yet my time.* It's finally clear to me in this moment. I recall that it's what you already explained to me before. With this reaffirmed knowledge, perhaps I will be more content when I return. Perhaps. At least I'll know why I feel what I feel. *This could be progress.*

Letter Forty-Seven
Faith and Magic

"I believe you have your answer, my child." B squeezes, then drops my hand, and so does Green. I nod and bow my head in reverence to this ceremony. We are standing around the crystals, but the plateau has disappeared.

"It is time to gather at the house," G states simply, turning toward an opening in the wall.

"The house? You mean O's house?" I ask with excitement, drawn to it like a magnet. I pull the robe tighter around me, feeling a chill. The recent experiences have been a lot for my system. I chuckle to myself. *That's an understatement!*

"Come this way," Green directs. Black and I follow through the branches. We're suddenly outside beside the creek. The sound of gurgling water is vitalizing. The sun has sunk low in the sky over the dunes in the distance. Together, silently, we start walking.

The air is golden from the setting sun. *Magic hour,* I whisper in my mind. It sheds an enchantment over the grasses and hills. I could not feel more magical, more spiritual than I do at this moment. I might as well be walking on air. And my bare feet on the sandy trail are as happy as if they *were*. The atmosphere, the Earth, the vegetation—all is one. I know Oneness doesn't manifest, but this is pretty darn close to it.

I hear your clear voice in my mind, to answer my musing. *"Yes, my new friend. This is Oneness. Look deeply at it now, this instant. You will see what it truly is."*

I look, and I *do* see. The Oneness I feel is implicit in the manifestation. It is in the underlying fabric of essence. It is within me and within all that is around me. It guarantees all the forms, all of existence. It's the creation platform, the stage upon which manifestation is the play, the scenes, the actors, the *game*.

O, can you hear me? I ask with a thought.

"Yes."

Why did you call me 'new' friend?

Silence. Deep silence. No answer. I feel the grass brushing my green cloak as we walk the path; there is some kind of energy exchange in the contact. I hear sea birds calling in the distance and smell salt air from over the dunes. Now I see others coming along other paths, converging, by twos, threes, singles—all the members of your group. Our group. Their forms move deliberately, yet lightly and quietly, through the golden-lit grasses. The scene is a ceremony in itself, under these pink and orange clouds. It is a perfect meditation, in a perfect, sacred moment—stillness in motion.

Your voice slides inside me. *"I said 'new' because you are transformed at this time, in this space. You know it to be true. You are the* persona clara, *clear mask, in our midst, representing your entire species to us. You have looked through the lens, the perfect seed-link. You now know both my species and yours better yet than we do. So shall we renew ourselves—vigilans—and learn from your perceptions. You will accelerate our own powers of appreciation. Walk the path with us today. Welcome."*

I see your house with no roof. My heart thrills. My appreciation soars. I know, in this moment, that I will be able to carry the feeling back with me into being human again. There will be a great gift to myself waiting there. I plant that seed-link inside, right into my own ego. It will take time to germinate, to sprout and grow. But I know it is planted. I know the soil has been prepared. G described it. It will liberate my ego, compassionately from within—with light and faith.

"There is no faith without magic," you whisper, as if keeping pace with me.

I like that. But what do you mean?

"We live by faith, in the moment," your presence responds. *"It is our link directly into the Holy Unknown and our destiny. For this we require magic, all around us and in us, at all times."*

We are standing before your house now. The whole form sweeps up with rainbow colors, out of the ground, into the sky. Waves of pastel light flow upward again and again like a waterfall of rising light. The waves become an aurora in the heavens. *Magic!* I look around and see all the group assembled, myself included, glowing and afire with the same cascade of light. Everyone is beaming—quite literally. Our hearts are open wide. I know all these souls so deeply, from the most ancient of times. They are my origin, my refuge. I sigh with a full presence.

"Please come into the house, just you and Green. The others will prepare the circle in the field with Black. I wish to talk with just the two of you for a moment."

Apparently my friends have received the same communication from O. Green veers away from B. She turns out into the field with the group, while he waves me ahead with him. I follow, through the sliding wall into your house.

Inside, the coursing light continues up the walls and into the sky. You are seated in your living room, on cushions in one corner. Except for the pulsing light, the room is dark. Yet it seems more *alive* than ever. We cross to you and are motioned to take seats beside you, looking out through the windows to the pond. The sun has set behind the trees, silhouetting them in brilliance; shadows envelop the water.

G embraces you and strokes your hands before sitting. You then turn to me and touch my hands warmly.

"It is sweet to have the three of you here," you say.

Green and I look at each other. "Three of us?" he asks.

"Yes. I've invited a friend of ours to join us." You wave a hand in the air and a shape begins to materialize out of the shadows. In an instant I realize it's the old man. I raise up with surprise and stare at him.

"You're here?" I start. "You all never cease to amaze me."

Green is more surprised than I am. He rises and stares transfixed at the small, wizened figure that has joined us from another dimension and time. "Excuse me, sir. Who are you?" he demands.

Suddenly G realizes who it is. He whispers, "This is indeed a rare honor." The two are strikingly different in form. G stands half again as tall as the old one. OM reaches out and touches G on the hands, then on both shoulders, finishing with a strong hug.

"Please. Let's sit and talk," OM motions to the cushions. "I asked to be invited to your portal ceremony. It concerns me greatly, even a thousand decades from now."

He turns to me and smiles. "I'm glad to see you here in this form, son. You've had some adventures, I see."

"Yes, quite. Not the least of which was you dunking me in the river." I feign a frown. "It's good to see you too."

"Think of it as a baptism." He smiles like a saint, then winks.

"Of course, indeed. Why didn't I think of that? And now you're talking about a 'portal ceremony'? What's that?"

You draw my attention back to you, and answer the question. "It is time to put some magic into our project, my soul brother. From where we are now, much groundwork has been laid. You have done all that *you* can do in that regard. But there is more that *we* can do from here. We can invoke the magical essence. It is now a time for *faith and magic!*

Old Man speaks, looking at me. "We ask you to return to your time and world, the old universe, and indeed to your old form— including your ego. But you will not go back empty-handed. You will return with faith. And as Orange has said, with some magical assistance."

He continues, "As you may know, faith is an energy and an entity of consciousness in her own right. But faith has waned in your time, as has magic. Skepticism, cynicism and distrust are rising like never before in humanity. This you can observe, no doubt. In times such as these, there is a need for magical invocations. They will draw breath up from deep instinctual levels. Such breath has brought forth the avatars of your age."

You glance over to me. "You likely still have some questions about the vision of avatars we witnessed at the Ends of the Earth."

I nod agreement.

"I will answer some of these in a moment. But first I want to address G's concerns. He's wondering why he's in here talking, when he could be outside, gathering wood and laying the fire."

He laughs, "You know me too well, love."

You smile. "And I know you better every moment, glancing over to Old Man with an almost-wink. I asked you in to help out with our temporal grounding. I've got my own younger incarnation here. It will balance the equation if we have *your* older one."

OM suppresses a smirk.

"Fair enough," G sighs.

You continue, "These are powerful forces we're holding together, G, over many thousands of years. I need you in this mix."

"I understand now. That makes perfect sense. You always make perfect sense, O... in the end." We all pause with G and then, looking around at each other, laugh. He does indeed know you as well as you know him. I'm starting to admire your relationship, whatever it may be.

You turn back to me after a quick look at OM. "So, ask me your questions."

"My questions? Well, I haven't really been thinking of any. I guess I was just assuming explanations would come in due time. Since you asked, this must be the time. So, there were symbols related to the avatars that I didn't understand. I mean I've heard of such images as the Tree of Life, the rivers flowing from it and so forth. Who is the child? What do the arrows and bows signify?"

I pause for an internal reading. The stream is catching up with me. "Also, regarding the avatars, how literally should we take them? Will these two individuals become more prominent on the world stage of my era? What will they do for us? Do they, in fact, know they're avatars? What can we expect to happen when they meet the child? Hmm. I guess I *do* still have some questions."

"I knew it." You grip me on the shoulder heartily. The others laugh.

Green is gazing up at the light show in the sky over our heads. He asks, "How did you do this, O? I'm impressed."

"Something I learned in Atlantis." You chuckle and squeeze my hand. "All right, let's start answering some of those mysterious questions. I'll take the first—*not* in order, of course. Do the avatars know they're avatars? Simply, no. But they have a deep sense of mission and destiny. Their mission is all they care about. It's not about them personally. These two have exhausted their self-examination period last lifetime. Now their focus is on service, pure and simple. If you told them they were avatars, they would probably laugh and change the subject."

G clears his throat. "Let me take one question. You asked 'what will they do for you?' My impression is that it's not what they will do, but what *you* will do for *them*. Avatars come to set examples, to infuse inspiration and energy into the populace and the Earth. It is up to people to accept their infusion or not. Their 'world stage' is you—humanity itself. Their prominence depends on your appreciation. The question I would ask is 'what will humans do, for themselves and for the Earth, under their influence?'"

"All right then. Let's ask that question," I accede.

Green goes on, "You will awaken to the shared destiny of your species. Some will get it quickly. Others will come along 'kicking and screaming'—an appropriately human phrase. Many in your world now are alert enough to sense what's happening. But as long as you're yoked to an ego, you will all have doubts about whether you've got it right. Your defensive side will not want to be led down the 'primrose path'."

Green chuckles to himself. "You can see I've been studying some human phrases. In spite of all your wariness, the inner evolutionary momentum will carry you on, especially as it becomes increasingly awake."

"I call that momentum, faith," you interject. "It is magical appreciation. This is why the avatar vision is metaphorical and not literal. It requires you to take that story into yourselves and give it meaning. It requires faith. In response to the downward spiraling, doomsday attitude of many humans, there is another option. It is to see the upward spiral of your own DNA. If you take this attitude—as faith—you will be blessed."

Old Man, as usual, has been sitting quietly, listening. Now he speaks. "Let me reflect on the Tree of Life. It appears in many ancient human traditions. The meanings are numerous and layer-upon-layer deep. The essence of it all is that there is a structure of wisdom, beauty and compassion lying within your living being. Your being is composed of an inner constitution—a tree, metaphorically—that links you with divinity. It's purpose is to bring growth and prosperity into manifestation for all—up from the Source roots. Is there anything more beautiful than a tree? Is anything wiser or more stable? Has any creature ever been more compassionate to the world than the tree?"

As OM pauses, G interrupts, "My home is in the trees, beside the river and ocean, in the fields and mountains. My whole life is devoted to feeling the continuous linkage with nature. I simply can't get enough of its essence."

The old one looks appreciatively into G's eyes, seeing his own eyes, from a former time. There is clearly a soul union here. Then he returns his gaze to me.

"In your vision at the Ends of the Earth, the Tree was the destination for the arrows of the avatars. The silver arrows, formed from the Earth, carry the vitality and potency of your species into the far reaches of inner sacredness. The arboreal symbol stands there—at the heart and inner sanctum of creation on Earth. These arrows are the messengers from your species to the locus of Life itself. They are the rebirthing agents, male and female, returning the seed to the ground vortex of the planet.

"The Tree of Life reaches from its deep roots in Earth up into the heavens, space, the *Akasha*. You were intuitive, friend, when you visualized the Hall of Memories as natural and tree-like. The Tree in your vision symbolizes the attractive and nurturing forces of nature, ready and waiting to take you—by your own volition—from the soil of this planet into high space. That force will move you from form into formlessness. The Tree draws all unto itself. It sends out all creative energies and Life into your lives upon the ground and in the air and water. It is both antenna and anode. It breathes electromagnetic spirit—in and out.

"There is virtually no end to the powerful symbols born in its flowers and leaves, its branches and roots. Its base is the birthplace of the *child* who is all children. It is humanity's birthright—to be born into the Oneness of spirit, as a child is born into the union of its parents, as the tree unifies Earth and sky."

The four of us fall silent for a while. Outside the sky is dark. The aurora continues in gigantic curtains of pastel color, curling and weaving slowly, ceaselessly, into full-depth formations one after the other. Below, in the Earth, I hear twilight insects and frogs beginning their vigil of the night. The darkness sparkles with fireflies. This brings me a smile; they didn't live here in human times.

I look at you in the dim light. Your orange robes are shimmering with a faint glow of their own. It dawns on me that the clothes you wear, as vigilans, are actually *alive!* What an idea!

Now your voice comes again. "Humanity is the metaphorical approach to this child, following the river and the avatars. All your species are being led on this path, whether they accept it or not currently. They are moving toward destiny, awakening and a finely tuned equilibrium with nature. It is the Peaceable Kingdom that awaits your faith.

"Following the river, symbolizes your journey back to Source. You must go upstream as a species. It has always been your lot. This time, however, the mountains are magically removed. The gods have smiled down on the likes of you. You have been invited to return into your original consciousness. You are the *prodigal* child becoming the *prodigy*. And so, what happens when humanity, led by the avatars, meets the child?"

Though you are in shadows, I feel your eyes upon me. I'm a little surprised that the question is directed at me. I muse and pause to listen to the stillness first. Then I answer, "I'll speak from my heart. I see that we will make our peace with nature, with our Oneness. We will focus our awareness through the lens of creation, the *vesica*. We will, in fact, generate the portal that all require for passage into the next species. When we meet the child, we will *become* the child, the children of a new age and universe."

"Well said, friend. Well felt," you acclaim.

Again, we all enter the silence, like it is our *true* living room. Muffled voices come from outside in the field as B and the others make preparations for the ceremony. I can *feel* out into the distance, intuitively, in a way I could not do as a human. I hear the heartbeats of all my brethren, their breathing, their continuous joy at being here together. *What a world this is! Who would not want to evolve into this?*

"I've been thinking," I say, emerging from my reverie. "What you said about magic in my world. It seems we actually have a lot of it already—in movies, games and fanciful stories. But it's like no one is allowed to *believe in* it. We treat it as mere fantasy—something we play with causally and then dismiss. We think of magic as childish."

"Isn't that interesting?" You stare into the brilliant sky. "Childish! As if that were inferior. Magic is a verb, actually. As I pointed out earlier, it comes from the same root word as 'to make'. The reason I'm linking magic to faith is that it is the means for manifesting faith's blessing. Your language uses the phrase, 'have faith'. In ours, we say *'make* faith'. What this means is that we participate in manifesting our destiny. Faith is the aspect of Life force that brings destiny to us.

"In your time, faith has been relegated to religious precincts. It has been captured, imprisoned even, within the concept of 'belief'. In our time, we have liberated faith into all our creative endeavors. The same phenomenon pertains to your perception of magic. You have relegated it to general amusement. Your handling of magic is just more of the *separation*, so characteristic of humanity.

"Faith and magic will not be expunged, however—even under regressive regimes. They are too closely allied with truth to be eliminated. Thus they live on in your art forms and entertainment, waiting for your species' awakening. Then they will return to full and open expression."

"I look forward to that." My voice cracks with awe. "So tell me, what do you mean? You will send 'magic' back with me?"

Old Man stands and turns toward us all. "Let's define magic first. The simplest meaning of the word is 'to bring spirit into matter'. If we accept this notion, then all incarnation is magic, all creation is. These letters use magic to manifest—from our time to yours. Our entire project—the transposing of time—is nothing short of magical. I stand before you this moment through the power of magic!"

"I certainly wouldn't deny any of that, revered friend," I affirm. "But what can this mean, in specific terms, about what you will send back to my world?"

He doesn't answer at first, but turns his face to you. *"What* indeed. There is a wide arc that we are following through our collective Earth experiences. It is the span of evolution in the Great Age—26,000 years of time. This span is embraced by another period of time, nearly as grand. Atlantis was at one pole, the midpoint of the last Great Age. My beloved River, *Isa Ber,* is at the other pole, midpoint in the next Age. These are another twenty-six millennia. The human race is now both at the center and at the edge. Either way, you embody a fulcrum point of galactic history—the point of a grand cross.

"What will we send back with you? Here is what we are sending: a figment of imagination, a form of communion, an open portal into our world. From the center and the edge, you will each decide which timeline, which species, which universe to follow. The choice you will make has already been made in eternity. This is the paradox—the making of magic, with both free will and pre-destination. We are spontaneously writing the 'script', and it is, at the same time, guiding what we write—all our choices. All things are possible in the realm of mystery, timelessness and formlessness. All actions are magical when taken from the basis of authentic being.

"What is about to unfold on our planet—in your time—is a wonderful transformation, up from the roots of the Earth, through your body and soul—from the soil—into the divine sky. Matter into spirit, spirit into matter. Thus, will Oneness be proclaimed and known within the population and in the individual. The events that bring this about will be clear and present magic for all to see. Only those with the most recalcitrant hearts will reject the obvious. And even *they*, end the end, will find no solace in their denial."

Your voice begins, almost melodically. "Magic, however, is already welling up from within your species. We do not send magic back *with* you. Rather, we send the silent song, from the still, small voice, as we have come to know it in *our* species. What we send is this: the stimulus toward recognition of the *vesica piscis*—the essential feminine—lying at the root of you. We send a way, for anyone who cares, to hear the silence that sings there.

"We are delivering back to your time the key to hear your own inner voice as never before, beneath your separatism and fear, and to resonate with that voice. It is a subtle note of music—of the muses—that will trigger the vibration of your DNA. This vibration will put you into a state of readiness."

OM Speaks, "What we are saying, in the most practical terms, is that the portal you're constructing is both the physical and *psychical* bridge. Once opened you will stand firmly at both ends of the bridge within your own selves. You will be both human and vigilan, alternating inside your own consciousness. Part of the time you will be human, with ego-mind still dominating. But during the other part, you will be free of ego, transformed, and indeed formless.

"For any human living today who has recognized the approaching mutation, there is the opportunity right now, to live with one foot in each universe. What does this mean in your daily lives? You may feel 'crazy' at times, torn between your divided natures. At other times, however, you will feel the opening into your destiny of freedom and peace and empowerment. You will feel both duality *and* Oneness—like never before."

I swallow hard. "I'm already feeling crazy a lot of the time. But I'm also feeling like there is a new world being born inside me. I have sensed what you describe on both sides of that bridge."

You reach out of the darkness and touch my arm with your long fingers. Your silver eyes are shining, reflecting the pulsing curtains of the aurora. They pierce into my eyes. I feel deep emotion in you.

"This is because you have found and created your portal. It is now active, as you know. You know also that I have asked you to remain in your ego world for a time longer. This will not be without its difficulties, I'm afraid. But you understand now why it is necessary."

"I understand. You need a *mailbox* for your letters."

Green suddenly laughs out loud from behind me. "And I too am a 'courier' for the other side of our equation. I understand as well. We reach across wide distances, our group."

Old Man leans down over G, who is sitting, staring into his face. "You and I shall meet in time, my friend—as one being. Yes, even *in time!* Come. For now, let us go to the fire. There we will find that link we've all been imagining."

Letter Forty-Eight
Fire

We file down the hallway under the stars and the aurora, then out into the field. Immediately I see a blazing fire not far off. I'm drawn to it like a moth. I start walking, but hesitate. Touching your arm, I pull you aside.

"There's something I don't understand," I whisper. "You said we can be in two universes as the same time. When I go home I will somehow be aware of both places inside me? This sounds rather schizoid to me."

You look straight into my being. "Everything is inside you, whether here or there, whether one universe or another. There is only Now, here, this space. The two universes are one, by virtue of the portal inside you. By awakening, you become the bridge. This is the realization to take back with you. You will begin to experience it more fully over time—now that you've been told about it. It is not for your mind to understand yet. It is a sensation, a deep *streaming*.

"Your craziness, as humans, is based on emotional feelings that your minds fail to interpret and appreciate. But emotions have deep inner potential, linking you to the soul and to formlessness. The insanity you may feel emotionally can open you to the sensations streaming from Source. Use your emotions from a state of wisdom."

I nod my head, trying to absorb your words. OM and G have moved ahead of us and now are taking places in a circle around the fire.

You watch the people assembling as you speak to me. "What you feel with your deepest sensations comes from the new universe. In the moments of resonance with that, you are a transformed being. You may still physically inhabit the old universe. But you have manifested the portal and the bridge in yourself. This is the key teaching of this second book. It is that you can live—right now, where you are—in *both* worlds, the old and the new, the ego and the evolved. The more you resonate with this understanding, the more you will invite in the destined mutation of the your species. The more each of you performs this function, the more others around you will as well."

"This makes sense," I reply. "I've already felt it occasionally in my time. Right now in fact, I can fee l the old, ego world still inside me while I'm here. But what's my role in this? Do humans need to hear this from us in order to open their portals?"

"No, they don't. They need only to pick up the resonance around them in the ethers. There are many ways to open portals; and the forms they take are myriad. Some humans have already opened their own portals and are now joining them to others in a grand network around the globe, without ever knowing these letters exist. They may not even call them 'portals'; they may not recognize a new universe as such; some use the language of 'dimensional shifts'. It doesn't matter; these are just words.

What matters is that the passage for evolution is within them, that they feel their beings moving from one state to the next— toward liberation. But alas, with this movement comes increasing discomfort for many. You will feel progressively more divided with-in yourselves. This, of course, is the Great Storm. From whatever belief system you may come, the essence here is to be open to the possibility of *already being your awakened self* in another realm. Waves of the old self will still wash ashore, to be sure. But brighter, finer waves there will also be, in their midst.

"As for your role in this, I've said before, do not worry about 'getting the message out'. The message has its own life and will look after itself. All that each of you need do is relax and feel the free-dom within. Detach from form and feel the space of Now. When you do this, you will be your authentic self. And from there, the ac-tions you take will be aligned with the *one soul*, and with *Conscious Evolution*. What more could you ask?"

"I guess that says it all!" I sigh. But I know my mind will always continue asking and worrying.

You take my hand and pull me steadily toward the flame. All the group is now assembled, standing in a circle around the blazing firelight. It is twisting and whipping high into the sky, dancing with the movement of the aurora. The fire is in the center of the great stone wheel that lies flat on the ground; it is some ten meters across.

Warm light dances on the faces of those assembled. Everyone is smiling, waiting with eagerness. They sway as they chant softly, staring into the flames. Directly across from me, my eyes meet a woman I have not engaged before. Those eyes are very familiar. I gasp, *Mestiphius*—in a vigilan incarnation; a female! Still, I can tell by the eyes. She smiles, seeing that I know. Then beside her, I recognize another figure—the man with long, blond hair. It is Allamorath! Both are members of the group. I bow my head in honor, racing with Atlantean memories. The emotion rushes through me as we merge back into the group rhythm. All is well. All is one.

Black leads the chant, punctuating it at intervals with her high sweet voice and words from some beautiful, sacred language. The others, in unison, either repeat her words or answer them in alternation, in harmonious expression. Words well up inside me, and I join the song. Occasionally our voices fall into silence and wait, listening to another, still voice, deep within us all. Reverence rides the radiance of the flames. It sweeps across the calendar inscribed in stone below us. It swells in the sensations of us all.

The chanting resumes, and there is an energetic breathing in it. I feel the groups' attention turning towards me. All eyes and hearts are focused here. It is nothing personal; all is symbolic. The group reaches out as one, and draws an essence out of my heart, and out of the very cells of my body. It breathes in the *human* nature from me. There is a long pause. And then the group breathes out it's own nature, back into humanity—back and forth, in and out, over a long period. The group's electromagnetic field expands and contracts with this ritual, becoming more resonant with each cycle.

I sense there is energy coming in from somewhere else. *Yes, I know.* It is being channeled through this small group from vigilans everywhere. Our group has coordinated with many others for this ceremony. And then my perception opens out. I see gathered vigilans across the entire planet, throughout the whole species. I know, without asking, this is the largest congress ever held on Earth. It is composed of every conscious being in the world. My imagination perceives them assembled by twos, threes, hundreds, in every nation, directing intention and appreciation into our midst. I am beyond awe. I am transfigured.

In faraway lands there are circles like this one, replicated or embellished by local custom. There are many who are not from Earth originally, who are participating as well. It is exhilarating to feel their intent joined with ours. People, by the millions, are focused on a single mission. They are projecting the force of their collective and individual power—the electromagnetic heart—back into this circle, back in time, to the heart of the human species. This is a mighty and pure filament, the likes of which no human or vigilan has ever seen. The purpose of this grand projection is unified and focused: to open the greater passage and to trigger the awakening!

I almost cannot imagine such a focus of living power. It stymies my mind to comprehend. And yet there is a center of appreciation in my heart that receives the image of grandeur. I can and do imagine this. This is the dream of a lifetime, nay, of a Great Age. And I, astoundingly, am at the very vortex of the force. It is all funneling though *this* fire, at the center of *this* circle.

I feel your hand slip into mine. On the other side, G's hand grips me. It is time for the group breath. Enormous bursts of vitality surge through our hands and bodies. My mind wonders whether I am strong enough, even in group-formation, to be a vessel for this vast force.

"This is not about you or me, friend," I hear your voice in my head. *"This is about* Conscious Evolution. *Let go, and allow the will of Life to manifest through us all. Accept this destiny. It is all our greatest blessing. Come alive, humanity. Come awake!"*

Suddenly I feel a great wrenching inside me. It is the light of all my chakras turning on at once. There is a bursting forth and a flowing of such brilliance that I could never survive it without the gift of Source itself to this purpose. I'm shaking like a violin string, plucked and played to a music only angelans could sing. Huge waves of raw energy are sliding through us all—from the Earth. It comes up, irresistibly, through each chakra portal, one by one. It pauses in each to register the full commitment to evolve. Earth, root, sacrum, belly, heart, throat, eye, crown—then up through the tops of our heads, into the sky, space, the *Akasha.*

The whirling begins. All in the circle are breathing as one. The waves of power sweep around, and sweep *us* around. We flow like a fiery liquid on the Earth and in the air. My vision merges with the others and extends around the whole planet. I recall the trip I took many months ago from this location. As rapid as that was, it was not instantaneous. Our joint vision embraces every corner of the globe at once. We see into the hearts and souls of every vigilan, every being here—including animals, plants and minerals. All are breathing this holy breath.

A great bell tolls somewhere in the Cosmos. It is heard through every fiber of existence. Suddenly the bottom drops out. The Earth opens and swallows us all, all the nations at once. Down we go, into the abyss, the Void, as one. I've never imagined such a thing. I'm at a loss again to contain what I perceive.

Source has called us unto herself. She has taken on a feminine presence for this. It is an act of surrender, sacrifice and rebirth. We are all in the presence of the ultimate Master-Mater-Mother. No words, thoughts or images are exchanged. There is nothing I can write here to depict or define what this is. *I invite the reader to go within your heart to visit, first-hand this presence. But no, I misspeak. It is not I, but Source who invites you. Come and feel the union of our shared destiny.*

"Feel the pull of the future Now—safe passage through the Storm. Let it draw you into your knowing. Let it realize, in you, its own awakening. Allow the cumulative gesture of the next species, the vigilans, to reach you, bless you with its timeless compassion and draw you out. Accept your blessing."

There is a powerful upward rushing sound in my ears. I feel as though I'm waking from a very deep sleep, refreshed, amazed at everything around me. There is, strangely, no confusion in my mind. All is stable and well, amidst the swirling up of energies. It feels like I'm riding a volcanic eruption, from far, far underground, up the granite channels of the Earth, up to the heights of the highest mountains. And higher still. We are exploding over the landscape in fire and fury. But all is as it should be. I accept this outrageous experience as perfectly natural. I'm flowing with it, rising and falling with it, into the air—ashes and dust, back to Earth, back in time.

I am at one with this paradoxical dissemination from the Great Mother. I feel myself to be as small as a molecule, an atom, even smaller. I also am as large as the planet itself. I am, fantastically, all sizes of all things. I am in each aspect of nature and creation. I am at the heart and cell of each creature. I am giving new Life to what I am, what I project. I am the Projector and the projection. I am.

Slowly, by eons, I recompose into the body of this writer. There are all the pieces of myself, from all the reaches of incarnations past and future, from all space and Earth. I seem to come to life at last as all the elements converge, slamming me into fullness. Here I am again at one with just *one* being, my little self. It is at once confining and confirming.

All in the circle break hands now and stand very still for one last moment. We have returned from our explosion, from the sending forth of communion into the stormy past of Earth. We are now individuals again, around a ceremonial table of stone and fire. We are back to some state of normalcy, if there is such a thing.

I look around at you and at others, blinking and smiling. Everyone is full of light, sparkling with resonance. We step back from the altar and begin to mingle. I rush over to embrace Mestiphius and Allamorath; their colors are Crimson and Tan. Without words we are fully aware together. We know that another grand circle is complete.

Turning back to the group at large, I sense a ceremonial meal will be offered back at the house. The group gradually moves away, in twos and threes, talking in low voices among themselves. Black is leading the procession. I hesitate, waiting for you. B looks back one last time and pierces me with a knowing eye, and an inscrutable seed-link.

Old Man stops us—Green, you, and me. "There is yet another part of this ceremony, friends. It is for us alone to proceed from here."

I look curiously at his beautiful, wrinkled face. His eyes twinkle in the firelight. I ask, "What now? What else could there be after that?"

He smiles. "It is now my turn. Please follow me, all of you. Do not be alarmed. All is well. All is as it is."

Not surprisingly, I'm mystified by his partial answers. He touches each of us on the forehead with one finger and turns toward the fire. We all step up onto the stone platform, drawing closer to the rushing, crackling flames that soar high above our heads. Quickly OM steps directly into them and disappears. I gasp and look at you. You smile and nod reassuringly at me. But then you follow OM into the furnace and are gone. Green pats me on the shoulder with a word of encouragement and follows suit. I am left standing alone, shaking my head in disbelief. *Where have they gone? What should I do now?*

I decide not to act immediately, but rather stop to appreciate the situation. This is clearly an opportunity to understand myself better. I look into the fire, at close range. The heat is surprisingly low. I can feel it, but it's like I'm much farther away than this. I turn my gaze into the darkness all around. I'm truly alone in this place, this future. *Alone in 500* for the first time. I smile to myself at this realization. It feels fine. It feels like home.

The crickets and frogs call from the dark; the spitting and crackling sounds inside the flame echo back. I'm mesmerized by the sensation of sound and silence, darkness and light, Oneness and aloneness. A faint breeze pulls against my cloak. The textile responds with a sensation of it's own, radiated into my flesh. It is a living part of me. What an amazing moment this is—at one with nature and self.

"All right. I'm coming," I whisper, stepping into the column of fire. A rush of silence comes over me.

Bright sun assaults my eyes. I stagger and fall to my knees. My hands touch a hot, glassy surface below. Reflection upward from it is blinding me. Squinting, with my arm over my eyes, I get up and take a few steps. There is an edge to this thing I'm standing on that I can just barely see. I manage to climb down to soft, sandy ground. There is no grass.

"O? Green? Where are you? Where am I?"

Out of the brightness, I feel hands grip my arms. They pull me a few steps into a shaded place.

"Sorry, friend," your voice is comforting. "We lost track of you for a bit. What happened? You must have hesitated before stepping into the fire."

My eyes clear, and I now see you and the old man. "You bet I did! It's not customary where I come from, to walk into raging fires."

You answer, "Ah. Well, we've been waiting here for half an hour. I was just about to come back for you. It's not always possible to transpose the way we just did—in single file. On this end, there was some temporal distortion. But, we're all here now. Very good."

I glance around and survey my surroundings. We're standing under an open-framed structure with a grass roof. Wooden poles and cross pieces form a kind of scaffolding. I start, "OK. How about some explanations? Where are we? Why is it so hot here? I'm sweating. Why did we have to go through a fire?"

OM is busy with some object in his hands, turning it around and pressing parts of it in a patterned way. It looks rather like a TV remote control. But when he holds it upright, it also resembles an old wooden flute. He begins an explanation; gesturing with the device. "Take a look out there. You will recognize this place."

I squint and look in the direction he's pointing. It's desert. Sahara Desert I would guess. And there in the distance is a thin band of green and the great river. "Are we back at..."

"Yes. We're back in my time. That's the *Isa Ber*."

I look at OM with concern. "Not the river again! Please. I've had quite enough of that."

He stares at me inscrutably for a moment, then returns to his work. "Don't worry. We'll keep you dry this time. Mostly."

I realize I don't really trust him. I'm feeling different; something's not right. I look all around now. We're in the middle of nowhere. Just yellow-orange, bright sand everywhere. Not far from our shelter, there's an odd-looking structure. It must be where I landed moments ago. It's a very large, ovoid dish made of glass, sloping up on the backside, down on the front. This gives it the appearance of leaning in our direction. A metal obelisk rises vertically from the center, perhaps 30 meters high. Sunlight glares at us from all the polished surfaces.

And now I realize something else confusing. There are only three of us. I don't see G. And I'm not in his green robes anymore. I'm back to my khaki shorts.

"Where's Green?" I wonder aloud.

OM murmurs. He stands erect and pats the center of his chest with a serene, mysterious look on his face. "He and I are *here* now, as one. The twins that we were, have merged in my time. This is our last vigilan incarnation."

I stare in disbelief. "Awesome. Um, so, what does that feel like?"

"It feels totally natural." He replies, again working on his little device. "The division of my soul, for long ages, has served its purpose. We evolved expansively through our times apart."

"So, you two were twin souls? Like the avatars?"

"Yes."

"Hmm. I guess I was thinking twins would be male and female."

"Often, yes, but not always. Green and I each had incarnations in both sexes over the ages, of course." He lifts his gaze to focus on my question. "The stages preceding merger can be characterized as balancing the masculine and feminine spheres. But this can be done in bodies of either gender."

"Doesn't it bother you that G is gone? I mean, even if he's there inside you?"

"He's no more gone than the child, you used to be, is gone inside *you*."

Suddenly the strange feeling that's been nagging me is more intense. And yet it is all too familiar. I feel a separation within my own soul. My head is feeling stuffy, compressed.

"O, something's happened. I don't feel so good. My head... my stomach... Something's not right." I moan, "Oh no. I know what it is. I'm back to being human again."

You touch my cheek and sigh empathetically. "Yes. I'm not surprised. Tell me what you feel."

"I'm feeling the weight of ego, literally. And my thoughts — there are so many! I never realized it before. All this mental busyness is such a distraction. It's truly painful to me now."

I can actually visualize dozens, even hundreds of thought bits, like mind fragments sweeping around my head. "I was so light as a vigilan. I'm so heavy now. I'm weighed-down by myself. It feels like a prison. I don't want this, O. This is terrible!" I slump to my knees in the sand, rubbing my forehead, groaning. I want to cry.

You place a hand on my head. "I hear you, dear one. We knew this would happen when we took you away from the group. I do know what you're feeling though. I had my own ego torment with Hunab Ku, if you recall. I know that separation. Losing who you are is the worst thing imaginable."

I feel a pressure to describe my anguish more, lest I lose the sense of it. "It's like the true awareness is squeezed into a tiny corner by all my thinking. My busy mind overwhelms the simple, still consciousness. All the incoherent thought bits float around and grab onto one another, forming blankets and trains of mental matter. They form a thick patina everywhere, and masquerade as consciousness. But it's nothing but a horrible mask, a woven fabric of illusion."

Taking a breath, I sigh, "Yet I remember the 'other awareness' is not limited, not extinguished or put into a corner at all. It cannot be. It's always there, beneath the cover—limitless and free. But it's all so upside-down in my mind."

You break in. "Indeed it is. The freedom beneath that blanket of mind-stuff is your true power, your authentic being. This is the real you. Claim back your power, friend.

"Perhaps I can ease your anxieties a bit. Go into your body memories of being free. There you know reality. Know that this is always your presence underneath the confusion. Let it be you—pure awareness."

I close my eyes to feel what you're saying, but I'm still on the verge of tears. The portal inside me has become a battleground. *Will it be a bridge or a blockade?*

OM leans over. Looking up from his work. "Let your true power—from Source—take over the bridge. Bring presence up into your personal dimension. This is what we have asked you to do before. Plant the seed of awakening in the core of your ego. Let it germinate and begin the path of growing."

OM sets his device on a small table, and reaches around to me. He now takes my shoulders in his hands, looking sternly into my eyes. "This is destiny, son. Do not shrink from it. Welcome it as your own path through the Storm. It is your greatest blessing to now know both worlds. Accept it. The more you can experience both universes simultaneously, the closer you will be to liberation."

I feel stretched and drawn, torn from old moorings. Yet in spite of it—indeed, *because* of it—there is an expansion happening. "You all keep saying that. It must be important."

My mind freezes. Something in me gives up and stops fighting. "All right, I accept." My voice drops to a whisper.

The words trigger memories of all my vigilan friends, and the ecstasies I have felt while being one of you. It was freedom beyond comprehension. Above all it was freedom from the incessant submersion in human thought; it was the ability to be still and pure. It truly is the greatest blessing I've ever received. *I do accept it.*

Streaming again. Going one more step, to my surprise, I accept my ego too. I see it suddenly as a kind of blessing—a gift of the bridging awareness. I rise to my feet and shake my head free. Like a newborn, I gasp and look around at everything. Pieces of some unseen puzzle inside me are tumbling down, into a new place. I grip your arm for support.

"Who knew I'd have such a reaction?" I sigh.

You offer, "Now you know why babies cry when they're born."

OM comments, not looking up from his work, "This might be a good time to take a look at what is really going on in your human psyche. All the answers are right there."

"Easier said than done!" I reply. "But I get the idea. Yes. Here I am back in the box. What does this box look like? How thick are the walls? Where is the lid? And the *id?*" I murmur.

You chuckle softly and gesture at the space around us. "Don't forget to look at what that box is made of."

An idea dawns on me, streaming in. "Wait. The box is made of *me!* It's something I have created. What I create is really not outside me; the walls are inside my mind. My ego too is inside me. I know I am more than it."

Old Man grunts acknowledgment and strides out to the large glass dish. He is bending low, touching the edge of it. Now, holding the small device in one hand, he moves it like a magician, slowly over the glass. You and I walk out to stand behind him. There is electricity in the air. OM sweeps his arms down and then back up, expansively. On the upward movement, something stirs in the sand around us. I hear a high-pitched whine from the dish and obelisk. Now the ground is vibrating. A light dust rises up from the Earth.

"What?" I jerk around, startled. Something's coming up out of the sand in front of us. *Wait, no.* It seems to be forming right out of the sand—the silica—before our very eyes.

Letter Forty-Nine
The Ark and the Covenant

Large objects are being formed around us amidst the rumble and whine and flying dust. It's pure magic! Soon there are three spheres sitting quietly on the sandy ground awaiting our attention. They stand slightly taller than me and are made of clear glass, inches thick. The globes have a slight orange tint, a product of the colored sand that made them.

"Come, friends. It's time." OM slaps my back and gives you a brush on the elbow with his hand. Then he pushes his hands through the wall of one of the spheres and steps in.

"Let this be a lesson to you about walls, son," he chuckles.

You look at the spheres, then at me quizzically and shrug. "I had no idea."

You approach one of the glass balls and repeat his movement, entering through the glass. I'm left standing outside, staring, wide-eyed. *All right.* I walk up to the remaining empty sphere. Timidly I put my hand on it. The surface is firm. There *is* a slight give; it feels more like hard rubber than glass, though it's very reflective. I don't see any door or entry through it.

I hear OM's voice, slightly muffled. "Use the key to enter."

"What key?" I demand skeptically.

"Your hands!"

You intervene, speaking to OM, "Remember, he's not so intuitive anymore. He's human again."

Then to me she says, "Use your hands as the key. Cup them together, like praying. No, not like that. Not flat. Leave some open space inside. Curve the fingers. Yes."

I realize my hands have made the *vesica* shape. I press them against the glass. Low and behold, they pass right through. My whole body passes through, and I'm inside.

"Wow. That's cool. That's the *key*, eh?"

I turn my head and see both of you looking at me as one would at a child, smiling patiently.

"Let's go," OM says. His sphere then lifts a meter off the ground, hovering. Yours does the same. Mine just sits here. Though it's vibrating in sympathy with the others.

"OK. D'you want to clue me in on how *this* works?" I grumble.

"We use the will to direct the globes, through the hands. It's all about eye-hand coordination," the old man says patiently.

"Is there a seat in this thing?" I ask, looking around at the smooth, clear surfaces. Suddenly a seat appears beside me, pushing up from the transparent floor and walls. It too is transparent. *Ah, I willed it to be! That's how it works.* I flop down and, right away, feel more comfortable. I put my hands together and imagine the sphere rising. After a brief hesitation, it rises, somewhat wobbly. But it is clearly following my unspoken command.

OM assures me, "You're getting it. Don't worry. I'll control both your vehicles from my module. It'll be more efficient."

With that, all three spheres begin moving slowly across the ground toward the river. There is nothing but a slight hum; I guess it indicates some kind of propulsion system. I'm sitting comfortably in a soft armchair, cruising a meter above the sand; and it's air-conditioned besides. *Now, this is the way to travel in the desert!*

Within moments we reach the river and proceed out to the middle, some hundred meters. The three glass balls stop and float in the air above the swirling current. I look down at small aquatic plants drifting by, along with leaves and branches torn away from their origins somewhere upstream. I glance at OM with a little suspicion. He looks back and laughs.

"You promised we're not going down there!" I remind him.

"Correct. We're not going down *there*," he replies cryptically.

"So, where *are* we going?" you ask.

"Up river," is all he says. "Moving over the water will be a little smoother than the sand. Let's get going." The sound of his voice is right in my ears—an amazing audio system.

In front of us, he turns his craft north and moves off at a rapid pace. The two of us follow, skimming along the water, with no sound and no wake. From a distance we must appear like three water sprites skimming the surface, heading against the current.

We pass islands, lush with vegetation and choruses of tiny frogs. Exotic birds call from trees along the banks. Beyond the intermittent line of trees on either side, lies the bright hot desert, stretching out over hills, cliffs and rocky promontories. The hills are dotted with sparse, pale vegetation. Near the bank, there are occasionally people in boats or in small settlements. If they spot us, they wave genially as we speed past.

We have seen hippos in the water in places and giraffes in the distance. Several lions were at the riverbank at one point, gazing out at us with interest. These are scenes that could have existed here at any time in the past 100,000 years or more.

OM is out in front a few meters. Directly above of us, the sun burns down fiercely. But the glass filters the brilliance and softens the effect. I look over at your sphere, smoothly floating beside me. Leaning in your direction, I ask a question that's been on my mind. "O, why did we need to walk through the fire to get here?"

"Ah, I'm sure you're aware of the symbolism of purification by fire. Well, that's more than mere symbol sometimes. We used that aperture because it had been opened by the collective will of our people. A very pure, undistorted message has been sent back to your race by its means. That fire will burn for a decade, sending continuous blessings. At the same time, many toxins from your side will be absorbed and cleared."

I stop you. "Does your fire link with some fire somewhere in my world?"

You explain, "Yes. It links with many flames, all around the globe. Any consecrated flame will be a channel for our message. You have many so-called 'eternal flames' at monuments, mausoleums and sacred sites."

"I like that," I reply. Then I wonder, "Could it be a temporary flame—like a candle or campfire? If it were consecrated?"

You smile over at me. "I suppose so. I hadn't thought of that. Yes, it would work, if the fire is aligned intentionally with Source."

"Good. I'll think of that every time I light a candle now."

You resume, "So, once such a vortex is opened, it can be used for other beneficial means. The aperture is available for transposition as well. It brings us through into a more pristine, focused sub-dimension. What we do here, under it's influence will have far-reaching effects. So, we must be at our best."

"You mean *I* must be at my best," I sigh. "I know *I'm* the one with the toxic personality. But that's all right. I understand. I'm back inside my ego. And on that subject, I have another question. I remember your advice about not having to *do* anything about ego; only *notice* it. Surely, that's not enough! What do we gain by just observing? No matter how much I look at my ego, it's still there, behaving in the same old disappointing ways."

Though I'm not close enough to see, I sense you smirking. "By noticing your ego you are building up an awareness of its qualities and proportions. You're cataloguing its proclivities and limitations. You learn to see it as it is—naked and unadorned by it's disguises and subterfuge. In observing, you are using the *other* awareness, stepping back from mere mental functioning. You are inculcating the new patterns of freedom with each observation.

"On the other side of noticing, you may also observe your state of *freedom*, its qualities and proportions. Just as you learn to observe the ego, you will learn to observe your state of awareness beyond ego. It's what's left of you when you take ego away. In the transition times, you are bridging the polarities.

"This is what opening the portal will afford you. You may observe both directions, both universes. You are opening the portal into awareness of all that lies beyond your ego patterns. The 'other awareness' is your authentic being—the essence of observation."

Silence flows between us for a time, as does the river. "I don't know... Wait." Then I begin again hesitantly, "Let me correct that. I see what my ego was just doing. It was trying to tell me I *don't* understand. I see that that's one of its little tricks. It tries to pull me back from using the *other* awareness."

"Indeed. That's one of its *chief* tactics. True awareness is anathema to ego. It thrives in the state of ignorance and manipulation. When you observe it, you are exposing it to an atmosphere it cannot breathe."

At that moment a great fish leaps out of the water just ahead of us. I marvel. But as we swoop past, I see the reason for the leap. An enormous crocodile is hunting it. Might it be Old Tijani?

The drama disappears behind us in a flash. I pause with the image of it frozen in my mind. "I see right here again an opportunity for my ego to distract me. My mind could veer off from looking at ego and start worrying about crocodiles."

You acknowledge, "Good observation."

The sun is arcing down in the sky, now straight ahead of us, leading on; we have turned due west. The colors of the desert are deeper red, yellow and orange along the river. The waters are greener. Our three bubbles cruise on.

OM has been silent for a long time. I wonder what he's been thinking. Then I realize, probably nothing at all. He has simply been feeling and noticing. This is the vigilan way that I came to know in my brief immersion. Thought comes into vigilan awareness only when invited and when useful—not as in the human mind. We are awash in near continuous thought. I muse, *It must be tiring for vigilans to have a human around—me, with my incessant thinking and worrying.*

"It *is* tiring," you answer my thought. "But we take no offense. It is part of what we signed on for in this project. Nevertheless, I would not like to live in your world, surrounded as you are by such a continuous barrage of thoughts, words, and information. The microwaves, radio and transmissions in the air would be very disturbing to us. Our world is a space of great peace by comparison."

Suddenly I realize I've never asked a very important question. "Is there a difference between your time and the *new universe?*"

"There *is* a difference. The world we are in now is still the *old* universe. Vigilans and humans alike live in both. Our collective species is being given the choice to move into the new, or to remain with the old."

"I'm confused. I thought you all lived in the *new* universe."

"Recall our passage through the *Jaws of Hunab Ku*. This happened for both of us, for all of us. It is the icon of *newness*. For humans, it is the magnet, drawing you to shift your consciousness. For us, it is the energy of awakening into new appreciation of *you*, humanity. We had grown attached to our distance from you. The new universe is a way for us all to shed limitation."

I sigh, "I guess I just don't really understand the new universe."

The old man's voice finally cuts in. "Don't try to put it all in your head, friend. Keep it more in your imagination. *Wonder* about it. Don't *worry* about it. Don't try to pick it apart. These endless explanations you humans require are fatiguing indeed."

"Say, isn't that fatigue a little like an ego reaction?" I joke.

He swerves his bubble back very close to mine, so I can see his piercing eyes. He says calmly, "A little. Now let's have some silence for a while, son. Let your thoughts absorb into the spaciousness."

I take my rebuke with good humor, as I'm sure it was intended, and simply watch the scenery pass by. *It is indeed tiring being human!* The great river has narrowed here, and we can see both banks clearly. For long stretches there is no vegetation. The desert sands come right to the edge, like a huge ocean shoreline—only reversed, where land is the ocean and water the beach. I fall into silence and peace, just watching, appreciating. An hour passes.

OM breaks our reverie at last and announces, "Here we're going to leave the river, *and* the ground. Our destination lies west of here. And as you can see, the river is turning south."

That's all he says. I examine my thoughts for a moment and decide to hold back the obvious question, of where we're going. *Why won't he tell us? I guess I'll know soon enough.* Our craft, under the control of OM, have crossed out over the sandy wastes and have risen a hundred meters into the air. Briefly, I feel queasy, dangling in this transparent sphere so far above the ground. Our speed has accelerated and the air is slightly bumpy. The sun is low in the sky. We fly directly toward it. Again the glass reduces the glare. The orb of the sun is serene, hanging, sinking slowly before us.

Finally, I can't resist asking another question that's been simmering a long time. "Sorry, O, but may I ask you something?"

"Certainly." Your voice is right next to me, inside the bubble.

"Just what is the real mission of the avatars? Can you tell me any more? Are they here to *save* us?"

"You know the general mythos of avatars. They come to Earth in times of great peril and need. But they do not come to *save* humanity. They come rather to initiate the species into its next quantum leap in evolution. They come to set the bar higher through the example of themselves—that is, in their degree of appreciation, equilibrium and authenticity. They are not here to accomplish great works necessarily. Their mission is to *project* more than direct. They do not build the future. But they inspire that future to build itself. They 'lead from behind', as the saying goes."

With a foot in the door, I continue asking, "I know you've said the vision we had was metaphorical. But what was going on with the people *attacking* the avatars, and the sharks all around?"

"There is always a vocal minority who are manipulated by the forces of regression. It is this block that wants to hold onto its beliefs and fantasies of the past, to find shelter in them. Hence, you have the fierce fundamentalist movements in every political party and religion of your time. It is natural and to be expected. The avatars entered the world knowing this; it was no shock to them. They were aware from the start they would find a grievous situation, and that they would be called upon to deal with considerable adversity.

"Nevertheless, the avatars are human beings, and they appreciate any support they may garner from the awakening populace. And many *do* offer assistance and empathy. Most of the people, however, simply stand by and watch unconsciously without becoming engaged. This too is to be expected. It is the very reason the avatars have come, the reason they always come. They are here in response to misery, apathy and despair."

"So, what can they actually *do?* What is the outcome of their incarnation?"

"They are acting out of destiny. Therefore, *Conscious Evolution* is guiding their course. When matters reach their absolute worst, the power within them grows in the greatest measure. Then their prominence soars, because they are seen—by those with eyes to see—to be beacons amidst darkness. They are beacons of magical transformation. They give us the essence of magic and faith.

"Again, it is not what they *do* that matters. It is *how* they do it. It is how they live in the midst of chaos and undeserved attacks. As the Storm rages around them, within the populace, they are calm and centered. Eventually, this serenity demonstrates the new ethic. It finally becomes the model for widespread behavior. Once this commences, the wholesale mutation of the species is not far off."

OM interjects, "The avatars of your age stand tall in our memories today, even 13,000 years later. We know their names and their presences as the foundation of our civilization."

He flourishes a hand dramatically before us. "And soon, my friends, we will approach our destination."

Ahead, I see the ocean on the horizon. *This is our destination?* Our speed seems to increase even more, and soon we're flashing past the beaches, out over open water. Staring straight ahead, we watch a most beautiful sunset through misty clouds, streaking long vermillion tendrils in our direction. Light sparkles across the water in great swaths.

I glance around and survey our three craft, moving relentlessly into the growing twilight. We bob on the wind and weave along. I watch you and OM sitting in your own vehicles, relaxed and poised. I have no idea where we're headed. But I still refrain from asking. I pick up a thought message from you: *"If he wanted us to know, he would tell us."*

Another half hour passes silently. "We're nearing the islands called the Azores, I can tell you that much," you whisper.

"We are here," the old man announces immediately. "We shall now descend."

There is still some light left in the sky, but even so I can see no land, no islands anywhere.

"Where are we landing?" I ask with some apprehension.

"No land, young friend. We're going down *there*, into the ocean!" The old man announces coolly.

On command, the three spheres turn and dive toward the water. I'm about to scream, fearing the sudden impact. At the last moment, the craft slow themselves. But immediately we're submerged, into the black waters of the Atlantic. I look at the two of you, your spheres streaming a trail of bubbles out behind. Our globes are illuminated, radiating a wide halo of light around them. We proceed downward without the slightest hesitation.

"Where are we going, OM?" I can't hold my question back any longer. But there is no answer. We simply continue to fall into the abyss.

Our descent proceeds for half an hour. I can only guess at the depth—*a mile, two miles? Maybe more.* As my nerves are about to reach their limit, the bottom suddenly appears in the range of our lights, about fifty meters down. It is eerie, a silent, blue and gray moonscape, surrounded by eternal darkness. Now we move swiftly over the sandy bottom just as we did over the dry desert not long ago. Boulders slide past under our feet and great chasms slice deeper into the Earth. The endless force of the unknown boils into my emotions. Vigilans may cherish the unknown, but it still provokes apprehension in me. We move on, over ridges and valleys for a time, until steep walls jut up on the perimeter of our vision. We are at the foothills of some underwater mountain range.

Gradually I notice rectangular rocks in the bottom silt. At first, there are only a few. But now they're in abundance, scattered chaotically everywhere. Here now is a broad opening, like an avenue, surrounded by great jumbled piles of stone. At first I think how similar these shapes appear to ancient ruins I've seen on land. Then I realize they *are* ruins! Finally, I get it.

"This is Atlantis!" I shout. "You've brought me back. What is this about, OM?"

Our spheres stop and hover a few meters above a field of rubble that was probably once a large building. Deep dust cloaks it all. OM turns his vehicle around to face ours before speaking. "This is where we will find the generator. It has been waiting all these 26,000 years. It is still here, still powered. I visited it not many years ago. I knew, as soon as I laid my eyes on it that this is where we would need to come to initiate the transfer. We would need to come here together, at this specific time."

"What transfer? Why this time?" I demand, still feeling very uneasy about being here at all. A moment's thought about the miles of water above us, and all the pressure just inches outside my bubble, sends a chill through my body.

You speak, "I know now. We are transferring our essences into the new universe. It happens within our bodies, to be sure. But we also need a physical portal in the Earth. This is the ancient center of all portals—into space and between dimensions—this lost island of Atlantis."

OM is back at the controls of our bubble craft. We begin moving, slowly into the blue, dark gloom. The illumination from our technology pushes open the black curtains as we go; they close menacingly behind as we pass on. Our path is along an ancient grid of streets and canals. They lie straight in places and make large curves in others. It rapidly becomes a maze to my mind.

"Are you sure you know the way?" I wonder aloud, and realize how weak my faith is.

"Don't worry, son. The globes know the way. They just need to get their bearings."

I whisper to you, "O, what is this thing—this generator—we're looking for? Why do we have to come all the way down here?"

I see you looking across at me, a calm smile on your face. "Because this is where it is! We must activate it here and nowhere else. Here is what I'm sensing: This generator will trigger the resonance across the ages, and across the boundaries of the twin universes. I spoke to you before about the difficulty of moving across those boundaries. We must have a holy alignment of spirit and matter for that. I'm certain this is the heart of the magic we need."

"Well, if you put it that way, I guess I'm just going to have faith." I chuckle and shake my head at my own disbelief. Then suddenly, *That's it!* I realize. *If I don't have faith, I'll just have to make some!*

After interminable minutes of winding our way through old channels that were once streets and alleys, we reach an area where there are actually some buildings still standing. They are amazing to behold. Gigantic pillars, ten meters in diameter, stand around an open square. This looks very familiar to my past life memories. Most of the pillars are toppled. But two at the far end of the square stand as they must have done for eons.

Reading my thoughts again, you say, "These pillars were first erected over 100,000 years ago. And *not* by humans!"

"By *whom* then?" I query.

Old Man insists in a low voice, "Let that be a story for another time, friends. We have business to attend to, here and now."

The three luminescent bubbles cruise up to the pillars. I stare in awe. They are perhaps ten stories high, made of a solid piece of stone each. They rise into an impenetrable inkiness above. Somewhere up there, I imagine, are the stars, the night sky. The air!

"Come now. Please retract your chairs and stand on your feet for this."

I follow his direction and feel a little wobbly. There's nothing to hold onto in this sphere now. I feel as though I'm actually standing on the bottom of the ocean. We drift between the columns and behold a gigantic staircase, as wide as a city block, heading down into more darkness. We follow it down, step by eerie step. I swear I can hear echoes. There's a dusty landing, then more steps, well wide enough to accommodate dozens of our spheres side-by-side.

At last we reach the bottom. It is covered with thick detritus. But in places I can see the patterns of stone tile—red, black and white in the floor, characteristic of Atlantean design. This patterned floor spreads out a hundred meters before us. We pass silently, reverently, over it toward something I recognize. It's another wide oval with an obelisk in its center, like the one in the desert. This is at least five times the size of that one, however. *It's the size of the Washington Monument!* The tip of the obelisk above is at the far range of our light auras.

"All right. We have arrived. The mystery shall now be revealed to us," OM states flatly. "I have not told you what we will experience here, because I do not know. We are in the embrace of the *pure unknown*. Honor it as such and exult in its primacy."

I look nervously over to you. You're staring straight ahead. After several more minutes of silence, you begin to speak. "I'm getting a resonance, an impression—an *image* now. I see us assuming positions around the obelisk."

"Do you mean on the dish itself?" OM sounds surprised.

"Yes."

"That could be dangerous," the old one whispers, as if we are on hallowed ground. "Bear in mind here, this object before us is none other that the legendary *Ark of the Covenant.*"

I gasp, "What do you mean? How can this be the Ark of the Covenant? How can it be here in Atlantis? And it's so large. How could the Israelites have carried this with them out of Egypt?"

OM sighs, "We don't have time now for lengthy explanations."

He sees the scowl on my face and then reconsiders. "I'll give you a brief synopsis of it. The arks that various groups possessed were replicas of this. They were links—remote terminals—of this central engine. Some were small enough to be portable. But this is the original. It has been in this place—both under water and above—for well over a thousand centuries."

"Whoa!" I persist with my inquiry. "Just what *is* it, this ark?"

"It is the repository for our testament and grand agreement—to be in existence here at all. It sends out the carrier wave—the *arc,* if you will—upon which all our forms and energies are delivered. It always has. It is a *very* powerful vortex and antenna, connecting our planet and all its life forms into the cosmic network of civilizations! It is an intensely focused nexus. And let me say, formidable forces guard this ark. It would not still be here otherwise. If the ark did not want us to see it, or be here at all, we would not have found it."

"You make it sound like it's *alive.*"

"Indeed I do. It is more alive than you or I. This is the cornerstone, quite literally, of all life on this world. It inseminates and vitalizes all physical creatures."

Old Man's gaze tells me he takes this all very seriously. His eyes bore into me, silencing any further questions. "I will tell you one more thing about this place. It has to do with the ancient myth of

Atlas, the namesake of Atlantis. That myth was handed down through many lineages before the Greeks. Finally, in Greek mythology it came to be described as the 'defeat of the Titans'. Atlas, a Titan, was commanded by Zeus to stand at the western edge of Gaia and hold Uranus on his shoulders. Gaia, as you know, is the living Earth; Uranus was the Greek name for the Cosmos. He was *not* ordered to hold up the Earth, as was thought in your times.

"The Atlas myth derives from this very place. It cloaks the fact that Atlantis holds us to the Cosmos—that is, links Earth with the physical *Akasha* and deep space network. The submersion of Atlantis 26,000 years ago was, in part, a means of hiding this generator from the world of men, as they entered the great dark age. All the karmic events associated with that cataclysm were woven together around the destiny of the ark.

"Now, with the passage of time and the awakening of humanity, its secret can be revealed again to the world. That is how important and transformative your period is. That is what is anchoring and empowering the Great Storm. We are here now—at the safe distance of 13,000 years—to pay homage, and receive guidance that will then be delivered back to your time."

He pauses and takes an even more earnest tone. "If we mount onto that dish, comrades, all hell might break loose. I cannot predict what effect it will have on us and on the entire planet. Take a moment to ponder the gravity of this. Then answer me if you choose to proceed. And, O, please reach down deep and be absolutely certain of the instructions you have received."

I feel the *crisis* of this moment—danger and opportunity—and hesitate in it, swept by a nagging fear. Taking a good, long look at the fear, I see it for what it is—simply an ego posture. It can no longer stand in the way. It will not. Destiny is upon us and will protect us all—or not—in whatever way is true.

I give my assent. You affirm your earlier guidance and likewise nod to our leader. OM bows his head gravely and moves us forward onto the dish. We halt at the base of the great obelisk. I gasp. *This thing was cut from one single piece of marble! Wait.* I remember my little silver marble! I quickly pull it from my pocket and hold it tightly.

You wink over at me and clear your throat, whispering, "Now I'm getting that we should separate ourselves and find positions of resonance around the pillar—a triangulation."

"Agreed. For this, I release control of your globes," OM incants. "We must each find our own point of prime resonance."

I feel my bubble lurch and quiver. It has been un-tethered, its movement now under my control. As my faith waivers, however, so does the stability of the globe. *I've got to calm my thoughts and touch into deeper powers. I know how to do this,* I tell myself. *But I need some help.*

I let go my resistance and quickly sink into the Void—down, down, within, into the timeless zone. I see flowing images of all my recent experiences. There is the Hall of Memories, the Threshold, the *Akasha.* Next I see my life in Atlantis, the descent to the bottom of *Isa Ber,* and floating above Lake Union. Images of my body in the field of portals and my first encounter with the *vesica piscis*—all these events flash back to me. At last, the Ends of the Earth, the avatars, the Tree of Life and the child come into view. I sense these visions are all a means to raise my confidence.

I take all the images, with their piercing feelings, into my heart. I feel all my chakras unite as one—bridging Earth and sky. This is the vehicle of Oneness, both deep within and now in my immediate environment. I ask for help. Unceremoniously, I find myself back in my craft. I realize how to maneuver it. This bubble is as alive as my green cloak was, as the house with no roof, as I am myself. It connects with that Life in me. And I sense more acutely the awesome vitality of the obelisk. It is at once alien and earthly, mysterious and familiar. *It knows we're here.*

The obelisk shows me, without words or thoughts, that the Life force in us is physically purer here than anywhere I've ever known. With no delay, it moves me to my position of alignment. Instantly, there is a strike of lightning stabbing me, head to toe, and into the ground below. I recall the time Old Man attempted a similar alignment with us. The force is enormously more now. But this time, I'm prepared. The lightning flows straight through me without damage, without disturbance or pain. I am where I must be, where I belong, at last.

I see the electricity arcing down from the tip of the obelisk into each of us. We have assumed our positions in a triangle around the base and it has responded. Each of you must be experiencing exactly what I'm feeling. Suddenly there is nothing. All is still and silent. The lightning is gone. We wait. Minutes pass. I wonder, *Is this all there is? Do we just turn and go?* Silence. Impenetrable stillness.

Something compels me to look up. Far above in the dark, watery sky, there is another light. A tiny point is descending. As we all watch, transfixed, it grows larger, brighter, nearer. Our eyes take it in at last. *It's another globe like ours. There's a figure inside. She's wearing black robes.*

As the craft pulls finally down to our level, we exclaim and welcome our friend. Black smiles through the shimmering surface of her sphere. "Something told me you might need a fourth element for your ceremony down here. In fact, the ark itself has summoned me—out of a sound sleep I might add."

"How did you get here, 13,000 years in the future?" I wonder aloud. "And where did you get that bubble craft?"

"The ark has her ways," she replies simply. "Actually, it called me to the desert site where you formed *your* globes. I was there just after you departed, and I've been trailing you all day long, just out of range. This ark is an amazing creature. It kept me out of communication with you until just now. It works in a dimension I cannot fathom. It has its own will and way."

You interrupt, looking across the fluid space at your mentor. "Why do you think the ark invited you here?"

"Because it needs a fourth element to make the cross—the balance—with the pyramid," Black answers. "Pyramids and obelisks are crosses when viewed from straight above. You were not given full information. The ark was somehow in touch with both of us, giving you and me each, only part of its instruction. It's as though she wanted you to begin without me. Don't ask me to explain. I'm only guessing."

OM takes over again. "All right everyone. Find your new places in a cross formation on this dish. Let's get to work."

We reposition quickly. The ark seems satisfied. There are the lightning lines again, channeled through each of us. This time there is more. A horizontal belt of light appears halfway up the pillar. Its glow washes the marble up and down. The ark commands us to move ourselves away now, and back off from the dish. We all hear it in our minds, even me. I comply gladly, much relieved. *My human form can only take so much of this.* As we move back, we can see the entire shape. We come together and stand as four-in-one before the enormous vision of power.

The blue ring suddenly divides in two. One band sweeps upward along the shaft, the other moves down. They leave crystal sparks spinning on the stone surface as they pass. As the two halves move apart, there is a film of indigo light, an envelope extruded between them. Once the bands have reached the point and the base, there is a single, slow motion flame between them, surrounding the entire column. It burns as though from some gigantic, unseen candle.

The indigo form slowly swirls around the column; the cold black water is its stage, all around. The gossamer fire then forms into a giant *vesica piscis*—the holy oval around the pristine pillar. It is a vision of absolute beauty—blending form and pure essence. Not quite physical, it straddles the boundaries of time and space. Somehow I know that the home world of this object is a far more pure than ours. But nevertheless, here it is in our dimension to bring us as much virtue as we can receive.

We each are shaken with awe—the greatest magic. Within its countenance is the inscrutable presence of the far *unknown*. The ark spreads a scintillating glow out into the ocean. I dare to shift my eyes and glance around us. Amazingly, the dark ocean abyss has become transparent. I can see into the distance of our submerged landscape. There is my former land—Atlantis—in ruins, cast about within the embrace of its native mountains. Its former grandeur is dashed, yet preserved, here in a sanctuary, the watery sepulcher of its Earth incarnation.

The beauty of this event, its brilliance and magic, has absorbed me. And I have absorbed it. I accept its blessing. In so doing, I play my part in *making the faith* that will emanate from this point and time. I bow my head to the gleaming ark, union of heaven and Earth, synergy of two species, concurrence of universes.

With that thought, that acceptance, my spirit is suddenly pulled out of me toward the ark, the *vesica* portal. The pillar—the *lingam*—is the lightning rod, the pointer and arrow. The *vesica* is the compass, the passage and the vortex. It is the opening—*yoni*—the birth canal of worlds.

I still my emotion and quell my fear. There are higher powers at play here than any feeble, personal anxiety. The mighty unknown is *alive!* I am pulled as though through a tunnel, a wormhole. The rush of transformation is beyond description. It is a simultaneous destruction and reconstruction of my presence. Memories of our passage through the Jaws of Hunab Ku flood back.

I realize our forms in the new universe have been mirroring our progress and guiding us to this reunion all the way. I'm in two universes at once, divided in half, standing on both sides of the portal, like a human mirror. My individuality nature still ties the two parts of me together. So that becomes a bridge for me between these two vastnesses.

I look through the giant *vesica* lens and see myself with my three companions on the other side. Now, instantly, here they are with me on this side as well. We all four have become the bridge! The tiny *vesica* portal within my own body is pulsing in resonance with the greater. I feel it. Together they are one. All portals are *one portal*. Finally I understand. I see how Oneness is indeed the vehicle of our transfiguration.

Breathing heavily, I'm suddenly back in the old world with my friends. Our bubbles tremble with the sensations coursing through us. We are each filled to overflowing with this volcanic essence. The ground rumbles. Holy energy holds us in its sway. Compassion floods me. I feel you three near—closer than close, in my blood and in my soul. I want to reach out to you each, and hug you hard.

But it is not to be. I feel water, cold and biting, turning around my ankles. Rising. I look down in alarm and gasp. *Is my bubble dissolving under the pressure of the great ocean?* I look around at you, allowing a fear to swell in me again. You hover nearby, but show no alarm.

You are safe. OM bows to me. Black is stolid, gazing straight through me.

You squint one eye, in your characteristic near-wink. But clearly, *my* bubble is dissolving. Panic floods my mind. *Is this my fate—to die here now, to drown again in Atlantis?* A part of me acknowledges it might be fitting. I look into your eyes, plaintively. They are at peace. That peace fuses into me. Alas, I must allow whatever this may be. My heart swallows up my mind, and accepts. The world blurs.

I close my eyes tight. A deep breath of air surges through me. *I'm not drowning.* Eyes wide now, I'm in open air, yet in *water* as well. *Wait. It's the stream again.* I feel the bottom, sharp with stones, on my bare feet. Fluid ripples past my ankles. The ark is gone. The bubble craft are gone. Atlantis is gone. My friends have vanished.

I look around, frantic. My eyes adjust. There's my car on the riverbank, below the maple trees. My sandals are exactly where I left them at the water's edge. *I'm back in my own time.* I don't know whether to feel relief or regret. I take another deep, deep breath. The sky above is clearing. It has just stopped raining. Only seconds have passed since I waded into the creek. I stare around, feeling hollow and profoundly alone.

That's where you and I sat, in my car, I reflect. *It's so empty now. You're so far away from here. Where are you? 13,000 years in the future, at the bottom of the Atlantic Ocean!* I'm overcome with melancholy. I miss you all intensely, like integral parts of me—bodily organs that have been torn away. Feeling cold, I wade toward the bank. I rub my arms to warm them, and the sun glints at me off the water, like an almost-wink. Hah. There! I see your face in the glint, in my eyes.

You are right here with me, within me, I start. *There's no real distance in time. Now is now, forever. You and I are Now!* I turn my gaze—our gaze—to the old stone bridge over the stream, feeling your presence sweetly. Above, a dazzling rainbow cleaves the passing storm clouds. The bridge arches up with grace and down to the opposite bank. Just below it, just now, the water is still as glass—silver glass. *I can't believe what I'm seeing. It's so magical and beautiful.* Appreciation bursts out of me, all around. I laugh. The bridge and its inverted reflection in the water have formed the shape of a horizontal *vesica*. *Of course.*

Epilogue
Why Souls Leave the Earth

"O, I've been thinking about this series of letters we've just finished."

"And you have a question?" Your response is quick.

"How did you guess?"

"Go ahead. I've been expecting you."

"Admittedly, this is my ego talking, but it seems all our talk about portals could be looked upon as a form of escapism, like trying to get away from the old Earth. Why do we want so badly to *leave* this place? After all, we've chosen to be here, haven't we?"

"Yes, of course," you reply. "But it is only natural to feel like it's all too much. Tell me what you think humans want to escape *from.*"

I muse, "Well, we have a frantic, dangerous, toxic world right now. It seems to be rapidly overheating and unraveling. But the bigger issue behind it all is obviously 'the ego'. We want to escape *it!* And yet, now that I think about it, the ego itself probably wants to escape too. It could see escaping as another means to create separation and stress. There's a lot of stress around this planet these days."

"And?"

"I guess I'd have to say it must be egos creating the stress that egos want to escape from."

"Good one."

"A world full of egos is a horrendous place," I continue. "It's crazy. You know that. I feel it even more acutely now that I've had the glimpse of awakening you gave me."

"Tell me what you remember of that."

My mind goes quiet at your suggestion. I feel energy streaming in. "You know, I'd have to say awakening is really not all that far beyond us. You said it from the start, of course."

"Yes?"

"It's basically *appreciation*, isn't it. What was so wonderful about being 'vigilan-for-a-day', was the continuous state of appreciation I felt. We humans are capable of something like that even now—just not the 'continuous' part. What serenity and Oneness that was!" Suddenly words fail me; I'm back in the vigilan awareness. Warmth and peace flood through my mind in a vigorous stillness.

You ask, "What is it?"

"It's the feeling of Oneness, of being at one with the moment. *That's* what I learned. What appreciation really gives you is the presence of *Now*. Or maybe it's the other way around. Having that sense of Now gives you appreciation."

"Just so. I'd say you've got it," I feel you grinning. "We vigilans do not rely on *time* to feel appreciation. Through your human eyes, I'm seeing more clearly what vigilans do. Appreciation is a timeless quality that we *stream* into time. Indeed, you have made a breakthrough in understanding the Now. If you would be in the moment, simply *appreciate what is*. If you want to appreciate, then be *in the moment*. They are one and the same."

"OK. That sounds good." My brow wrinkles. "But 'what is' includes *everything that is*, right? Good and bad both? How can you appreciate unpleasant—or worse—harmful or evil things? Can you actually value that?"

"Yes, we can. For appreciation to work the way it does, it must link us with Source, with the origin of every manifested form. In the ego world, there are many forms that are unhealthy and unconscious—and yes, *evil*. We can appreciate these forms as necessary elements in the parade of evolving consciousness. We do not have to condone or engage them to appreciate their place in creation."

I wince inside. "But we can't just allow horrible things to go on happening in the name of evolution."

"Nevertheless, these horrible things *do* happen in your world. Awareness of them moves all consciousness forward. Appreciation means looking deeply into the essence. It allows evolution to adjust itself to more benign expressions. That is basic duality. Resistance produces freedom, when it is brought into awareness."

"Whoa. O, you've always said *don't resist*."

"There is *natural* resistance, built into the evolutionary process. It is opposition to what is untrue and inauthentic. There is also the resistance within any duality system—a creative tension that propels growth. This comes from the interplay of any two polarities, masquerading as opposites. Polarities are, in reality, just two sides of one coin, two ends of the same axis. Finally, there is *discursive* resistance that is generated by ego and mind, attempting to enhance their sense of separateness from creation. This *blocks* evolution. It is poisonous to your system.

"When I recommend *not resisting*, I'm talking about this third form. I urge you not to apply resistance within yourself. Do not identify with it or put it out into your environment. Your environment is *you*. Each individual is a conduit for universal creative force. Each person takes on a share of this energy and becomes a co-creator of all that is around them. If you pour your share of energy into resistance, you are increasing separation within your own being, your *environmental self*."

"But how does resistance produce freedom then?" I puzzle, fully back in my human self and not understanding. "Can we use resistance without identifying with it?"

"To say 'no' to something that doesn't resonate with your authenticity, is not adding resistance. It is adding clarity. It is appreciating the *natural* resistance to what is false. This promotes Oneness, not separation. For humans there is a fine line, however. It is very easy for you to slip over that line from conscious assertiveness into unconscious identification with opposition. It is easy for you to confuse your opinions with truth, and easy for you to condemn what is not aligned with those opinions.

"If you become identified with your opposition to anything, even with very noble intentions, you have moved away from appreciation. Your true identity is not opposition, not division; it is wholeness. For this reason, the teachings on non-resistance are among the most *critical* of your age." You smile. "Sorry about that pun. True understanding of this element of awakening is rare—and difficult for me to communicate, I must admit. I will continue to remind you of its place in your practice, in hopes of finding the right words."

I chuckle. "And I will do my best not to *resist* those reminders."

"We have all moved our beings through those dark states into brighter realms over the course of our individual evolution. That movement is what true awakening is. All events and forms in creation are necessary to produce the inevitable *Conscious Evolution*.

"Appreciation ultimately means to notice *what is*, without internal resistance, and to do so in the presence of your authentic being. This will have transformational powers. It brings both the light and the dark into Oneness. Even what seems to your mind as negative or evil, will eventually reveal itself as part of wholeness, once you no longer identify with your resistance."

"I yield to your wisdom," I sigh. "But I still have misgivings about appreciating evil."

"I accept that in you. Allow me now to show you how this relates to our initial subject, *why souls leave the Earth*. We all come and go, whether human, vigilan or angelan. This is the principle of *cycling*. It is a basic function of duality in motion, within Oneness. That which enters duality must leave; that which leaves must return; what is born must die. And while we are here, we all must move through both shadows and light. The mind sees the end of a lifetime as the greatest separation, something to be resisted and feared. But that is illusion. The heart sees the truth.

"Leaving the Earth is one of the most profound ways of heightening our appreciation. As we cross the threshold back into soul consciousness, we experience a period of divine fusion. This applies to all creatures—vigilans, humans, ants and atoms. It is a blessed, blissful perspective, granted to all those who return. It is a state of pure grace; it is part of cycling. We see the authentic depths of our being; and we are reacquainted with *its* view the world. The more awakened a soul's vehicle is, the longer and deeper this post-lifetime exposure lasts.

"The transition period after leaving Earth has been called the 'life review' by some. Some religions have viewed it as Judgment Day. The *judgment* that transpires is simply the clarity of spirit descending into our presence. And it is not limited to just one lifetime. During this period, we see the greater patterns of all our lives, and the lives of all the souls we associate with during our incarnations.

Surrounding us during this review are our guides, angels and elders who offer us expanded insight and suggestions for improvement. It is conducted in a powerfully compassionate manner.

"The post-incarnation sessions are the most focused and energized guidance we have as souls. All informative resources are brought to bear here in one place and time. Whether you realize it or not, your soul is looking forward to this encounter with great joy. That is a prime reason to leave the Earth plane, to receive this intensely focused love and appreciation, and to see how to steer your course in the most creative directions.

"Once the soul has completed its sojourn of lives on Earth, or a similar planetary situation, there is a *final* leaving. This takes place at the end of our last angelan incarnation. It is always an ecstatic, sacred celebration among vast numbers of peers and elders. This is truly a major cosmic *initiation*. It merits and receives widespread attention, from far beyond the little Earth. This tiny planet has always produced great wonders in the Cosmos."

I feel a surge of appreciation just hearing you say this.

Your voice continues. "Graduate souls from the Earth Series are operating in influential and beneficial ways throughout all the universes and dimensions. They are masters of wisdom and creation. This is what we all are evolving toward, through our lives here. And there is no end to this evolving after we graduate. We are part of a timeless spiral of unfolding consciousness and service. If you pause and feel—as in right *now*—you can stream into your heart the connection to that spiral. It is *you*, your eternal birthright. Thus we play our part in the great game."

"I want to say, 'unbelievable', and yet, inside me I know you're right. It *is* believable. I've always known it—as a soul. I can 'stream' that knowing and appreciation into my mind. But, you know, as a human I can easily fall back into doubt and disbelief."

I feel you shrug. "So be it. That is the way of your species. If you did not cycle back into that, you would no longer be human. It is, again, the cycle of dark and light. Let me remind you to accept yourself *just as you are*. Accept *what is,* just as it is. Only from this acceptance can you appreciate and see through the illusion. Only then may you take authentic action to evolve and to promote your own conscious evolution. Take it as a stepwise process, from the moment into the Moment, from the present into Now."

Other questions are bubbling up now. "This whole book has been about building portals, or rather just one *grand* portal—the passage through the Great Storm. You put a lot of ideas in my head about what portals are and where to find them. But I'm a little unclear about what's next. I can imagine readers wanting more guidance about just what they're supposed to do. Would you please summarize the instructions for us?"

"Yes, of course. First, I will say that building the portal is an *imaginal* journey. The true portal does not exist in the physical realm, and needs no construction here. Our project is an invitation to use trans-physical means to move beyond your current physical and mental dilemma. It is not a problem-solving exercise for the mind, however. As with all aspects of being, it is not something you can just *do*. You must allow it to *be* within you first."

"Fair enough," I react. "But I'm concerned that this 'imaginal' journey is too weird and personal for many potential readers. How are people going to relate to this?"

"These most recent letters are put to you as stories, to stimulate the imagination of the reader—and *your imagination* as well, I must say. In many cases, you are remembering events that have *not yet happened*. In these stories you have resonant forces at play that can be absorbed directly from the morphic field. They are a 'silver lining' to the Great Storm. The gestalt of the whole is what will trigger a response within others at the most fundamental levels. This is where the most important actions are taking place—the ones that will transform your DNA. Awakening comes from within, and remains forever within."

I sigh, "All right then. I guess what you're saying is that we must just 'grok' this process. But isn't there something else you could say to summarize what you want us to know?"

"Yes. Once you are in tune with yourself, both as a persona and as a soul, you will be able to hear what I say, but not before then. Those who do not resonate with these messages are not resonating with their own being. Look first to that work within yourself. Then the way of appreciation will open to you. Find a method to realize *who you really are.* There are many teachers in your world today who are providing this guidance. Hear them.

"When you are resonating with your own essence, or even just glimpsing it occasionally, you're ready. Now go within, to the deepest levels of your physicality, to the tiniest subatomic structure in your cells and biochemical makeup. Sense your way there. That is where my voice is entering your world. That is also the primary portal for communion with Source.

"You are using your imagination to listen within the Threshold. There you may continue and find the aperture, the *vesica.* Imagine it. Look through it. Pass through it, from both directions; this invokes the principle of cycling. Set your intention to activate the *vesica* portal. Let go of any fixed ideas you may have about what this is, or how it works. Let go of any desire to control it. Allow *it* to empower *you.* Accept its empowerment. Set the intention to evolve. Invite *Conscious Evolution* to move within you, according to its will.

I interrupt, "OK. That's all good. I follow you. It's all about imaging the things we've written about to actually be happening inside us, inside the reader. But what will this do to alleviate suffering in the world? What is going to change in our lives? How will we know if it's working? And what are the practical techniques, the practices, that we can use to keep this awakening moving forward?"

"The only practices I recommend are the ones you've heard many times now. They are 1) notice *what is,* 2) do not put your identity into resistance, and 3) be and act from your own authenticity. These, each and all, trigger *appreciation.* Notice when you are appreciating; do not put resistance in the way of appreciation; realize who and what your true nature is in the moment of appreciation."

I reflect, "Well, now that you mention it, just last week and again yesterday, I found myself feeling very appreciative—with no apparent cause. There wasn't really any specific thing that was making it happen. I did acknowledge it in my mind. I even realized how it made me aware of just being in the moment. It was so simple. On another occasion, I might have just let it slip by without actively paying any attention."

You reply with amusement, "On *many* other occasions you *have* let it slip past. This new development of yours is a sign that awakening is happening—moving gradually forward. All that you really need to *do* for your 'practice' is to acknowledge appreciation when it comes to you. The more you feel it, the more *it* will feel you, the more it will *enter* you and live there creatively.

"Other than this, I do not promote any complex of practices for awakening. They are too often mere crutches for the mental-emotional nature. Methodologies here stand in the way more than they facilitate during the Storm. They imply that you must 'accomplish' something before you can 'achieve' awareness. I remind you, there is nothing to *achieve*. Rather *receive*, and be aware. This will open the portal to you.

"Any effort, no matter how well-conceived in the mind, will only take away from receiving what is already there by grace. Effort has nothing to do with enlightenment. If you feel you must have a spiritual practice and are drawn to it through inner resonance, I would advise you to treat it like an *accompaniment* to awakening, not a 'gateway'. Practice is appropriate for worldly experience—for the mind, emotions and body on Earth. It enables you to live a proper life and perform the functions of incarnation, to 'improve' yourself. It is how you navigate the physical planes. But it does not apply to matters of grace.

"You see, there is always the risk of losing one's identity in form—especially for 'spiritual seekers', who usually stand on uncertain ground. The *seeker* is looking for a shift, a deliverance, a new identity—a *form* in the end. Identity with form creates and perpetuates the trap of ego. Attachment to any spiritual practice is an ego function. Ego will always want to *delay* awakening. You will find its so-called 'gateways' are only labyrinths of delusion."

I ponder this for a moment. "These are rather harsh words, I think. Many people feel that spiritual practices, and seeking, are an *essential* part of the path to enlightenment. Religions and devotional approaches are filled with practices and techniques. Many see them as a prerequisite."

"I understand. But there is no 'path to enlightenment' from my perspective. Awakening is the natural course of evolution—when you are ready. To be ready means releasing attachment to form, including attachment to practices. This is all I'm saying. You may have your practices if you must. They may be quite enjoyable and helpful to your physical-emotional-mental well-being. Just don't look at them as the path to enlightenment. And don't attach your identity to them."

"Thank you for that. I know, however, some people will not agree with what you've just said."

"So be it."

I'm still wondering. "Back to the topic of portals one last time. What about the ones we're building. What do we do about them? How urgent is it that we get the message out?"

"With the publication of these books, the message *is* out! That's all it takes. Hear the message. See the message. Feel the message. It is streaming into the world all around you. Do not think you have to *do* anything. Do not think you have to *push* the message out into the world, or into anyone's mind. I've told you before that the *Letters* have a life of their own. It really is true. Their life is Life itself, welling up from the eternal spring of being in every creature. Allow that Life to determine how, when and where the message will flow."

You chuckle. "*Conscious Evolution* will not be delayed or enhanced by any initiative of your *marketing strategy.*"

"All right. I surrender," I sigh. "I'll stop asking for further instruction on that matter. I will trust inner guidance to *live* this into existence. But it's going to take a lot of patience."

"Excellent. I have one last comment. The portals are all around you, in myriad forms. The key point of this second book is not actually to get everyone busy *building* portals, though it may appear so. The real core message here is to be *aware* of portals at all, however they emerge. Be aware that ultimately there is only one portal that binds them all. This portal is the vehicle of Oneness. Through that opening will come your precious awakening."

I smile. "Now that really does help me. *Just be aware of portals!* Thank you. I'm having one of those moments of appreciation right now. Cool."

I feel a subtle shift in your position. You say, "I know that you have other questions. Why don't you go ahead and ask them? But please be brief."

"Well, you probably know I've just finished reading through the whole book again. Doing that has brought up several new questions. For one, I'm feeling a little strange about the name you have for yourselves—'vigilans'. It feels almost like *I* made it up somehow."

"You are sensing that we have 'made it up' together. We did that for purposes of communication. We actually use no name for ourselves in my time. There was a period, however, earlier in our development when we did employ names, both for our species and our individualities. There was never just *one* name though. Some of the names were imagined by humans for a species evolved out of themselves, such as *homo noeticus*, *homo spiritus*, *homo divines*, *homo illuminatus*, etc. 'Evigilatus' was one such attempt to describe us."

"Very interesting. That rings true. Thanks. But for us humans, I think it makes sense to keep using the name."

"I hear you."

Now, I have another question. "Here's one that comes from people who have read the first book and our Internet blog. It has to do with when we can expect the 'transition' to happen. People keep asking about dates. I know what you have said before, and this is truly not so much my concern. But I feel I must ask it again. When is the year 'zero'?"

"There is *no* year zero. The same was true of your Christian calendar—an exact time for year 'zero' was never known. Zero symbolizes the Void that came between your time and mine. If you wish to conceive of the Void as 'zero', then it is a fair approximation. But it wasn't a year; it wasn't *time* at all. As to when it will happen in your time, it already *has*. The shift *has happened*. It is happening right now, and will always *be* happening. The only thing that keeps people asking that question is that they have not yet awakened to its presence. If this were not so, there would be no conversation about it at all. If your readers are asking that question, they are sensing the shift within themselves. It only remains for them to accept what they already know."

"OK. But I think they are also wondering about the world. When will the world change? And in the population at large?"

"I can only go on repeating myself. The shift happens for the world, just when it happens for the individual—when she or he realizes it's already happening. I will give you a date if you insist. 1776. There it is. You want another date? 2001. Still not happy? 2012. How about 2020? Do you see? It's not about numbers and *quantities* in your mind. It's about spaces and *qualities* in your heart."

"Whew. For me that's plenty. Enough. But I'm afraid people will keep asking."

"There's no harm in asking, only harm in not hearing the message that lies within your own consciousness. The mind goes on asking. But it is spirit that must answer."

"Here's something else. I know we talked it about the new universe already, but I'm still wondering. Why did we spend almost the whole book in the old universe? At the end of the first book it seemed we were never coming back."

I sense a sympathetic smile from you. "It is a mystery I don't fully understand either. It's not possible to have a conversation like this with our counterparts there. But they are living in correspondence with us, as we witnessed in Atlantis. They have parallel lives to ours, and they will always be guiding us, transmitting energies of assistance and appreciation. My best answer to your question is that *here* is where the real action is for now; it is where the greatest need lies. It appears that the story of this book is in the old universe because this is where the Great Storm is. Our focused attention is to bring the old into the new, so that the new will come into the old."

My mind is chewing on that. Another thought slides in. "OK. Speaking of 'old': What about 100,000 years ago? Who built the obelisk in Atlantis? There wasn't time for an explanation before."

"That is a very long and very old story. I won't do it justice here. But I will give you a brief overview. The human spirit comes to Earth through the soul realm, as we discussed in the epilogue to the first book. The human *form* likewise has come to Earth from another realm. In fact our form is a composite from many other places in the Cosmos. It is through the interstellar web of conscious evolution and civilization. We have roots in the systems of Sirius, Orion, Draco and the Pleiades, among many other dimensions and galaxies.

"In the beginning, humans on Earth were simply an experiment of exploration at the far edge of intergalactic settlement. The intentions were quite limited. Some of your scientists have conjectured about a so-called 'slave race'. This is partially accurate. The early forms, later to evolve into humans, were simple-minded creatures. They were put in place by mixing genetic components from particular extraterrestrial species with those existing in Earth hominids.

"As millennia passed, evolution exerted its prerogative, and new, more adaptable forms became available for incarnating souls to inhabit. This made the game of Earth life increasingly interesting—to both discarnate life forms and extraterrestrial races. Our intellectual capacities expanded, as did our connection to general unfolding consciousness.

"The Covenant and its Ark were put in place when it became clear that the Earth evolution deserved it's own contract with the galactic systems of governance. It is their way of assuring that evolution will be allowed to follow its deeper mandates, without undue manipulation from interlopers.

"Your race and mine have a guarantee within that covenant that we are a recognized part of the cosmic evolving civilization. Once you realize this and make it truly conscious, your awakening proceeds apace. This is why it was essential that we conclude this book on that note. It is time for humanity to recognize it's rightful place in the Cosmos."

"Wow. I'm sure there's much more to be said on that subject." I can't resist a follow-up. "What do you mean by 'interlopers'?"

"There are those—with their own egos—from other places and dimensions, who come to Earth and attempt to influence our planet to their own ends. The Ark safeguards us greatly from this tampering. But not entirely." You fall silent.

"Do you want to say anything more about that?"

"Not at this time. It is far too large a subject for this book. I will only add, as a hint, be alert to the rings of power—as in Tolkien's *rings.* They play a major role in the interplay of dark and light forces on the planet in your time. They are portals of great mystical force, both light and dark."

"Hmm. That makes me start wondering. Perhaps there will be more about this in the next book?"

"Perhaps," you say enigmatically.

I shrug and turn my attention back to a concern that's been bothering me. "On several occasions you've described the Earth experience as a 'game'. Isn't that a little glib? Doesn't it make rather light of all the suffering and turmoil in the lives on this planet?"

"Exactly so," you respond, to my surprise. "The point *is* to 'lighten up' a little. I do not use the word 'game' in a compassion-less or condescending sense. To call the Earth experience a 'game' is to point out that it does not need to be taken as seriously as most humans take it. Yes, there is great suffering, cruelty and ignorance in your world. Many games countenance such outrageous behavior. Just look at your human video games, for example.

"The stakes in this 'world game'—to quote Buckminster Fuller—are very high. No question about it. They are 'life and death' stakes. But life and death are what we do here on this plane, in any case. If these stakes are unavoidable, why not choose to *play* with them, rather than fear and anguish over them? The origins of the word, 'game', imply the *joy of people getting together.* Let this be the sense of your life experience and you will profit therefrom."

"Well, O, I sense this dialogue coming to close now. But I have one more request for clarification. Can you speak a little more about what you said earlier, about 'falling back into formlessness? I feel there is something to be said on that subject."

"Yes, there is, as always. And this will be a fitting way to close. 'Falling back' is a way of opening to space. Formlessness is the Void, the Now. It is also the Absolute, the Source, spirit, God. Each of these words carries its own quality as a pointer. But each is only a form.

"Form is all the mind can ever know. There is much conscious-ness beyond form, however. It is infinite. Falling back into form-lessness simply means letting go and realizing the beneficent sim-

plicity of your origins, of who you really are. It means allowing the embrace of peace and presence.

"Your true nature is not form-bound or form-generated. It is a nature that can choose to create forms if it likes. It can enter and immerse itself in the realms of form. It may even, for a time, accept the illusion that it *is* form, that it *is* the mind—and *only* that. To 'fall back into the formless' is your release valve into awareness. It is your ultimate and intimate way of *leaving the Earth*. And it is what brings all our *projections* full cycle.

"I advocate falling back into the formless at any time, especially at those times when you feel the weight of forms pressing upon you, stressing you—when you have lost sight of the *Projector*. It will bring you peace and joy and timelessness. It will bring you into the Now. And you know I must say it again. It will bring you into *appreciation*."

"O, so are we ready for the next book yet?"

"I am, yes. However, you my friend, are not. Not quite yet. Have patience. I love the irony of a human expression I once heard, 'Patience is a waste of time!' It's funny, but there is great truth in it. Time is your prison. It needs to be recognized as the illusion it is. In order to realize patience, time *must* be wasted, removed from the equation. Without time, there is no distance in space, no need to move from here to there. You are already everywhere. And yet, paradoxically, you must wait for the cycle of expression to come to you. This is where you must be patient. Be timeless. Lay waste to time. The next book is already written from that space."

"I'm happy to hear it. Thank you, dear friend and guide, O. With that I will sign off for now."

"Blessings of endless abundance to you all."

Who Are the Authors?

Robert lives in Chester, Pennsylvania. He is one we have asked to transcribe and translate our messages for your world and your time, given his training and previous experience. He informed us of his willingness to participate before he was born. For our part, we are a group of twelve beings, living 500 years from your time, who are charged with a mission of alerting you to the great adventure that lies just ahead for you. And, ah, the muses; for their part, they live forever inside us all.

Made in the USA
Middletown, DE
19 November 2024

65032975R00156